Finding Hope

*A Practical Guide for Families Affected by Mental Illness
Drawn From the Experience of Families Like Yours*

Donna Kay Smith
in collaboration with Susan Willey Spalt

with contributions from Chris Blue, Chief, Chapel Hill Police Department,
Grace Hubbard, DNP, PMHCNS-BC, Jim Huegerich, M.Ed.,
John Poetzsch, Dawn Woody, and others.

Copyright 2019 © Donna Kay Smith & Susan Willey Spalt
All rights reserved.

This book or any portion thereof may not be reproduced or used in any manner whatsoever without the express written permission of the author, except for review purposes.

Some names in this book have been changed to protect privacy.

The Mole by John Haines, published in *Winter News* (Wesleyan University Press, 1966), reprinted with permission.

Cover & interior design by Sable Books

ISBN: 978-0-9987810-8-2

Sable Books
sablebooks.org

There are no words to describe the world when your child is different. It all hurts. When I saw other people his age, a voice in my head asked: "Why isn't my son like that? Going to college. Working. Making friends. Hanging out. Going through all of the things that we all go through at that age. At any age." I do not know what is worse. This, or seeing young mothers with young sons. I remember being a young mother with a young son doing the things that mothers and their children do. Living a normal life—whatever that may be. I remember wooden blocks, Tonka trucks, the powdery smell of moist diaper wipes, polished, smooth, warm baby skin, and silky soft hair against my cheek. "I want to eat you up," I would tell him, gazing at his round, red cheeks and chubby baby arms, his double baby chin. Kisses were never satisfying enough. I remember school plays; pictures taken on the first day each year while waiting for the bus. I remember going about the daily business of life when my son was my son and I could talk to him without having first to enter the world of delusion. The days when baggy pants and big T-shirts were our worst conflict. I see mothers and sons now and I remember being one of them. I remember that life. I remember my son and me. I remember how it was.

I have since entered into a private club. Others can look in through the window. They can feel sympathy, or empathy, or horror, or whatever it is that the sight of us evokes. But they can't come in. They do not know. There is now and forever an invisible wall between us. I can never step back from this world into that, into the life we once inhabited. The only ones who know are those who share this strange existence. We recognize each other. It comes in the first words, "my mother, father, sister, brother, child…." And then we look into one another's eyes and see our own life there. We don't say anything more. We don't need to. We know. We live it. For that moment, I am not alone. I have found "another." There is nothing to explain and it's too damn painful to talk about. What would it accomplish other than the affirmation that we have entered into the hell that never ends? It is hell to love someone, to keep the body, the voice, the eyes, the face, and to have lost them nonetheless…..

We belong to this private club. We have lived its experiences. We have wept its tears. We have fought for the hope and the possibility that exists here. Yes. Even in this, there is hope, and there is possibility. Most of all—there can be success. *We want you to know this.* There is a way through the journey your family is on. It is not an easy journey. It is often painful. It is a journey where few may seem willing or able to help—not least of all, the system that is supposed to treat this. But it is a *journey*. And there are things we can share with one another that will make this journey easier.

The purpose of this book is to share our collective wisdom. It is for use by families with who want help negotiating the confusing journey through mental illness. Tips for dealing with immediate crises can be found at the beginning along with important phone numbers. Part 1 covers general information about mental illness, Part 2 addresses specific situations, and Part 3 provides guidance on how to navigate the treatment system and get someone the care they need. There is a description of specific illnesses in the appendix along with other resources and information, but the guide itself focuses on helping your loved one and taking care of yourself. We have included personal stories to help you better understand your own experience and know that you are not alone. We hope you find this book will help you on your journey.

       Most of all—we bring you hope.

Finding Hope

*A Family's Guide to Mental Illness
From People Who've Been There*

Mental illness can be difficult to understand. It is difficult to cope with. The treatment system is often difficult to navigate, confusing, and can fail on basic levels. This guide is a tool for families dealing with the complexities and challenges of mental illness.

TABLE OF CONTENTS

QUICK REFERENCE

CRISIS PHONE NUMBERS	2
IMMEDIATE HELP: WHAT IF SOMEONE MAY BE SUICIDAL	7
IMMEDIATE HELP: WHAT IF SOMEONE MAY BE DANGEROUS TO OTHERS	9
IMMEDIATE HELP: WHAT IF I AM NOT THERE AND I BELIEVE SOMEONE MAY BE IN CRISIS	10
INFORMATION YOU SHOULD PROVIDE TO THE POLICE	11
Strange Gift / *Susan Spalt*	12

PART ONE: MENTAL ILLNESS

INTRODUCTION	14
Sidebar: Mental Illness or Distress?	16
What We Wish Someone Had Told Us	17
HOW DO YOU KNOW IF SOMEONE NEEDS PROFESSIONAL HELP?	20
IS PROFESSIONAL HELP NEEDED: KEY QUESTIONS TO ASK	24
If You Suspect a Problem: Where to Start	26
Reflections on Our Family's Experience With Mental Illness, *Elizabeth*	29
MENTAL ILLNESS AND REHABILITATION	31
DM's Story	36
Adjustment to Mental Illness	37
Adjustment to Mental Illness for Those Experiencing Symptoms	42
Sidebar: Chronic Sorrow	48
Supporting Rehabilitation and Symptom Management	49

PART TWO: SPECIFIC SITUATIONS

Tips for Speaking With Someone Who Is Psychotic	52
Tips for Speaking With Someone Who Is Depressed	56
Anger in Your Loved One	58
Helping Someone Having an Anxiety Attack	60
Drug and Alcohol Addiction	61
Being an Addict, *Stephen*	64
Drug and Alcohol Use in Conjunction With Other Mental Disorders	66
Sidebar: Choosing a Treatment Facility	67
Drug and Alcohol Addiction: A Family's Thoughts, *Dawn Woody*	69
Child Mental Health, *Grace B Hubbard, DNP, PMHCNS-BC*	72

Siblings	77
If Children Are Still Living at Home	78
When an Adult Child Has a Mental Illness	80
If Your Adult Child Lives at Home	82
Estrangement	84
The Elderly	86
Violence and Mental Illness	88
Missing Persons	90
Homelessness	95
Joblessness	96
INTERACTING WITH THE POLICE	
Guess Who's Coming to Dinner: When Police Respond to a Mental Health Emergency, *Jim Huegerich*	98
Our Family's Experience With the Police *John Poetzsch*	101
Insights From Law Enforcement *Chris Blue, Chief, Chapel Hill Police Department*	103
A PRACTICAL GUIDE TO SELF-CARE	105
CARING FOR YOUR MARRIAGE	107
Step-parents and Marriage	108

PART THREE: THE MENTAL HEALTH SYSTEM

To My Service Provider / *Donna Kay Smith*	**114**
A Tale of Three Diseases	115
INTRODUCTION	116
Robert's Story, *Ruth*	119
CONFIDENTIALITY	121
PROFESSIONALS: WHO ARE THEY AND WHAT DO THEY DO?	124
Choosing a Professional	127
TREATMENT OPTIONS	130
Alternative Treatments	134
Sidebar: Evidenced Based Best Practice	138
SERVICE DEFINITIONS	
Inpatient/Residential Services	139
Community Based/Outpatient Services	143
INSURANCE AND FINANCES	145

AN IDEAL CARE SYSTEM: DIAGRAM ... 154

TREATMENT MANAGEMENT
    Putting a Treatment Plan Together ... 155
    Treatment Walls and How to Get Around Them ... 159
    Advanced Psychiatric Directive, Guardianship, and Power of Attorney ... 163
    Advocacy ... 166
    Medical Records ... 168
    Sample Excerpt: Family/Psychosocial History ... 173

INVOLUNTARY COMMITMENT: Not Just Suicidal or Homicidal ... 175
    Step 1—The Petition ... 179
    Step 2—The Evaluation ... 183
    Step 3—Admission and Initial Treatment ... 186
    Step 4—Second Examination and Treatment Pending Hearing ... 189

VOLUNTARY ASSESSMENT AND/OR INPATIENT ADMISSIONS
    Admitting a Minor ... 192
    Adult Voluntary Assessment and/or Admissions ... 195
    A Letter to My Family, *Anonymous* ... 198

The Mole / *John Haines* ... 200

APPENDIX

Types of Mental Illnesses ... 203
Symptoms: Terms to Know ... 206
Suicidal Thoughts: How to Support Someone, *Rethink Mental Illness* ... 211
Dealing With Unusual Thoughts and Behaviors, *Rethink Mental Illness* ... 221
10 Tips From the Depression Alliance ... 231
Reference Forms ... 233

RESOURCES
    Books ... 273
    Online ... 277
    NC Agencies & Organizations ... 281
    NC Facilities ... 284

QUICK REFERENCE

CRISIS PHONE NUMBERS

This is a list of phone numbers you may need quickly. It is not comprehensive. For more information about what is available in your area contact your LME/MCO.

Because areas may be served by several or different providers, <u>highlight the numbers that you may need BEFORE you need them.</u>

We have provided space at the end of this list to write numbers you want easy access to.

National Suicide Prevention Lifeline: 1-800-273-8255
- The Lifeline: Twitter: @800273TALK

Crisis Text Line: Text 741741

NAMI NC Helpline: 1-800-451-9682

NAMI National Information Helpline: 1-800-950-NAMI

Mobile Crisis Teams
- Alliance Healthcare (Durham, Wake, Cumberland, Johnson Counties): 1-800-510-9132
- Asheville: 1-888-573-1006
- Burlington: 1-336-538-1220
- Catawba Valley Healthcare: 888-235-4673
- Easter Seals (Edgecombe, Wilson, Lenoir, Greene, Wayne, Sampson, Duplin): 1-866-241-7245
- Forsyth Behavioral Health: 1-800-718-3550
- Greensboro: 1-855-459-9507
- Integrated Family Services (Beaufort, Bertie, Brunswick, Camden, Carteret, Chowan, Currituck, Dare, Gates, Hertford, Hyde, Martin, Nash, New Hanover, Northampton, Onslow, Pasquotank, Pender, Perquimans, Pitt, Tyrell, Washington): 1-866-437-1821
- Mecklenburg County: 1-704-566-3410 (Select Option 1)
- MHA: Mecklenburg and Cabarrus: 1-800-939-5911
- Orange and Person Counties: 1-877-967-8844
- Regional Mobile Crisis Management (Buncombe, Henderson,

Madison, Mitchell, Polk, Rutherford, Transylvania, Yancey): 1-888-573-1006
- RHA Health Services (Brunswick, Carteret, Craven, Jones, New Hanover, Onlsow, Pamlico, Pender): 1-844-709-4097
- Wake County Crisis and Assessment: 1-877-626-1772

North Carolina Suicide and Crisis Hotlines
- Ahoskie (Bertie, Gates, Hertford, Northampton Counties): 252-332-4442
- Alamance, Caswell Counties: 336-513-4444
- Alliance Behavioral Healthcare, (Cumberland, Durham, Johnston, Wake): 1-800-510-9132
- Brunswick, New Hanover, Pender Counties: 1-800-672-2903
- Cardinal Innovations (Alamance, Cabarrus, Caswell, Chatham, Davidson, Davie, Forsyth, Franklin, Granville, Halifax, Mecklenburg, Orange, Rockingham, Person, Rowan, Stanley, Stokes, Union, Vance, Warren): 1-800-939-5911
- Carteret County: 252-247-3023
- Clyde County: Teen Education and Crisis Hotline: 1-800-367-7287
- Cumberland County: 1-910-485-4134
- Daymark Recovery Services
- Crisis Hotline: 1-866-275-9552
- Suicide Prevention: 1-800-273-8255
- Durham County: 1-800-510-9132
- Eastpoint (Bladen, Columbus, Duplin, Edgecombe, Greene, Lenoir, Robeson, Sampson, Scotland, Wayne, Wilson): 1-800-913-6109
- Elkin (Iredell, Surry, Yadkin Counties): 1-888-235-4673
- Greensboro Teen Crisis Line (4-midnight): 1-336-387-6161
- Halifax: 252-537-2909
- Hopeline (Raleigh, Durham, Chapel Hill): 1-800-231-4525
- Hopeline Teen Talkline: 1-919-231-3626
- Johnston County: 1-919-934-6161
- Lee, Harnett Counties: 1-919-774-4520
- Mecklenburg and surrounding areas/Alexander Youth Network: 704-377-0602

- MHA: (Mecklenburg and Cabarrus): 1-800-939-5911
- Mooresville: 1-704-664-4357
- Orange, Person, Chatham Counties: 1-800-233-6834
- Outer Banks Hotline: 1-252-473-3366
- Partners Behavioral Health: (Burke, Catawba, Cleveland, Gaston, Iredell, Lincoln, Surry, Yadkin): 1-888-235-4673
- Pitt County: 252-758-4357 (TTY)
- Pitt County Teen: 1-252-758-1976
- Salisbury: 1-704-633-3616
- Sandhills Center (Anson, Guilford, Harnett, Hoke, Lee, Montgomery, Moore, Randolph, Richmond): 1-800-256-2452
- Statesville: 1-704-872-7638
- Trillium Healthcare Resources (Brunswick, Carteret, Nash, New Hanover, Onslow, Pender, Beaufort, Bertie, Camden, Chowan, Craven, Currituck, Dare, Gates, Hertford, Hyde, Jones, Martin, Northamptom, Pamlico, Pasquotank, Perquimans, Pitt, Tyrrell, Washington): 1-877-685-2415
- Wayne County: 1-919-735-4357
- Wilson: 1-252-237-5156
- Wilson Teen Help Line (4-8 p.m. M-F): 1-252-243-6444
- Winston Salem: 1-336-722-5153
- Winston Salem KidsLine: 1-336-723-5437
- Winston Salem Teen Line: 1-336-723-8336
- Vaya Health (Alexander, Alleghany, Ashe, Avery, Buncombe, Caldwell, Cherokee, Clay, Graham, Haywood, Henderson, Jackson, Macon, Madison, McDowell, Mitchell, Polk, Rutherford, Swain, Transylvania, Wautauga, Wilkes, Yancey): 1-800-849-6127

NC DHHS: 919-733-7011, https://www.ncdhhs.gov/divisions/mhddsas

- Crisis Services Information: https://www.ncdhhs.gov/assistance/mental-health-substance-abuse/crisis-services
- Deaf and Hard of Hearing Mental Health and Substance Use Disorder Services: https://www.ncdhhs.gov/divisions/mental-health-developmental-disabilities-and-substance-abuse/deaf-and-hard-hearing-mental
- Discounted Medications: https://www.ncdhhs.gov/assistance/low-income-services/discounted-medications

- Customer Service and Community Rights Team, 919-715-3197 or 855-262-1946. Email at: dmh.advocacy@dhhs.nc.gov

NC LME/MCO

- Vaya Health: 1-828-225-2785. Crisis Line: 1-800-849-6127 (Alexander, Alleghany, Ashe, Avery, Buncombe, Caldwell, Cherokee, Clay, Graham, Haywood, Henderson, Jackson, Macon, Madison, McDowell, Mitchell, Polk, Rutherford, Swain, Transylvania, Wautauga, Wilkes, Yancey)
- Cardinal Innovations: 1-704-939-7700, Crisis Line 1-800-939-5911 (Alamance, Cabarrus, Caswell, Chatham, Davidson, Davie, Forsyth, Franklin, Granville, Halifax, Mecklenburg, Orange, Rockingham, Person, Rowan, Stanley, Stokes, Union, Vance, Warren)
- Partners Behavioral Health: 1-704-884-2501, Crisis Line: 1-888-235-4673 (Burke, Catawba, Cleveland, Gaston, Iredell, Lincoln, Surry, Yadkin)
- Alliance Behavioral Healthcare: 919-651-8401, Crisis Line 1-800-510-9132 (Cumberland, Durham, Johnston, Wake)
- Sandhills Center: 1-910-673-9111 Crisis Line: 1-800-256-2452 (Anson, Guilford, Harnett, Hoke, Lee, Montgomery, Moore, Randolph, Richmond)
- Trillium Healthcare Resources: 1-866-998-2597, Crisis Line: 1-877-685-2415 (Brunswick, Carteret, Nash, New Hanover, Onslow, Pender, Beaufort, Bertie, Camden, Chowan, Craven, Currituck, Dare, Gates, Hertford, Hyde, Jones, Martin, Northamptom, Pamlico, Pasquotank, Perquimans, Pitt, Tyrrell, Washington)
- Eastpoint: 1-800-913-6109, Crisis Line: 1-800-913-6109 (Bladen, Columbus, Duplin, Edgecombe, Greene, Lenoir, Robeson, Sampson, Scotland, Wayne, Wilson)

Other Numbers I May Need

IMMEDIATE HELP: WHAT IF SOMEONE MAY BE SUICIDAL

**For more in-depth information on suicide please see the factsheet in the Appendix*

If you think someone may be suicidal you must act. Everything takes second place to life and death—including your need to be 100% sure or your concern they may be angry with you.

If someone tells you they are thinking of suicide—believe them.

Do not be afraid to ask, "Are you thinking of hurting yourself?" No one starts to think about suicide because someone raised the subject.

If you believe someone may be thinking about suicide:
- Ask them: *Are you thinking of hurting yourself? Are you thinking of suicide?*
- Ask if they have a plan for how they would harm themselves. Ask what their plan is? Ask: *Have you thought about how you might hurt yourself?*
- Try to find out if they have the ability to carry out a plan. Do they have the gun? Are there pills available?
- If the answer is yes—WITHOUT PUTTING YOURSELF IN DANGER—ask them to give the weapon, the pills, or whatever they would use to you, another trusted person, or to put them in another room.

If they have a plan but no way to carry it out, the crisis is not as urgent but they are still in need of immediate help.

Someone may be at greater risk if:
- they have attempted suicide in the past
- they have hurt themselves or others in the past
- they know someone who has committed or attempted suicide
- they use drugs or alcohol

DO NOT TELL SOMEONE
- to cheer up
- that everything will be all right
- that they will feel better
- that they are being selfish.
- Try to persuade them that they have a reason to live.

When life seems hopeless it does not *feel* like things can or will ever get better.

DO

- Express concern. Tell them they matter to you.
- Tell them you want to help.
- If possible, tell them you will stay with them and support them
- Encourage them to call the suicide hotline 1-800-273-8255, a local crisis line, their therapist (if they have one), or a trusted clergy person. If they are more comfortable texting they can text "HOME" to 741-741. You can offer to accompany them to the local Emergency Room or Assessment Center. Assure them you will be with them if they are afraid to go alone. If they won't call and you do not believe the situation is urgent you can call the suicide hotline or a crisis line yourself for direction and help.

Call 911

- if you believe someone has done something harmful
- is at immediate risk of doing so, and
- if they are not willing to get help.

Ask if they have a Crisis Intervention Team (CIT). Ask for a CIT officer to respond. Provide as much information as you can including things which have helped or made things worse for this person in the past or any people that they may trust to talk to them. Let the police know if there are weapons that the person may have access to.

** CRISIS INTERVENTION TEAMS are officers who have specific training on identifying and responding to mental health emergencies.

If you believe that someone is suicidal and unwilling to get help, and you are able to leave them or send someone else, you can ask a magistrate to issue an order that they be taken for assessment. For more information on this see the section on Involuntary Commitments on **p. 175.**

Suicide Hotline: 1-800-273-8253

IMMEDIATE HELP: WHAT IF SOMEONE MAY BE DANGEROUS TO OTHERS?

If you believe you or someone else is in danger, you must get immediate help.

Get to a safe place. Leave the home or the location of the person you fear. If others are at risk, you must warn them.

Call 911

Ask if they have a Crisis Intervention Team and if so request that a CIT officer respond. Give the police as much information as possible including why you believe you or others are at risk and whether the person has access to any weapons. Let them know if the person has ever been violent in the past, what has made things worse and what has made things better.

** CRISIS INTERVENTION TEAM officers have specific training on identifying and responding to mental health emergencies.

If someone is an immediate threat to you or others, you can also go to the local magistrate and ask to take out Involuntary Commitment papers. For more information on this see the section on Involuntary Commitments on **p. 175.**

IMMEDIATE HELP: WHAT IF I AM NOT THERE AND I BELIEVE SOMEONE MAY BE IN CRISIS?

If someone is in crisis and you are unable to check on them

1. You can ask the local police to do a well-being check. A police officer will go to their location and check on them. If they determine there is a problem, or they are in danger the police can get them help.

   If you need to call the police you should always ask if they have a Crisis Intervention Team (CIT) and request that a CIT officer respond. *CRISIS INTERVENTION TEAM officers that have specific training on identifying and responding to mental health emergencies.*

2. Many communities have trained crisis response teams. These are mental health professionals who can make contact, and determine if someone is at immediate risk and what interventions may be necessary. A list of local Crisis Teams can be found on **page 2**.

When is it a crisis?

It is a crisis when:

- Someone is threatening to harm themselves or someone else

Someone is not able to care for themselves: they are not eating or drinking, caring for their personal hygiene, able to meet their basic needs, or keeping themselves safe.

- Someone's ability to keep their housing is at risk due to behavior they cannot control.
- Someone's use of drugs or alcohol places their life at imminent risk

INFORMATION YOU SHOULD PROVIDE THE POLICE

Tell the police:

- about any possible weapons—what they are and where they are kept
- about any threats to harm themselves or someone else; what was threatened; if they have the ability to carry out the threat; if there is any history of them trying to harm themselves or others
- if they are impaired or using drugs or alcohol.
- what will help them to feel safe, calm and to trust others and what things make the situation worse.
- if there is someone they respond well to and/or trust
- if they have had problems in the past, tell the police what you know works to help and what things have not worked.

Strange Gift

The hot wind blows
across islands
of frustration and hope
we rise, astonished,
in a world filled with sadness,
bearing in our joined hands
the determined gift
of ourselves.

Susan Spalt

PART ONE

MENTAL ILLNESS

INTRODUCTION

The term "mental illness" is often misunderstood. What is meant when we say someone has a mental illness? Do they have a physical disorder, like cancer, diabetes, or heart disease? Are they struggling because of a traumatic experience or the difficulties of daily life? Professionals may speak of a mental health continuum. On one end lies the healthy person who functions well. At the other end lies the person with mental illness. Those in the middle are struggling to cope because of a situation that is particularly difficult, challenging or traumatic. The idea of a continuum can be misleading. It suggests that mental illnesses are the consequence of not being able to function rather than a cause. In reality, even people who are capable of excellent coping skills can develop a mental illness. Mental illnesses are not the necessary consequence of poor coping skills or difficult life situations.

In general, *mental illness* is a physical disorder that impacts the brain. It affects how people think, feel, and act. Mental Illnesses cannot be fixed or controlled by will-power. They cannot be overcome by developing new and better coping skills or changing our situation. Mental illnesses are known to have a genetic component. They are biological. The emergence of symptoms can sometimes be linked to experiences, but mental illnesses are not caused by environment alone. Just as lifestyle can contribute to heart disease in someone with a genetic pre-disposition, experiences can contribute to the onset of mental illness. Examples of this might be prolonged stress, use of drugs that alter the brain's chemistry, abuse, or trauma.

It is important to note that for many individuals who develop symptoms of a mental illness there is no precipitating event. It may not be possible to point to something and say "this is why it started." Many people ask "Why me?" Why someone in my family? There are no easy answers. In the end, it may be impossible to know why someone developed a mental illness. What is important is understanding that mental illness is not willful bad behavior. It is not something that someone can control. Mental illness is *not their fault nor is it yours.*

Common mental illnesses include clinical depression, anxiety disorders, schizophrenia, bipolar disorder, obsessive-compulsive disorder, ADD, ADHD, some forms of addiction, eating disorders and schizo-affective disorder. These disorders are NOT the same as going through a stressful or distressing experience, sadness or transient struggles. We all experience difficult life situations and occasional problems coping. While these experiences can even be debilitating, they are not the same as having a mental illness.

There is no medical test for diagnosing mental illness. Diagnosis is made by observing the symptoms a person experiences. This is a complex process. Illnesses may share the same or similar symptoms. Different people with the same diagnosis may have different symptoms. The same person may experience different symptoms at different times. People who do not have a mental illness can appear symptomatic when they are struggling. Diagnosis should always be made by an appropriate professional. A competent professional will take as much time as they need in determining someone's diagnosis. The diagnosis is not, however, as important as finding what combination of treatments will best manage their symptoms.

If you or someone you love was diagnosed with cancer, heart disease, or any chronic condition, if you or they were in a significant accident, no one would expect treatment or recovery to be accomplished in just one day, one week, or even one month. You know this is going to take time. You would expect ups and downs, successes, and setbacks. The same is true when treating mental illness. Time, support, education, appropriate treatment, experience, and patience are all required. The two most important words to remember are *patience* and *process*.

> ***Remember: regardless of diagnosis and symptoms, human beings are incredibly resilient. Recovery, stability, and rehabilitation are always possible. <u>Rehabilitation is a process</u>. Treatment of mental illness is not as simple as taking a pill. Even when there is a pill that works, medications have side-effects. Some are quite significant. Learning to manage symptoms is a process that has many stages, involves many factors, and takes time.*

Mental Illness or Distress?

Matthew Miller, age 20, has fallen apart in recent months. He had to drop out of college and is now living at home. When Matthew returned, he was quite angry and blamed his parents for everything wrong in his life. He could not sleep. He became disruptive to the lives of everyone in his family. Matthew often did not change his clothes or shower. He stopped eating and had lost weight. He became pre-occupied with damage to the environment and would speak about this incessantly. His parents finally got him to see a family doctor who referred him to a psychiatrist. Several months and appointments later, Matthew was diagnosed with Bipolar Disorder. He was hospitalized and put on medications. He is more stable and seems to be making progress but is still moody and still blames his family, especially his mother. He continues to have frequent angry outbursts.

Matthew's mother, Marjorie, has been having trouble sleeping. She has felt tired and very sad. She also has lost weight. There are mornings she has called in sick to work because she can't make herself go in. She sometimes finds herself snapping at her husband and other children because of minor things. She knows the holidays are not far off and she dreads having to explain to family and friends why Matthew is not in college. She blames herself and can't stop thinking what a bad mother she is and is sure that this is what others also think. Marjorie's physician recommended counseling for Marjorie and prescribed an anti-depressant. She has followed through on these recommendations and is doing much better.

While Matthew's diagnosis may or may not stay the same, it is likely he has a mental illness—and with persistence, love, and support he and his family can learn to manage it. Matthew's mother, Marjorie, on the other hand, is most likely suffering from situational depression. Dealing with a family member who has a severe mental illness is stressful, exhausting— and depressing.

What We Wish Someone Had Told Us

1. The first symptom of mental illness is often behavioral: moodiness, trouble sleeping, changes in eating or appetite, extreme reactions. It may be difficult to know what is causing the changes you see. It is not always clear that someone is developing a mental illness.

2. The name for the disease is not critical. If you go to five doctors, you may get five diagnoses. Diagnosis is a clinician's best attempt to summarize symptoms and the problems they cause. What is essential is how symptoms affect someone's function and what works to treat them.
    a. Symptoms may vary from person to person or over time in the same person.
    b. Different illnesses may share signs or symptoms.
    c. The effect of symptoms on function may vary.
    d. Some people have more than one illness.
    e. Diagnoses can change.

3. No treatment works for every person in the same way. The treatments that work for any person will be specific to them.

4. This is a process. Some symptoms resolve quickly with medication. It can take up to a year for other symptoms to resolve. Learning about symptoms and the combination of treatments and lifestyle changes that best manage them takes time. It will involve trial-and-error.

5. People who have a mental illness do best when:
    a. They have strong, consistent support from people that understand learning to treat and live with a mental illness takes time and that there will be setbacks.
    b. Their treatment is individualized, flexible, and makes use of a variety of services.

6. There are things you have no control over. You cannot control how someone views their illness. You cannot control whether they accept treatment. You cannot make someone well and you cannot make them understand they are not well. You can only control your response in a situation that is often painful and difficult.

7. If you are part of someone's support system, it is critical you find support. Support from friends, your faith community, a therapist, or a supportive organization such as NAMI, will help you help your loved one.

8. You can do everything humanly possible and still have your family member get worse. Agnosia is a symptom that leaves people unable to see there is anything wrong with them. This is not within their control—or yours. Sometimes all you can do is to try to maintain a relationship and give support. Sometimes a family member is so resistant to treatment that they would literally rather "die than get help." Sometimes they may choose to not take care of themselves. Sometimes they may die of suicide. It is important to remember:

- The best we can do is not always enough
- This illness is painful and frustrating illness for the family and for your loved one
- You are not alone and you must get help and support for yourself
- Learn what you can. And repeat to yourself: I did not cause this illness and I cannot cure it.

People who have mental illnesses can and do get better. There is hope. People with mental illnesses have good lives and relationships. Mental illnesses are not death sentences—even for those who experience severe and persistent symptoms. Symptoms can be managed. It is not quick. It is not easy. It can take many years. Those years can be harder than anything you imagined. But rehabilitation is possible.

- I wish I knew better coping strategies
- I wish I knew not to be afraid to seek help for symptoms
- I wish I knew not to be afraid to go talk to doctor about medication (and get genetic testing to determine which one might work)
- I wish I knew that people with mental illness are just like everyone else with hopes, dreams and aspirations
- I wish I would know there is solution that can make the hurt go away
- I wish I knew whether there was an end
- I wish I knew that what I experienced was mental illness—that it is common, no shame
- Everyone has some connection with mental illness; don't be afraid to speak up or out
- I wish I knew that mentally ill people are required to ride in a police car with handcuffs on way to hospital. Should be an ambulance
- I wish I knew more about mental illness
- I wish I knew how little control parents/patients have
- I wish I knew that at 18 years old, even when a teen is hospitalized the laws prevent parents from getting info from doctors right away.
- I wish I knew that the first therapist may not be a good "fit"

HOW DO YOU KNOW IF SOMEONE NEEDS PROFESSIONAL HELP?

In early stages, mental illness can be difficult to distinguish from other difficulties that someone may have. The symptoms may involve changes in behavior. This is often true when people are struggling, even when no mental illness is present. It is vital that we not think "mental illness" every time a problem arises. No one handles everything well all of the time. No one can claim a life free from difficulty. Everyone struggles at times. When we confuse going through a difficult time with being symptomatic, everyday experiences may look like illness.

On the other hand, early intervention can change the course that mental illness takes. The average time between first experiencing symptoms and treatment is one year. As some mental illnesses are progressive, intervening early on can change the severity of the symptoms that will be experienced. Because symptoms can intensify over time, the later someone first receives treatment the more likely much of their life will have been damaged: relationships have fallen apart, jobs have been lost, they have dropped out of school, they have lost their home, etc.

When someone is struggling, it can be difficult to know if professional assistance is needed. There are no hard or fast guidelines, but there are two key questions you can ask: 1) How is your loved one functioning? 2) Do you think there is a problem? In answering these questions, there are three key areas to consider: Relationships, Self-Care, and Responsibilities.

Interpersonal Relationships

We all are involved in many types of relationships. We interact with others every day: teacher, co-workers, people at our local stores and banks. We are parents, children, partners, friends. Human beings need relationships. We need to interact with others in a way that is affirming and nurturing. This is not to say that we don't experience conflict, or go through painful periods in relationships. They are challenging. Both intimate and professional relationships may challenge us to become more skillful in our interactions with others. When relationships are consistently marked by conflict, failure to communicate, or when they provide few rewards or healthy interactions, it is cause for concern.

Situations which may indicate a problem include:
- ending established relationships <u>and</u> not developing new ones;
- becoming or feeling disconnected, isolated, and alone;
- social and personal interactions that are marked by conflict;
- failure to communicate or work effectively with others;
- choosing only relationships with problematic shared interests such as drug or alcohol use, suicide, weapons, sex, etc.

It is not unusual for people to have problems with parents, teachers, co-workers, or even with friends. However, consistent and ongoing issues in all kinds of relationships, regardless of the degree of intimacy, are a clear indication that someone is struggling.

Activities of Daily Living

Activities of Daily Living is a term used in Occupational Therapy. It refers to the things that we all need to do every day to take care of ourselves. This includes eating, getting dressed, bathing, grooming, changing clothes, caring for pets, cooking or cleaning. When someone who has done these and similar activities/tasks without problem becomes increasingly unable it is a sign there is a problem. Mental illnesses can alter an individual's cognitive abilities. Two examples of functions which mental illness can affect are initiation and task sequencing.

Initiation

>Everything we do must begin with an initial act. This may literally mean moving, such as standing up to get something to eat, or it may be something as simple as thinking of dinner and what we might like to eat. As someone with mental illness becomes more symptomatic, they can lose the ability to begin activities. They literally cannot get started. This is often mistaken for laziness, disinterest, or irresponsibility. It may be particularly difficult to parse this out in adolescents for whom this can be a common challenge.

Task Sequencing

>All activities require a sequence of steps, often in a specific order. This is called task sequencing. People are often completely unaware that their brain is moving them through a logical sequence of steps. For example: when someone wants

a drink of water they must: 1) open the cupboard, 2) choose a glass, 3) take the glass from the cupboard, 4) turn on the water, 5) check the water temperature, 6) adjust the temperature, 7) check the temperature again, 8) put the glass under the faucet, 9) fill the glass, 10) turn off the water. To brush their teeth, they must pick up the toothbrush, get the toothpaste, open the toothpaste, put toothpaste on the brush, put the brush in their mouth. Mental illnesses can interrupt the brain's ability to lay out these steps or follow the steps all the way through from beginning to end. This interruption can be so severe that even things someone has done since they were a toddler become too overwhelming, or the steps too complicated to follow.

Having difficulty with initiation, task sequencing, and other cognitive changes impair an individual's ability to carry out activities of daily living. Someone may develop poor hygiene. They may not wash, shampoo, change their clothes, or brush their teeth. They may not eat properly and begin to lose weight. They may stop engaging in activities or doing things for themselves or in their home which they have always done without a problem. Other symptoms such as disorganized thought, poor memory, loss of reasoning skills, or confusion also negatively affect someone's ability to do all of these things. When a person stops caring for themselves or becomes unable to do things they have done with no difficulty this is an indication that something is wrong.

Responsibilities

Everyone has responsibilities. For someone in school, responsibilities include showing up for class, studying, doing homework, and completing projects. If someone works, they are responsible for showing up and carrying out the duties of their job. The symptoms of mental illness can interfere with someone's ability to carry out responsibilities. Apathy or difficulty with self-initiation and depression may make it difficult or impossible to focus or have the energy needed to work. People suffering from these symptoms may even have difficulty just showing up. Disorganized thoughts, confusion, and negative symptoms make it difficult to carry out the tasks that are required.

Summary

When the ability to function becomes impaired or deteriorates, life begins to fall apart. Friendships and other relationships become filled with conflict and may fail. People find themselves failing in school or losing their job. Self-care and home life suffer. As these things happen, people often do not understand why. Most importantly, they find themselves unable to do the things needed to stop the downward spiral.

Your knowledge of the person you love is critical and valuable. Do you believe something is wrong? It can be challenging to put our finger on exactly what is not working—why it is that we sense things have changed. Trying to identify symptoms—especially if you are not familiar with mental illnesses—is difficult. There can be many reasons why a person seems to be struggling, and it can seem extreme, even as we worry, to jump to the conclusion that there is something psychiatric going on.

The bottom line is this: listen to yourself. You know and love this person. If, at the end of the day you just feel something is wrong—even if you can't say what or why—trust yourself.

> You will find a list of common types of mental illnesses and symptoms that people may experience in the Appendix on **p. 203**.

> Parents know that behavior changes among teens are common. Young adults can be impulsive, and moody. Tempers may easily flair. Teens often experiment with different interests and ways of interacting with others. Not all of these attempts are pleasant or successful. This is quite simply a difficult time of life. Some young people go through this period with minimal difficulty. Many will experience problems at one time or another. Reactions to the pressure and changes faced by youth can be mistaken for the early symptoms of mental illness. And vice-versa. Sometimes you cannot tell what is going on until time has passed and more information is available.
>
> It is important to keep in mind that applying a magnifying glass to every struggle or examining every mood change or conflict for signs of impending mental illness will place unbearable stress on parents and children. It will not prevent mental illness. If you are concerned and your efforts to help your teen through whatever difficulty they face aren't working, help your teen to find the support that they need. Most problems will not be because of mental illness. If a mental illness is involved, that inevitably will become clear.

IS PROFESSIONAL HELP NEEDED?
KEY QUESTIONS TO ASK

1. Do you believe something is wrong?
2. Has my loved one's personality changed in a negative or harmful way?
3. Are there problems with daily functioning? Are personal care and hygiene good? Have eating habits changed? Are there relationship problems? Is there increased isolation? Are there problems handling the normal daily stresses and responsibilities?
4. Are any combination of the following consistently present: aggression, anger or joy which is extreme and/or not appropriate to the situation, withdrawal, isolation, flat affect (the absence of emotion), extreme or rapid mood changes, difficulty concentrating, impulsivity, extreme emotional responses, depressed or consistently sad mood/tearfulness, emotions which are inappropriate to the situation and/or circumstances, concerning drug or alcohol use, lack of interest in activities they enjoyed, confusion, memory problems, detachment, fear, odd or disjointed speech, illogical thought or perceptions, intolerance to stress or change, striking out physically at others, self-harm, threatening others or self, pre-occupation, obsessive thoughts, compulsive behaviors (washing, locking doors, rituals with activities that do not require them), changes in sleep, in eating, confusion, disorganized thought, lack of judgment and reasoning where once present, placing one's self in dangerous situations without awareness of or concern for danger.

It is important to consider how many of these things are happening, how often, and how long there have been problems. The impact these things have on someone's ability to function is key. Answering yes to any question does not mean there is mental illness. It can indicate you should seek a professional's help.

When you believe something is wrong seek outside or professional assistance. It is hard to sort out what is really going on alone. The person having difficulty may not see it. Honor your sense of yourself and of those you care about.

**Any time you believe that you or someone you care about are in danger you must seek help.

We are all familiar with the mantra: suicidal or homicidal. If someone is in danger of harming themselves or others then intervention is necessary. There is no benefit in waiting. A person may also be at risk if their judgment is so impaired they place themselves in danger and are unable to see danger exists or protect themselves. Someone is at risk if they are unable to care for themselves: to eat, sleep, wash or clean themselves. Finally, someone may be in danger if drug or alcohol use places them in immediate risk of dying.

When <u>there is the imminent potential for injury or death intervention is needed.</u>

If You Suspect a Problem: Where to Start

There are many things you can do if you suspect that someone you love is having a problem. Below are some suggestions to get you started.

**Do not attempt to diagnose someone yourself. Diagnosis is a difficult process that requires training and experience. If you think someone may be symptomatic the best course of action is to seek professional help.

1. If you are concerned about someone, talk to them. While they may not know what is wrong or see what you see, they are probably aware things have changed and/or that something is wrong.

2. If your loved one is in school, consider speaking with the school guidance counselor, nurse, or trusted teachers. They may have also noted changes and/or problems. They are likely to have some experience with the situations that young people face as well as knowing resources available to you.

    **Many schools have *student assistance teams of specially trained staff. They can evaluate student behaviors, meet with parents, make recommendations and provide in-school support.*

3. Leaders of faith communities are a good resource for discussing concerns, obtaining support, and seeking information on resources.

4. Don't underestimate the value of talking to a friend. Often friends not only know our family and us, but they are also removed enough to help put our concerns in perspective or validate them. They are also an invaluable source of support.

5. Educate yourself: speak to organizations that provide information on mental health issues, mental illnesses, and offer guidance for family members and friends. Do an internet search. Use resources like the ones listed in the appendix of this guide.

6. Make an appointment for your loved one with an appropriate professional. Psychologists, Psychiatric Social Workers, or Clinical Nurse Specialists are good starting points. They can offer counseling and support. They are trained to recognize mental illnesses and distinguish them from other difficulties. For more information on types of mental health professionals see the section on **p. 124.**

7. Local mental health organizations and your local LME/MCO (see **p. 145**) can assist in finding the resources available in your area, including crisis and assessment centers. They can also advise you on financial resources that may be available.

8. Speak to others whose lives have been impacted by mental illnesses. Organizations such as NAMI offer support groups for family and friends. They have people who you can talk to as you sort out your experiences and determine what options you have.//

9. You may find it helpful to seek help yourself. Helping someone cope with a mental illness is very stressful. Getting support is critical—and sometimes you need more than the valuable support friends can give.

****A Note on Finding the Right Professional

Not every professional is right for every patient. Shopping around is okay.

You want a professional who
- Your loved one trusts and who treats them with respect and dignity.
- Values their voice in the treatment process and listens to their unique concerns, needs, and goals.
- Will take time and partner with your loved one before determining a diagnosis and who is willing to change their diagnosis over time. It is not possible to diagnose someone in an hour.
- Believes that rehabilitation and a full life are possible.
- Will work to help your loved one learn how to manage their illness.
- Recognizes the importance of the family in treatment and recovery.
- Supports a healthy, ongoing relationship between their patient and h/her family/loved ones.

Not every auto mechanic is right for you and not every professional is right for every patient. Shopping around is okay.

For more on finding the right provider for your loved one see **p. 127.**

Reflections on Our Family's Experience With Mental Illness

Elizabeth

We were a typical suburban family with two active, happy daughters who loved sports and fun family outings, and enjoyed a close relationship with supportive grandparents who lived nearby. In elementary school, our younger daughter began to struggle with emotions and fears that sidelined her from school and extra-curricular activities, and we couldn't seem to find a way to help her. She was tested for learning disabilities and the school offered extra support, but her symptoms gradually grew more puzzling and more debilitating through her middle school years.

Meanwhile, our older daughter suddenly began having waves of uncharacteristically wild behavior in high school. We assumed this was normal teenage rebellion until we realized she had become paranoid. A doctor diagnosed her and immediately sent her to the psychiatric hospital. Our family was in shock. We did not understand what was happening to either of our daughters. While our older daughter responded quickly to medication and went back to school, our younger daughter continued to get worse even with multiple medication changes until she was hospitalized as well.

Many years and multiple hospitalizations later, we have learned quite a bit about how the mental health system works in this state. We have worked with many school counselors, therapists, and social workers who have helped advocate for our daughters. We have worked with many doctors who helped them—but some who didn't. We learned that keeping a log of everything was helpful, especially any major symptoms and medication changes. We also learned that all the best parenting advice in the world does not work when a child is suffering from symptoms of mental illness.

The hardest part of our journey for me has been that as much as we love them, we could not nurse them back to health in the same way as when they had the flu. There was no blood test or x-ray that could diagnose their illness so, at times, they did not believe they were sick and saw no reason to take medicine. Medicine does not work the same way on everyone's brain, so some medications made one daughter worse before we discovered a genetic test that determined which drugs were likely to be effective.

We want other families to know that mental illness changes the behavior of a person so much that it may be difficult to recognize your family member, but that person is still inside. With appropriate treatment, recovery is slow but the brain has an amazing ability to grow and heal. We also hope that other families do not isolate themselves from their friends and community, as we did at the beginning. Mental illness is so common that most people know someone who has suffered or had a family member who suffered from mental illness. They just don't talk about it, until they hear someone else's story.

MENTAL ILLNESS AND REHABILITATION

Margaret's son, Dylan, had a severe, persistent mental illness, and he was actively symptomatic. He believed his life was the subject of a television show broadcast across the world by the United States government. He thought his family was aware of this but hid it because if they told the truth, he would be told they had died. In reality, the government would remove them from the show—his life.

Dylan's psychosis was fueled by unrelenting mania. He paced day and night. He could, at most, sleep for 2 hours here and there. He chain-smoked. He stood in the shower several times a day until the hot water ran out, letting it pour over his body as he tried to relax while he sobbed. He could not eat. He did not trust anyone—even the family he believed was trying to protect him. He thought cameras were always on him. In his mind, the people around him in public, strangers, all knew who he was. They saw him on TV. They could tune in 24/7 to the video that broadcast his every movement, every conversation, every thought. The stress of this was becoming unbearable. There was no place he could go where he could be alone even for one moment.

When his family hospitalized him, he was furious. He was being punished for trying to break away from those controlling his life—from the prison the government kept him in. Misguided, thinking they protected him, his family had become government pawns to keep him imprisoned.

When Margaret visited Dylan, he would yell at her. She was betraying him. She was harming him. She had left him to others to force medication on him that would numb his mind, rob him of his will, and make him compliant. Dylan wanted his life back and she had handed him to people who would drug him to keep it. He would never forgive her. On this day he had been particularly brutal. His pain was palpable. His anger against her the only weapon he possessed. When it became clear her presence was only making things worse, Margaret left.

A nurse followed her—unlocking doors—unlocking the elevator in the small foyer. He stood with her as she waited. She tried to hide her tears. You know, the nurse said to her, I was just like him. <u>I was as bad as he is right now.</u>

The nurse explained to Margaret that he too had a mental illness. He told her that he had been just as symptomatic, as delusional, as psychotic. He had been as sick as Dylan. He too had been in and out of hospitals.

He can get better, the nurse told her. <u>Don't give up on him.</u>

Margaret has never forgotten that nurse. Of all the people—the doctors, the nurses, the social workers, the case managers, the counselors—he was the only one who had said, He can get better. And he had stood before her—living proof. Don't give up.

When we hear that someone has recovered from illness, we picture them healed. The illness is gone. However, recovery can mean that symptoms are controlled even though the illness remains. One way that the symptoms of a chronic condition are controlled is through rehabilitation. Rehabilitation is the process of learning to manage long-term, chronic illness. This includes helping people make changes that will help them to live a life that is satisfying and rewarding.

Mental illnesses don't go away. Some symptoms do resolve so that treatment is no longer needed. There is always some risk that symptoms will re-occur, though and people may need to make changes in different areas of their life to prevent this. Many people need ongoing treatment to manage symptoms. Even severe and persistent mental illnesses (SPMI), known for debilitating and severe chronic symptoms, can be managed. Symptoms may recur or worsen necessitating lifestyle changes. Sometimes symptoms recur even with treatment. It will take time to find appropriate treatments and to adjust to the impact of symptoms. Most people, however, can do so.

The ADA (Americans with Disabilities Act) defines disability as an impairment that substantially limits one or more major life activities. This includes people who have experienced impairment in the past *even if they are not currently impaired*. While the term disability may have negative connotations, people with disabling conditions live very well. The recognition that someone can live and function with a disability as well as someone who is not impaired has significantly shaped our social landscape. Technology has given us the ability to change the way that we do things. This and other progress has re-defined what is meant by impairment. These changes and the way they affect how we view disabling conditions mean that we no longer consider many disabling conditions negatively, with pity, or without hope.

The exception is mental illness. Unlike just about any other disabling condition, these are associated with a distinct lack of hope.

Our mental health system often does not view symptoms with the expectation that they will be well managed. There is no anticipation that those who experience symptoms will have fulfilling lives—especially when symptoms are severe. Mental illness is often viewed, even by the professionals treating it, as a dismal terrain laden with disaster, loss of potential, pain, and unremitting failure. The world expects those with mental illnesses will have symptoms that are never managed or controlled. The image of a person with a mental illness is that of a homeless psychotic person rooting through trash cans and yelling at strangers. It is no surprise that for many, a diagnosis of severe mental illness feels like a sentence of death.

We often deal with these illnesses as if they are tragedies that can only be contained and controlled. This is, in part, due to how recent the use of medication still is. It has only been 60 years since the advent of medication and the realization that symptoms could be controlled or ameliorated at all. However, this is also due to the failure of the mental health system itself.

The treatment system can be fragmented and services offered in a piecemeal fashion. The system is structured to respond to crisis and ill-equipped to provide the long-term supports that sustain stability and continued gains. Service providers are often over-taxed and unable to meet any but the most basic needs of those they serve. The difficulty faced in obtaining just basic medical care makes it difficult, if not impossible, for anyone to improve in a meaningful way. The focus of treatment is often medication because this is the easiest and most simple service to provide. The consequence of this, however, is that the range of treatments and supports needed to live with a chronic disabling condition successfully are neglected. Treatment providers all too often fail to engage those they treat. They may not encourage people to identify for themselves what their needs, their priorities, and their best lives look like. Nor are they responsive to what people say. If mental illnesses stand alone among disabling conditions in their lack of hope, it is in part because the mental health system stands alone in its inability to provide it. The medical system does not understand, view, or approach mental illnesses as it views other disabling conditions: with an eye to rehabilitation. It does not embrace the basic premise that *he can get better,* nor convey the message, *don't give up.*

Rehabilitation from any chronic or disabling condition means utilizing treatments that manage symptoms and adapting how things are done so the condition interferes or creates as few problems as possible. Learning to live with a mental illness requires identifying limitations and developing methods for dealing with them. It requires exploring and discovering the best ways to manage the symptoms that someone experiences. A person who wants to learn how to live well with a disability may need to find new ways to do things. They must explore and identify treatments that suit them. Even when treatment provides relief from symptoms, there may be situations or times when symptoms become exacerbated. They will then have to learn how to identify and manage those times. Rehabilitation depends on someone being able to recognize and appreciate their own talents and skills and use them to build a meaningful life. Each person who is trying to live well with a chronic condition must come to understand their unique condition, situation, what works for them, what causes difficulty, and then develop effective skills for managing all of these things.

When someone you love is diagnosed with a mental illness, your role is no different than if they were diagnosed with any other disabling condition. You are their support as they learn how to cope and live well with it. The challenges you face will be compounded because the mental health system is not oriented this way. Especially when someone has a severe and persistent mental illness, you may be told early on that they are always going to be like this; that some people don't get better. You may be reminded that agnosia—the inability to see that one is symptomatic—is a key part of mental illness. You may be told agnosia makes these illnesses impossible to treat. You may be advised to expect relapses in drug or alcohol use or have statistics cited to you about how many people don't take the medications. In other words, as you try to figure out how it is that someone learns to live well with a mental illness, you may be told not to get your hopes up because often, they don't.

This is terrifying. It is terrifying to envision your child or anyone you love living homeless on the streets, incoherent. It is heartbreaking to imagine a solitary, isolated existence spent in a one-room walk-up battling depression for anyone you care about. It is chilling to worry about drug-overdoses, missing persons, lost opportunities, violent encounters with the police. What is most horrifying of all is the fact that it does not have to be this way. A diagnosis of mental illness, even severe mental illness, does not mean there is no hope. You are facing this diagnosis in a system that does not work well.

Rehabilitation-based-recovery is not the overarching vision of the mental health system today. This means that <u>you</u> must provide this focus, and you can. This does not mean you are responsible for your loved one's treatment but rather that your support is necessary to provide what the system will not.

One point is essential here: whether a toddler, teen, young adult, your child, sibling, or spouse—your loved one will pick up how you view this illness, them, and the prospects for their life. If you find this illness shameful—they will feel that shame. If you consider their illness something that must be hidden, they will believe they embarrass you. If you find them noxious, they will see themselves this way—at least through your eyes. If you believe they cannot recover, that is the direction they will be shown.

The greatest gift you can give the person you love is the knowledge that this is a medical condition which they have no control over and it is not their fault or their choice. The understanding that there is nothing shameful in them or in their symptoms. The belief that this illness can be treated. The expectation that it will be treated. And the hope for a life which is good and meaningful. Know. Understand. Believe. Expect. Hope. And convey this in everything you do.

The question is not whether these things can happen—the question is how. There will be many things you do not have control over when it comes to the person you love and mental illness. One thing you absolutely control is **how you choose to define what it means to have a mental illness.** What do you want most for those you love– in the way they see themselves, in how the world sees them, in what they achieve? Believe that and convey what you believe in everything you do.

Today, Dylan is a college student who maintains a 3.9 GPA. He lives on his own and is self-supporting. He did get better.

DM

I was in graduate school when I was diagnosed with depression and prescribed Prozac. I struggled mightily against the diagnosis; did not want to take medication; did not believe I could be depressed. I was a happy person; a normal person; not a crazy person. But I started taking Prozac and within a couple of weeks, I realized I hadn't had a clue about what it meant to be happy. Suddenly, life seemed much easier, much more manageable, and I was able to sleep a full night's sleep more than 3-4 times a week. I finished my master's degree and decided to pursue a doctorate. About 7 years after being diagnosed with depression, my diagnosis was changed to bipolar II.

My earliest memory of depression was when I was five. My earliest memory of an episode of mania was when I was 16: I woke up one Saturday and decided I wanted to learn to bake bread. I got out several of my mom's cookbooks, found a recipe for white bread, a recipe for whole wheat bread, a recipe for raisin bread, a recipe for pumpernickel bread, and 3 others that I can't remember. I proceeded to make 16 loaves of bread that day, and no one in my family seemed to think that was odd!

But I am really lucky. I have a cocktail of medications that work for me. I have never attempted suicide although I have been close many times. I have never been hospitalized. Given that I have a mental illness, bipolar II is a pretty good one to have. Bipolar is treatable and with the cocktail of medications, I am very stable. I haven't had a severe depressive episode in over 5 years.

I've always eventually found a way to climb out of that abyss of depression. I've always had someone to hold on to me or found just a little bit of something to reach out to someone. I've always found a handhold in the wall of that abyss.

I would venture to guess that no one in my life would ever imagine that I have a mental illness. I live a normal life, hold down a job, and am in a wonderful marriage with the love of my life.

Adjustment to Mental Illness

Chronic illness affects those who live with it and those who love them. The exact impact will be shaped in part by how everyone adjusts to the realities of this illness. Those who find hope are able to come to envision a life that is good, valuable, meaningful, and fulfilling while living with a chronic illness. Someone who lives with a chronic illness and those who love them do best when they can see the potential for managing the illness and meeting the challenges it brings. This often means that first they must let go of *who they have been.*

Think of it this way—a person's identity—who they believe themselves to be—depends on many things. It is a product of what they do, their work, education, faith, relationships, how they understand themselves, their family, what is important to them, and what they picture for the future. When a chronic illness occurs, it can change any or all of these things. Everything that person thought they knew may no longer be true. That includes who they thought they were. Consider the parents who envisioned how their child's life might unfold: school, friends, work, marriage, grandchildren. When their child develops a disabling illness, it may cast doubt on everything they expected to happen. They must come to know the person they love in a new way. The life they expected very likely will change in some way. Family members may suddenly face the possibility that their loved one is going to need long-term help, or is not able to carry out their responsibilities or obligations any longer. The need for money or insurance may change plans for work or retirement. It may be possible to do things still, but many things may need to be done differently now.

For the person who develops mental illness, the changes are more life-altering. The child at college may need to come home to live. The person who worked two jobs may only be able to work part-time. They may have to take medication several times a day. They may not be able to do the things their peers do. Medication may make them sleep a lot. They may gain weight. They may lose weight. All-nighters, early meetings, or first shift work may become impossible. They may feel different from the people around them because of their experience and the way they have to do things. Symptoms may change the way they interact with others and the way others respond to them. Relationships may change or disappear. They may find dating or social interactions awkward and difficult.

The beliefs or images that you, your family, and your loved one have about mental illnesses and the people who have them get poured into this mix. Some people believe that dealing with symptoms is a matter of willpower and when this fails that it is because of a lack of self-control. Individuals with mental illnesses may be seen as "the crazy ones," weird, even frightening or dangerous. Some people believe the mother or the father is to blame if a child develops symptoms. They blame poor parenting, lack of rules, neglect. They think things like, "Great parents have great kids." How you, your family, and your loved one have viewed people with mental illness and what you believe about why people develop symptoms will impact how all of you respond when someone becomes ill.

As someone learns how to live with a mental illness, they must re-define their identity and what they expect for their life. Breaking this process into stages can help us to understand our experiences and what to expect. People go through the same identifiable stages in their own unique way anytime they face major changes in their life. These stages are shock or disbelief, denial, bargaining, guilt, anger, grief, and acceptance/hope. They can be very helpful in understanding what someone who has developed a chronic illness is going through. They can help us to understand our own response. Adjustment to profound life events requires a process of internal struggle and change. On the other side are acceptance and hope.

The process of adjusting to and accepting a chronic illness and/or disabling condition involve recognizing, adjusting to, and accepting the impact that this has on our lives. It impacts how we see and know ourselves. There are things that have changed, will change, or will be lost. We have to grieve the things that are no longer before we can feel positively about what will be. The emotions, and thoughts we struggle with during this process are hard and sometimes less than noble. That is common, and it is okay. There are things you may resent, and things you may hate. It is hard to let go of what was familiar and what we always understood. It is important to understand that no one goes through these stages in a strictly linear way or in the same way. One person may move through a stage only to find that they return to it three stages down the line—more than once. Another may seem to skip that stage altogether. Someone else may experience two stages at the same time. The way that you and/or other family members go through this process will be unique to each of you—your personality, your experiences, your situation, the nature and severity of the illness you face, your ability to cope, how well those around you cope. As symptoms change, as someone's condition or circumstances change you or they may find yourselves going through all or any part of this process again.

- **Shock**: Shock can be described as a feeling of being disconnected from our emotions or from things which are happening around us. Our first response when something unexpected, profound, or shattering occurs is to experience disbelief. We may not have any emotion or feel numb. It can be hard to feel that what is happening is real. We may seem to be just going through the motions as we respond. It is impossible to know the impact that mental illness will have at the onset: all of the things it will impact, what challenges there will be, how things will change. Even if you have been living with someone who is symptomatic for a while, when you are first told definitively what is wrong it opens the door to more questions than answers. Furthermore, anytime the situation significantly changes—when new and unforeseen challenges present—you may be taken off-guard and feel stunned, surprised, in shock, once again.

- **Denial:** Denial is an inability or refusal to believe what is true. This may be intentional as when someone decides: *I refuse to believe that he isn't in control of how he is acting.* It can also be the result of forces, beliefs, or circumstances that cause us to question the truth. Someone in denial about mental illness may reject the diagnosis or the necessity of treatment. They may deny that mental illness is present at all or minimize the impact of symptoms or their severity. They may attribute what is happening to other things. People deny what hurts because they desperately want life to be the same or they at least want to be able to control what is happening.

> I wish I had known how easy it is to blame a child who's experiencing mental illness for his/her difficult behavior—even while knowing it is not their fault. The guilt it generates is tremendous.

When dealing with an illness it is sometimes hard to know what is prudent caution and what is denial. Doctors have been known to misdiagnose people. The literature is full of stories of people who persisted in the face of medicine telling them something was true only to be vindicated when it was found to be false. How do you know? In the end, if it is a mental illness, it is a mental illness. No amount of not wanting it to be, or not wanting to need treatment will make it go away. If you or a loved one struggle with a diagnosis or the treatment that is needed and must try to find another answer or solution—this is what you must do. And this is ok. If someone is going to live well with a mental illness, they must fully understand and accept all the dimensions of these illnesses. There is no halfway. For some people, this may require making sure there is no other way.

- **Bargaining**: Bargaining is an attempt to negotiate with the realities that we face hoping that in doing so we can change something. Bargaining may take the form of trying different ways to manage symptoms when we know they must be managed but do not want to do what works. Family members may be bargaining when they suggest giving someone money, letting them live at home again, or whatever it will take if doing these things will make them not be sick. They may wonder if someone could just find new friends, a new job would it stop them from doing things that are harmful? Bargaining can also be an emotional or even spiritual phase. We fantasize that if we do this, give that, change ourselves, then things will change. If faith is important, this can be a time when someone tries to make deals with their God: making promises or asking for miracles. It can be a time which leads any person to re-think everything that they believe about life and their role here.

- **Guilt**: Someone who is experiencing guilt blames or holds themselves responsible for something that has happened. Every parent knows that there are infinite ways that their decisions can lead to guilt. Parents can feel guilty over what they did and what they did not do. Overacting or failing to act. They feel guilty about things that they did not have the power to cause or prevent. When anyone makes decisions it is often without the clear information that comes with the consequences—and yet many people feel as much guilt over as if they had absolutely known the outcome. It is very easy when someone we love becomes sick for us to wonder if we had any role in this happening. Did we somehow cause this to happen? It is even easier for us to feel guilt over how we treated someone who was developing symptoms before we knew what was happening. Oddly, feeling guilt can give us a sense of control that we have lost. If we caused this, or if we made it worse, if somehow we are a part of what has happened—then maybe we also have the power to fix it.

- **Anger:** Anger or frustration are natural responses when someone finds that something is very wrong and it cannot be fixed. Anger is also a way that many people experience or express hurt, fear, and powerlessness. Sometimes people who are angry must find someone or something to blame for what has happened. They blame God, themselves, the person who is ill, their family, even life. Mental illness is a life-changing condition. It changes everything for the person who has a mental illness and for the people closest to them. It is normal to be angry about what has happened, what has changed, and what may be lost. Anger or frustration is not wrong. These can be helpful emotions when they tell us something is wrong. What may be problematic is the way that anger is expressed. It is easy for an angry person to do or say things which are hurtful to others and to themselves. Screaming or yelling, throwing things sometimes feels like a great idea that releases the tension building up inside of us. Whatever relief someone feels for the exact 2.5 seconds those actions take will be made many times worse by the consequences. When you feel anger accept your anger and your frustration. Don't try to change the way you feel, or make it go away. You have a right to feel angry. Find a way to express the anger you feel that is not directed at someone else or yourself and which is not going to harm anyone.

- **Grief:** Grief is a process people go through when they experience a loss. People can grieve many types of loss. The process of grieving certain kinds of loss never ends. It changes. The sadness or pain is not as intense or acute. People feel joy again. But there are some losses that always in some way, hurt. Grief is a mix of emotions that include feeling pain, sadness, anger, fear, powerlessness, disorientation or a sense of things no longer being known or familiar. When someone's life is unalterably changed, it can be painful. As people adjust to the reality of mental illness, they may go through a period where they grieve. They recognize that they cannot control this. They cannot make it go away. This just hurts.

- **Acceptance:** It is possible to find peace with mental illness. This does not happen quickly. People do not come to this at the same time or even in the same way. You may find peace when your loved one does not. One member of your family may continue to struggle long after others. Even when each of you find peace there may be moments or situations when you are plunged into this process all over again. However, whether symptoms are managed or not, it is possible to come to a place of understanding and accepting life as it now is. It is possible to make the changes need to manage living with this illness. There is hope. There will be happiness again.

Adjustment to Mental Illness for Those Experiencing Symptoms

Family members are not the only ones who must adjust when a mental illness develops. Someone who becomes symptomatic will go through the same process of adjustment but in a way that is distinct. Recognizing this is important. It means that not everything they do, say, or feel is the result of symptoms. Every struggle is not because of agnosia-fueled resistance. Consider how you would react if you were told that every day for the rest of your life you had to take a medication with significant side effects that will impact your ability to do things. Would you feel frustrated, angry, resentful? Would you grieve? Would you fight that diagnosis? Try to seek an alternative? Would you try to prove to others—or at least for yourself—that you could manage without treatment?

There are certainly unique challenges your loved faces as they adjust to living with a chronic illness:

1. **Resistance to treatment**
   Medications must be taken daily and may have unpleasant side-effects. Some treatments are not viewed favorably in some cultures, by peers, or in individual families (for example: in some cultures, counseling is considered to be a sign of weakness—especially for men) Treatments may affect the kind of life someone can live. People may be resistant to undergoing a specific treatment or treatment at all because of the problems that result. They may refuse or not adhere to treatment or experiment with alternative therapies.

   The most important consideration for treatment is how well someone is able to function. It is helpful to draw a line for yourself and the person you love. What do you consider non-functioning? What would signal intervention is needed? It is fair to tell someone you support their exploring how best to manage their illness but that you will step in if they become at risk.

Avoid power-struggles over treatment. Easier said than done, especially when the failure to treat symptoms this can have devastating consequences. The goal is that your loved one develops skill in choosing the treatments which will be best for them. What they want may not be what you prefer. They may choose to live with some degree of symptoms because side effects interfere with their ability to achieve their goals. They may choose treatments considered alternative because these fit their life, their image of themselves, or their priorities better.

2. **Feeling a loss of control**
   Americans place a high value on being in control. They value independence and autonomy. When someone develops a chronic illness their feeling of being in control and their sense of what they control is severely challenged. They experience symptoms that they cannot make disappear just by changing their attitude or the way that they think. They may require a specific treatment whether they want that treatment or not. They may be unable to do things due to symptoms or the side effects of medications. They do not control the way that their body functions and they may have no choice or only choices that are undesirable. For many, having to take medication is in itself a sign they are out of control.

   The idea that someone cannot control their behavior or their mind is one that is particularly difficult to grasp. While most people accept that they cannot always control what happens to them, they believe they do control how they act. If someone's responses seem uncontrolled at times, they are told they just need to try harder. All of this is, in fact, something of an illusion. One of the greatest struggles that anyone can face is reconciling just how little control anyone really has—even over themselves. Someone dealing with the loss of control caused by chronic illness may try to regain control in any way possible—controlling treatment—including medication—or refusing treatment altogether, emotionally controlling those around them. They may express anger, frustration, experience a loss of self-esteem, apathy, lack of motivation. They may give up dreams or nitpick at small things to try to control anything they can.

We wouldn't give a peanut butter sandwich to someone who has an allergy to peanuts and then tell them they can eat it if they just control how their body reacts: don't scratch and keep on taking breaths. Someone with a mental illness is no more in control of the symptoms they experience.

Support your loved one in controlling the things they have control over. This is not the time to argue about clothes, hairstyles, or the choice to listen to music 24/7. Acknowledge and empathize with them about the things they cannot control. Recognize and make allowances for the things that are out of their control—like how much their medicine makes them sleep. Help them to figure out ways to compensate: if their medicine means they have to sleep 12 hours they can still get to work by 8:00 but they need to go to bed earlier. Ask, don't tell. Suggest, don't order. And accept it when your suggestions are not taken. Provide options. Be open to someone doing something differently than you or everyone else, or the way it has always been done.

Everyone faces things we do not control. The task is not to gain control of these things but to find ways to accomplish our goals despite them. Your task is to support your loved one accepting what they cannot control, discovering what they have control over, and figuring out how to live their best life in light of both. Empower them to be active participants in their lives and in the world and to figure out how they can do this given the limitations of their illness. It may not be the way others do things, but that is not important. Support this in every way and on every level possible. And when nothing can be done, empathize with the frustration and grief they feel. Your job is to always believe in and support their resilience and power in a world where no one has complete control.

> *The Serenity Prayer*
>
> *God grant me the serenity*
> *To accept the things I cannot change;*
> *Courage to change the things I can;*
> *And wisdom to know the difference.*

3. **Vulnerability**
    Mental illnesses can affect mood, emotions, perception, and the way that someone processes information. The person living with mental illness may rely on others to affirm what they experience. Once symptoms are controlled someone living with mental illness may not be sure that they will know when symptoms begin to re-emerge. All of these things can make navigating the world a fearful thing. It requires a trust in others most people do not have to consider. Humans rely on their own capacity for interpreting the world around them. When illness impinges on someone's ability to interpret the world, they may feel worthless or incapable. Fear may lead them to withdraw or become isolated. It can also lead to distrust of others or defensiveness.

    Acknowledge how vulnerable someone might be when they cannot trust their own mind. Help your loved one discover ways to compensate for what their mind cannot do. This may include identifying someone they can trust to be truthful when they need to check their perceptions or beliefs. It may mean developing a checklist that will tell them when there is a problem. They may struggle with if, when, or how to share with others that they have a mental illness. Help them to develop ways to handle this. Help them to explore ways to feel safe so that they are able to have healthy relationships with others. Your loved one needs to be as independent and able to rely on themselves as possible. They do not need rescuing or someone who takes over for them.

4. **Identification With Their Illness**
    When speaking of persons with mental illnesses people often will say something such as: "The mentally ill...." 'He's bi-polar," She's depressed." The tendency is to conflate the person with their illness or symptoms. However, this reduces them to the details of their illness. It also disposes others to see what the person says, thinks, or does as a product of the illness. What would it mean if people referred those with breast cancer as cancerous?

    Someone living with a mental illness can begin to lose sight of who they are apart from their illness. Symptoms identify what they are like. A diagnosis determines what their life will be like. Everything else carries less weight or importance. Someone living with a mental illness can believe the negative images associated with their illness reflect who they are. The mental illness outweighs everything else. Consequently, they may lose self-esteem or identify with the illness itself. When someone loses sight of the qualities, goals, desires, and beliefs that they have apart from the illness and assume an identity that is viewed as bad or negative, they lose hope.

When someone is identified by their illness, it can cause frustration, anger, and alienation. When others do this, they easily can attribute everything that is felt, said, or done to illness. The experience that someone who lives with a mental illness has come to be discounted. However, not every passion is due to mania. Not every hurt a sign of depression. People living with mental illness are affected by life just as those who do not have a disease. When others do not distinguish between someone and their illness, they risk not seeing and not, even more importantly, *hearing* them. They also risk not trusting that the individual with mental illness can effectively act in their life even when they are not symptomatic. This will undermine a patient's ability to see themselves as competent and act accordingly.

Recognize, remember, and remind yourself that your loved is a complex person who experiences life fully. There will be bad days, bad moods, and also great moments, too. There will be frustrations and experiences of every kind. Listen to the person you love. Remember that even when they are symptomatic that things completely unrelated to their illness can result in them feeling upset, excited, angry, or hurt. See the person with hopes, dreams, feelings, and experiences distinct from symptoms and connect with them over and again.

5. **Stigma**
   Despite significant effort to change public perception negative images and false beliefs about mental illness continue. The political and media-led tendency to over-emphasize violent acts which are directly attributable to the symptoms of severe mental illness further hinder substantial progress in changing peo-

ple's perceptions. Imagine being told you have a disease that evokes fear or loathing. One about which the predominant images are of ranting, homeless madmen or mass shooters. How do you present this to a potential employer—especially when you may need some accommodation due to your medications or symptoms? How do you tell a new friend? A potential love interest? It is not unusual for families to even have difficulty sharing the fact that someone has a mental illness with extended family members. There are far too few positive images of mental illness, and most of them involve dead artists from ages past.

Support your loved one through countering stigma wherever and however you and they find it in how YOU act—what you express, believe, expect. **"The stigma is most damaging not when others see it in a certain way, but when we see it that way ourselves."—Michael Landsberg.** *Always be the voice that counters the illusion and affirms the right of the person you love to determine for him or herself what it means to have and to live with a mental illness.*

Chronic Sorrow

Years ago there was a Broadway play called "Joe Egg," about a couple whose child had a severe disability. The play centered on the difficulty this child encountered and how her parents' lives consequently fell apart. At intermission, the young actress would come out as herself—a child without a disabling condition—and announce the break. This poignantly illustrates what many desperately wish for, when faced with a condition that is disabling. Chronic Sorrow is a term used to describe the ongoing grief someone may feel in the face of a loved one's disability. It is an ongoing process of mourning.

When there is a death in the family, grief is intense. There is a defined beginning to the situation and more importantly, a clear end. The outcome is certain, allowing people to adjust, heal, and move forward. This does not mean grief is easy. The feeling of loss may never go away. What is mourned, however, is a time-limited event. When that event has ended, people can move on to find closure.

When someone becomes disabled with a condition that brings pain to them and those they love, the grieving process can be very different. The nature of mental illness means that the problems, the situations or events that must be dealt with, the things that are going well, and those which are going miserably, all change unpredictably and continually. There may be progress. Then there are setbacks. There are things to celebrate. And there are new losses. Symptoms vary. Their impact changes. How well the person is able to handle the changes. Emotions like anger, frustration, fear, hope, excitement, doubt, and elation are experienced over and again intensely and randomly. There are so many aspects of this illness that a person cannot ever fully or entirely prepare for. Once they think they understand it, everything changes again. It can be difficult to find steady ground or to predict what tomorrow will bring. Finding closure is difficult because events are not finite. There are no clear beginnings or ends. The process of grieving can't be completed when it is interrupted, and the process of mourning must begin over again.

Most family members learn to live with a sense of sadness that is not always obvious. It is not the primary or even the most prevalent emotion, but it is still there. Coping with the chronic sorrow of mental illness requires a lifetime of adjustments. It often means that you will need to support yourself. It is essential, however, that you remember you are not alone in this process. Chronic sorrow does not mean there is no happiness. It does not mean there is no hope.

Supporting Rehabilitation and Symptom Management

Chronic illness has taken away everything about who I always thought I would be, and replaced me with a stranger I have no choice but to get to know and somehow learn to embrace.
I still love me, but I miss every single part of who I was before.
— Chris

There are ways you can help the person you love adjust to and manage their illness.

1. Promote a positive view of living with mental illness. This does not mean faking it. Mental illness is not *happy*. It is possible to be happy while living with a mental illness, though. It is possible to manage symptoms and live a good life. Mental illness is not a sign of weakness or bad behavior. Good, strong, intelligent, capable people have and live with mental illnesses. It is a medical condition that can be treated. It is not a flaw or fault. Approach and deal with this illness as you would any serious disease. Believe this can be managed. Convey this and support them as they work toward it.

2. Honor the process of adjusting to a chronic illness. Be kind. Accept the significant emotional turmoil that comes in being diagnosed with a chronic illness or having this happen to someone you love. Distinguish between symptoms and the process of adjusting. Allow for anger, frustration, grief, and denial and help express these feelings in ways that are not destructive.

3. Help your loved one:
    - explore treatment options and available services.
    - navigate the system and advocate for themselves.
    - determine the qualities they want in the health professionals they will work with and find providers who embody these traits.
    - establish a treatment plan uniquely tailored to them.

4. Help your loved one learn about their illness, identify limitations and explore ways to deal with the problems they encounter.

5. Support their learning how to make good decisions about treatment by being able to answer questions like these:
    - What do they want to be able to do? (Ex: Do they want to work, school, form meaningful relationships? What are their daily and long-term goals?)

- What problems/symptoms are preventing them from doing these things?
- What do they want treatment to achieve? Is this realistic?
- What treatment options are available, what will each accomplish, what problems could each cause? How can side-effects be minimized or handled?
- What qualifications should a provider have?
- How will they know a treatment is effective or is not working/failing?
- What signs would indicate a specific treatment is harmful?
- Are there combinations of medications that might be more effective?
- Is there someone they trust to give feedback on how they are doing?
- Which healthcare professional can coordinate treatments and help explore them safely?
- When stopping treatment or trying a new one, what safeguards can be put in place to minimize any risk?

PART TWO

SPECIFIC SITUATIONS

Tips for Speaking With Someone Who Is Psychotic

"Seek first to understand—then to be understood" Dr. Steven Covey

Delusions are beliefs not based in reality and/or which may use faulty logic. While delusions can center around one specific belief, they are often complex and involve how a person perceives, understands, and interprets the world. Hallucinations are the perception of tangible things that are not real and can include visual, auditory, or sensory perceptions. Psychosis is the experience of delusions, hallucinations or both. Symptoms of psychosis can vary widely among different people and for the same person at different times. The type of delusions or hallucinations that someone experiences can affect their mood, what they perceive happening, and even how they understand others' motives and actions.

When someone experiences delusions or hallucinations, he or she does not know that is what is happening. What they experience is as real to them as anything that they or you or I experience when we are not symptomatic. If merely explaining to them that a hallucination is not real, or using logic to debunk a delusion were effective then they would not be symptomatic, just misinformed. The fact that these are symptoms of illness means that their perception is literally altered. Trying to convince them of the error of their perceptions is equivalent to someone trying to convince you that the sky isn't blue. You know it is. You can see it.

All of this is especially true when someone is becoming psychotic for the first time. The patient has no idea that they might have a mental illness and no understanding of symptoms or their impact. They haven't experienced psychosis or how treatment will cause symptoms to subside. Even people who have experienced these things may be unable to tell the difference between symptoms and reality when they are symptomatic.

Delusions and hallucinations are just as likely to be unpleasant and frightening as not. Even when they are not unpleasant, the person who is symptomatic may experience discomfort and fear. This is due to the dissonance—the disconnect—between what they perceive and the way others are responding. We process the world around us by using many sources of information. One source is the response, observations, and perception of others. When others do not see the same reality or react in a way consistent with what we perceive to be happening, the effect is disorienting and confusing. It can also lead to isolation, fear, sadness, or anger.

1. Speak slowly in soft, gentle tones. Use short, clear sentences.
2. Be calm and keep body movements to a minimum. Either move to a setting that is calm and quiet or to surroundings that are open.
3. Do not try to use humor.
4. Do not express fear or anxiety as this can create fear or anxiety.
5. Honor the personal space of the person you are speaking with. If they are agitated, angry, or their behavior frightens you give them breathing room. Try not to have more than two people present other than the person you are talking to, and avoid having children present.
6. Listen non-judgmentally. Do not tell them they are wrong, nor try to change how they think or feel. Try to understand what they are thinking and experiencing without trying to change it. You can't.
7. Listen more than you speak. When you do speak, reflect back what they have told you. You can reflect the facts, details, or emotion they have shared. Ask if they can try to describe what they are experiencing to you. Repeat what a person says but in your own words (i.e., don't parrot). Example:
P1: "I can't stop crying ever since my grandmother died."
P2: "This hurts a lot," or "You have been upset and it's hard to feel calm."
8. Do not be critical, confrontational, or try to be the voice of reason. Frame the things you say as your opinion. Use "I' and "me" rather than "you." Say something like, "I am confused. I am not sure what you mean," not "you are making me confused. You don't make sense." Say something like, "I am concerned," not "you are sick."
9. Don't threaten. Especially if you are a parent, it may be second nature to issue a consequence for someone's behavior. When someone is psychotic, it's not a good idea to use negative repercussions for behavior. Your loved one's behavior is because of symptoms, not a lack of discipline. Furthermore, when someone is psychotic, trying to rationalize them out of their behavior is not going to work.
10. Do not make diagnosis, medication, or treatment the focus or reason for the conversation. You are trying to provide

support. You want to understand what your loved one is thinking, feeling, and experiencing so that you can help as appropriate and needed. You want your loved one to see you as on their side, and not an enemy.

11. <u>Do not argue with someone about their beliefs or perceptions.</u> Do not try to change their mind. Accept that their reality is different. You can ask them to talk about what they believe or perceive so that you can understand better but do not do this so you can change their mind. Insisting someone is wrong may strengthen delusions.
    Do not play along with delusions or hallucinations. Don't agree with something you know is not true. This can support the delusion or hallucination becoming more deeply entrenched. Focus instead on what the person is feeling. Reassure them and let them know they are not alone, and that you are there for them. When we reflect others' emotions, it helps to build empathy, trust, and rapport. This is especially important in situations when someone is frightened, in distress, worried, or feels threatened.
    You might say: "I know you are experiencing (……) and I don't see that/hear that, or I don't fully understand, but I do understand why you feel confused/scared/hurt." Avoid saying "That's not real. You're making things up. You're crazy. I know you are wrong!" Likewise do not say, "I hear those voices too. The voices I hear say the same things to me."

12. Let the person know you take them seriously and support them. Say: "I don't know what you are going through and I can't pretend to understand, but I'm happy to listen. Tell me what is happening." You can also tell them, "I think that is something you should talk about with your doctor."

13. Remember, not everything someone perceives or feels is a product of one's symptoms. Do not dismiss information until you have had the opportunity to consider its validity.

14. Don't be afraid to ask someone how they are feeling, if they feel safe, or if they have been thinking of harming themselves.

15. If they ask you to be honest—be honest. Do so gently. Do not imply that there is shame in what they are experiencing. You could say, "I know the voices are real to you but I just can't hear them." or "You believe_____. I don't believe that" not "You are delusional. That is not right."

16. You may be able to redirect someone through questions

(not interrogating!). If they are fixated on something and cannot move past talking about it, or become more agitated or upset, ask an unrelated question. Find areas of common ground—things that both of you can agree on. Choose things which are innocuous: the weather, something they did recently or plan to do.

17. Respect it when someone does not want to talk, or does not want to talk about specific things.

18. Do not make promises you cannot keep.
    You might say, "If you go to the hospital they will talk to you about how you feel and what may help you to feel better," not "I promise if you go to the hospital they will let you come home right away" or "I will only share what you tell me if I think you are going to be hurt," not "I promise I won't tell anyone."

19. Try not to take the things that your loved one says personally. Remember that they are symptomatic and that their perceptions are skewed. They are not talking or behaving as they usually would.

20. Do stay positive and encourage help. The emotional turmoil that psychosis brings is very real and often frightening. Psychosis can make life seem overly dangerous, dark and threatening. Try not to add to this. Being comforting and positive is important.
    Say something like "how would you like to be helped?" or if this has happened before, "what has helped you when you felt like this before?" Your loved one may have someone who he or she prefers to turn to during this time, (e.g., they may find their therapist more comforting than his psychiatrist or vice versa). Knowing who your family member trusts is an integral part of finding the right intervention.

For more guidelines and information on speaking with someone who is symptomatic, please see the Factsheet: Dealing with Unusual Thoughts and Behaviors on **p. 221** in the Appendix.

Tips for Speaking With Someone Who Is Depressed

Depression is not the same as feeling sad. It is not caused by how someone perceives them self or their situation. It cannot be fixed by getting up and getting active, changing their routine or our attitude. Depression is the result of chemical changes in the brain. It may cause someone to see themselves or their lives differently and in a way that is not realistic.

When speaking with someone who is depressed the most important thing is to honor how they feel. You should not offer quick solutions, accuse them of being manipulative, or try to cheer them up. You want them to know you are there for them, that they are not crazy and that their inability to just "snap out of it" is not because they are flawed or wrong.

1. Speak in soft, gentle tones and remain calm. Don't be critical.
2. Do not argue, threaten, or take an offensive posture. Do not imply that there is something to be ashamed of in what they are experiencing.
3. Move to a setting that is calm and quiet, or to surroundings that are more open.
4. Listen non-judgmentally. Do not tell them how they are wrong, or to try to change how they feel. You are listening to understand what they are going through without trying to change it. You can't.
5. Be a reflective listener. Listen more than you speak. When you do speak focus on what they have told you. Reflect the facts or details of what they have said or what they feel. Say something like, " Tell me what's going on," or "You feel......"
6. Don't be confrontational. Frame what you say as your opinion. Use "I' and "me" as much as possible, rather than "you." Say, " I am not sure what you are saying," not "you are confusing. You're not making sense." Say, " I'm concerned," not "there's something wrong with you."
7. Don't try to persuade them they have a lot to be grateful for or should feel happy about. Let them know you take them seriously and support them.
You could say: "I haven't gone through what you are going through, but I want to understand. I care, and I will listen."

8. Remember everything someone perceives or feel is not because of symptoms. Feelings may be valid responses to actual situations.
9. Don't be afraid to ask someone if they have been thinking of harming themselves.
10. Do not make promises you cannot keep. Say something like, "I will only share what you tell me if I think you are going to be hurt if I keep it to myself," not "I promise I won't tell anyone."
11. Try not to take the things that they say personally. They are symptomatic. They are not talking or behaving as they usually would.
12. Do stay positive and encourage help.
    Ask, "what has helped you when you felt like this before?"

You can find more tips from The Depression Alliance in the Appendix on **p. 231.**

Anger in Your Loved One

Anger is a common reaction to the frustrations of living with a mental illness that is not easily talked about. Anger can result from feeling out of control, frustrated or afraid. It can be triggered by symptoms such as anxiety or paranoia. Anger also occurs easily in interactions among family members. It is common for someone to feel that others do not understand what they are going through, that their feelings or perceptions are dismissed. Sometimes families attribute everything that someone experiences to symptoms. This can result in them feeling they are not listened to, or not heard. Your family member, the one you love and badly want to help, may blame you for their problems. When anger erupts, it can be hurtful and at times even frightening. When anger becomes a way of coping with what cannot be controlled it becomes a destructive cycle.

While you may not be able to do anything to change your loved one's anger or the way that it is expressed, you do have control over how you respond. It can be incredibly helpful to seek professional support. This will help you to have a safe outlet for the frustration you feel. A professional can help you to sort through what lies behind your loved one's anger and better understand them and their response. Most importantly, a professional can help you to develop effective ways of responding and handling situations when anger erupts.

It is also important to assess the safety of everyone in the household: Does your loved one have a history of using violence? Have they threatened to harm their self or anyone else? Do they have access to a means to carry out such threats? If the answer to any of these questions is "yes," it is important to talk with professionals about what to do. Contacting law enforcement before there is a crisis may be important to how any response is handled should they be called. You should review the section on interactions with the police beginning on **p. 98**. A therapist and law enforcement can help your family develop a plan for anticipating and managing outbursts.

Tips on how to talk with someone who is angry

- Speak softly and in calm, reassuring tones.
- If there is a weapon present ask them to put the weapon down or give it to you.
- Tell them that you love them and that you want to help but that you cannot talk while they are calling you names, shouting at you, etc.
- Do not argue with them. Do not back them into a corner, physically or psychologically
- Say "I can see that you are really angry right now. I really care about you and want to talk about his when you are calmer."
- Recognize your limitations. You can't reason with someone who is out of control.
- Sometimes sitting and listening is the best you can do
- Suggest taking a walk. Sometimes moving can help defuse a situation.
- Do not be afraid to call for help if you feel threatened.

Helping Someone Having an Anxiety Attack[1]

Anxiety attacks, also known as panic attacks, feel and seem like a real medical emergency. An individual may experience shortness of breath, palpitations and racing heartbeat, and other symptoms. It is important to take these symptoms seriously while reassuring the person that they are safe and that you will support them. It is important to point out that in rare instances, what seems to be a panic attack, may be a medical emergency. Symptoms such as severe, crushing chest pain, severe head ache should be evaluated by a professional.

1. Listen without judgment. You want to understand what your loved one is going through.

2. Validate your loved one's fear rather than trying to brush it off. Individuals with anxiety often worry incessantly or become excessively fearful of things or situations that may not seem scary to others, such as being in a crowd or having to eat in front of someone. No matter how you may feel about the fear/worry, remember, to your friend or relative, this fear is real.

3. Let your loved one know you are there to help. Your loved one needs to hear that you are there no matter what: you will hold their hand, stand by them and be supportive. Your support can help reduce feelings of anxiety.

4. Ask your loved one what you can do to help instead of assuming you know the right thing to say or do. Your loved one may want to talk about something else to help keep their mind occupied or may wish to find something to do unrelated to the situation causing anxiety. Before pushing your ideas, ask what will best help

5. Help your loved one keep things in perspective. This may be tricky because even merely reminding your loved one that anxiety attacks are temporary may end up sounding as if you are trivializing their feelings. Stay calm and be supportive. Remind them that they aren't dying although it may feel that way; they will keep breathing; they are not having a heart attack.

6. Ask them what has helped them before. During a panic attack, anxiety sufferers may not remember what to do, such as taking deep breaths and/or focusing on each breath. Or he or she may forget that taking an anti-anxiety medication will help. Asking what normally helps can remind them of what to do. Then help him or her take the needed steps to calm the attack.

---

1 Taken from: Eileen Bailey, "What To Say When Someone is Having An Anxiety Attack," Anxiety Disorders, August 29, 2012

Drug and Alcohol Addiction

Addiction is a mental illness. Those who have other mental illnesses may also use drugs or alcohol to deal with the symptoms they experience. These are two different things. Some people have an addiction and another mental illness. This is called a *co-occurring disorder.* Determining whether someone is addicted to or using drugs and alcohol to manage symptoms is a complicated process. When co-occurring disorders are present treatment becomes more difficult and complex.

Addiction can occur because of a genetic—or hereditary predisposition. It can occur because someone uses a substance which is physically or psychologically addictive. People can become addicted because of long-established family behaviors. Contributing factors can affect the success of any treatment. They can determine what other areas of function are affected when someone is not using. The brains of those with a genetic or hereditary predisposition to addiction may function differently *even when they are not using.*

When addiction exists, the ability to stop use is not a matter of willpower. People who are addicted require a support system made up of many different components. The point where someone stops using is not the point of success. It is the first step in what is a lifelong process. Those who are addicted may need a range of treatments that will help manage the way of thinking and processing information which accompanies abuse. Those who have other mental illnesses may find themselves engaged in a process of determining the impetus for their drug use. They may have difficulty finding the right treatments AND the right balance of treatments for each illness that they face. What is required to treat addiction may pose the potential for harm in managing other illness. Treatment for other mental illnesses may place someone at risk of relapsing.

The behaviors that are needed when a family member is dealing with an addiction are often counter to the way that we expect families to behave. They can be especially difficult for parents who may face the possibility that their son or daughter may die if they continue to use.

In the language of addiction, family members may try to "rescue" a loved one. Those who continually pick up the wreckage of another's addiction are called "Enablers." Although they believe they are doing what is needed to get their loved one to quit, their actions actually enable them to continue use. There are several ways someone can enable another's use unintentionally:

1. Trying to manage someone's drug or alcohol use: hiding drugs or alcohol, trying to convince others not to use at events so that the loved one won't be tempted to use, making deals about use—if you don't use all weekend then I will reward you by... When they do something to manipulate, convince, encourage, or make it more difficult to use for someone who has not chosen to quit, they are trying to manage that person's use. No one can make another person use or not use. No one can control the decisions another person makes. While it is true there are things which make it easier or harder for someone to use *in any given moment,* ultimately, the choice to use drugs or alcohol wholly belongs to the person using. Ironically, when someone steps in like this, the addict is able to use the controlling behavior to place blame and sometimes to justify continued use.

2. Trying to protect someone from the consequences of use. Use can impact a person's life in devastating ways. Loss of work, relationships, self-esteem, money, livelihood, a home, school. Anything that a person can possess, earn, or build up in their life can be lost as a consequence of drug or alcohol use, even life itself. People who care for an addict may spend a significant amount of energy and time trying to clean up the messes that addiction makes. They may help to hide use from others, lie to the boss about someone being sick. Do homework to prevent a bad grade or failure in school. Cover up in any way possible for the mistakes that the person using has made. The problem with doing this is that when there are no consequences for use, the person using has no reason to quit. If someone always steps in and picks up the pieces, alcohol or drug use has no price—for the person using. The price for the person picking up the pieces can be extreme. The most difficult of all decisions is the one which risks someone becoming homeless or even dying as a consequence of use.

3. Behaving passively. A passive family member may not actively cover up someone's use, or aggressively try to help sweep away the consequences. Nor do they acknowledge use or its impact on the user. When the addict using doesn't live up to promises, doesn't show up for planned activities, becomes angry and abusive while using, the passive family member suffers in silence. They work around everything that the person using does or does not do as though it is normal and has no impact. This enables the person using because, again, there are no consequences for their use. They are able to behave how they want, without regard for others, without consequence.

No one can control whether someone else uses drugs or alcohol. No one can make another person else stop. Family members can best support a loved one's health by refusing to engage in behaviors which support the addiction. This does not mean not acting in a loving way, but it may mean learning how to love in a new way. The best advice that can be given to someone who is involved with an addict is to get help for themselves, ideally through attending a family support group like Al-Anon or Alateen. These organizations provide the opportunity to learn how to respond to a loved one who is dealing with addiction in a way that is healthy and supports their ultimate health. It also assists the family in maintaining their own well-being regardless of whether their loved one chooses to deal with their addiction.

Being an Addict
Stephen

What is it that makes me so different? Why is it that others can sit down once in a blue moon and smoke a joint, enjoy it, and then put it away for any number of months or whatever amount of time before they partake again? If I were to smoke a joint I would spiral quickly. Within just hours I become fixated on finding my next high, placing that need above even food. I checked myself into inpatient treatment for this problem in 1986. I have not used marijuana or any other illegal substance since. How have I done it?. First, I had to come to grips with the reality that I was different. That joint seems to be enough to start me "chasing a high" forsaking all else. Second, admitting this is a physical issue. I react differently to mind altering substances. I am more likely to become addicted than the average person. This is a medically proven reality. No matter how I may wish it, for me given just these two factors I must abstain completely just to give myself a chance of success in life. The mental component is easier for me to come to grips with than the physical. Since I have been a very young child I have had two very distinct mental issues to deal with. In talking to thousands of other addicts in meetings over 30+ years I have come to realize we all feel the same.

    A. For some reason we don't feel like a part of the community of humans. We feel separated. No matter what people say or do this painful separateness exists.

    B. We cannot successfully associate any consequences to our behavior. Since we cannot associate consequences we do not have a very important check on our actions.

We struggle through life disconnected. On top of that, society hammers at us because we seem selfish. We seem to act with no regard to consequence.

How did I resolve these issues? The short answer is that I haven't. In order to become a happy, productive person, daily I have to remind myself:

    1. I have a connection to human kind as strong and as deep as any other human.

2. I am of as much worth as anyone. That my actions, while selfish on the surface, are driven by my inability to place internal controls on myself. In order to combat this I must always consciously think of the potential action and consciously play out the results in order to consciously associate the consequence with the behavior.
3. I admit to myself that since I seem to metabolize mind altering drugs differently, I will have a very hard time not abusing them. Total abstinence is needed in order for me to be able to learn to function in society.

Drug and Alcohol Addiction in Conjunction With Other Mental Disorders

When someone experiencing the symptoms of a mental illness uses drugs and alcohol to manage their symptoms it is called *self-medicating*. Often, this is not an intentional or conscious process. They only know things feel wrong and a substance helps them to feel better. Self-medication can result in habit and habit in addiction. When this happens, the addiction becomes a problem in and of itself. Because it is so common for people who are symptomatic—especially in the early stages of mental illness—to self-medicate, family members may blame drug and alcohol use for the mental illness. Likewise, addiction is easily blamed on the symptoms of other mental illnesses. Would someone have used and become addicted had there been no symptoms? Did drug use bring cause another illness to emerge? There is no way to know. And like the proverbial chicken-egg, it matters little once someone is dealing with addiction as well as another mental illness.

Correct diagnosis is the most important consideration when someone is showing signs of both addiction and another mental illness. Heavy drug or alcohol use can cause symptoms consistent with other mental illnesses. Such symptoms can include hallucinations, delusions, mania, depression, unstable moods, poor judgment, and poor self-care. Accurate diagnosis can require that a person be drug- or alcohol-free for a long enough period of time to determine whether symptoms change or even disappear. If other symptoms resolve, the then addiction is the only illness to be dealt with. There are also people who stop using drugs or alcohol without difficulty once other symptoms are adequately treated. These individuals clearly do not have an addiction.

Questions that should be asked: Is this person addicted to drugs and alcohol? Is there another mental illness or psychological disorder present? Are symptoms due to drug and alcohol use, due to another illness or disorder, or to both? Do drug and alcohol use stop when other illnesses are well managed? Do symptoms subside when drug or alcohol use stops?

Choosing a Treatment Facility

There are several types of treatment for addiction. These are based on different schools of thought or philosophies about what makes someone successful in managing their addiction. Before choosing treatment, it is important to learn about the philosophy it is based on. Some treatments are based on the premise that addiction cannot be successfully managed until the person stops all medication use—including psychiatric medications. Facilities that adhere to this philosophy do not allow anyone being treated to take any medications—even those legitimately prescribed. *Programs based on this philosophy can be dangerous to individuals who experience hallucinations or delusions, or who require medication to treat their mental illness.* When a co-occurring illness is not treated, it can also severely hamper efforts to treat addiction successfully.

It is also important to know if addiction exists in conjunction with other mental illness, and if so, which is the primary illness (the latter may be difficult or impossible to determine—especially early on). One of the key ways this is determined is the presence and severity of psychiatric symptoms when there is no drug or alcohol use. Whether someone continues to use when other symptoms are controlled is also an important consideration.

When another mental illness exists, traditional treatments for drug and alcohol use can exacerbate symptoms because of the stress placed on the patient, who may be ill-equipped to handle it. Traditional treatments often take the position that one must reach rock bottom—be truly broken—before true recovery can begin. This can be dangerous for those suffering other mental illnesses, as withdrawal of support can lead to a worsening of their condition and precipitate a crisis which is neither helpful nor desirable.

If you suspect a person may suffer from both drug and alcohol addiction AND another mental illness, there are rehabilitation hospitals and treatments which specifically work with the needs of persons with co-occurring disorders. These facilities understand that a different approach to recovery must be undertaken when other mental illnesses are present so as to not exacerbate those conditions. You will need to do your own research and talk to outreach professionals at each treatment facility you uncover to find out their philosophy and if this is a concern. Ask the facility about what they are equipped to handle, and what medications they allow.

Note: There are medications available that may assist with managing certain types of addiction. Medication is not sufficient in the absence of a desire to cope with addiction and may not be a good option for every person. Medication use will need to be closely supervised.

The opioid epidemic is something that is consistently in the news. Narcan is a drug that you can have available to you, if a family member uses any class drugs that pose a potential for a deadly overdose. If an overdose occurs, Narcan can save their life. For more information, speak to your family physician.

Drug and Alcohol Addiction: A Family's Thoughts
Dawn Woody

What do I wish we had known?

- that adequate treatment takes much longer than 30 days
- that fees are negotiable and that there are scholarships available for long-term treatment facilities
- that our whole family had to enter into recovery not just our daughter
- that rescuing our daughter by doing for her what she could do for herself simply prolonged her traction and enabled her addiction

What do I wish we did not know?

- that relapse will always be a possibility no matter how much time she has been sober; that relapse is statistically probable
- that many addicts overdose and die after lengthy periods of sobriety
- that our family will always be in recovery

What was/is most difficult for our family?

Continuing our lives without the consistent participation of our daughter has been the most painful aspect of our journey. We have celebrated many milestones without her presence. We have had to create a "new normal" for our family dynamic. We have had to confront and acknowledge that her future and her very presence in our lives is completely out of our influence or control. I have allowed myself to accept the grim fact that she might not survive her illness.

We want other families going through this to know

- Pride is not your friend. Share your family's struggles and need for help in the same way that you would any other illness. Don't be afraid to ask for help
- Celebrate the daily victories. A day that your child stays sober and doesn't hurt herself or others is a very good day!

- Addiction is a chronic illness no different than diabetes, asthma or arthritis. Speak of it with the same dignity and compassion. It is not a choice or a moral failing.
- Seek professional help for yourself and other members of the family. Therapists who are experienced in addiction can help family members avoid enabling and provide support when difficult decisions must be made.

What might help others to avoid or to navigate some of the pitfalls we encountered?

- Aftercare is essential. Completion of a 30-day program can provide a foundation and traction for recovery, but long-term treatment which often includes medication, housing and accountability is key to sustainable mental health and sobriety. Demand a sustainable aftercare plan before discharge.
- Financial assistance and scholarships are often available for clients who advocate for themselves. Our daughter received the most support and achieved her greatest success once we relinquished "control" over her recovery.
- Sharing our story as a family in recovery brought emotional support that we needed and freed us from the internal guilt and shame that we were carrying in isolation. We discovered that we were not alone.

A recurrent mistake that we made throughout the early years of our daughter's recovery was the ownership that I felt in creating the "perfect" aftercare plan for her once she completed inpatient treatment. I spent hours looking at sober living houses and IOP programs. I called intake specialists and referral agencies. I generated lists of local AA and NA meetings, volunteer opportunities and potential jobs. I knew that once she was released from 24 hour supervision my anxiety would resurface. The sleepless nights and fear-filled phone rings would return. I threw myself into creating, what it took me far too long to realize, a false safety net.

I typically allowed myself 14 days of respite before I began the all-consuming search for next steps once the 30-day program was complete. After three years and approximately 18 of these short-term inpatient programs, I began advocating on behalf of our daughter for our insurance to approve longer-term care and more intensive aftercare treatment. Sometimes it worked; however, another year passed with additional relapses and my patience, resources and motivation were depleted. I shared my desperation and frustration with one of her therapists. With two simple questions, she completely changed the way in which we now engage with our daughter, HER treatment and HER recovery. The therapist asked, "Why don't you trust (your daughter) to make decisions regarding her life and her recovery? Why are you impeding her motivation to become a sober adult?"

It was a turning point for me. I began to relinquish control over what I thought she should do. I encouraged her to advocate for herself and to ask for help. We provide clear boundaries with regard to what we will and will not support both emotionally and financially, and then we let her work with her professional support team to create a vision for a sober future. We have redefined what we consider success and we have come to accept that set-backs, mistakes and even relapse are all part of recovery. We no longer do for her that which she can do for herself. And we don't focus so much on the "fall" as the "bounce".

Child Mental Health
Grace B. Hubbard, DNP, PMHCNS-BC

A note about my context—I conceptualize my work with children in the context of development—developmental theory and an individual child's unique developmental trajectory. My experience teaches me it is the context of the child's life (factors he/she is born with and external factors) that influence the developmental trajectory. From this vantage point, I consider strengths in the child/family, barriers to development, unique responses of the child and family, and gaps within the context of their lives.

Introduction

Children have their unique style of following very typical developmental stages. They move at their own pace to develop physical, emotional, social, and cognitive skills. The child's development cannot be hurried along, but it can be slowed. We can predict the major stages of development, but each child has his or her unique pace for moving through that stage. Circumstances can support the child to move at his or her chosen pace, or circumstances can pressure a child to acquire specific skills prematurely. The promotion of mental health relies on acknowledgment of the individual child's natural pace for development and recognition when obstacles or challenges occur and influence that natural pace.

Stress is a response to real change or to anticipated change. Healthy stress occurs when a child feels challenged, yet believes he or she is capable of managing the challenge/issue. Unhealthy stress occurs when the challenge seems "too big" or overwhelming, resulting in frequent or ongoing worry. It is unhealthy stress that often creates obstacles to aspects of development. Unhealthy stress can impact children in several ways: requires the use skills he or she may not have developed, creates a sense of insecurity, and/or eliminates established skills causing a return to previous behaviors (bed-wetting). Stressors faced by children are often ones their parents did not face (social media, cyberbulling). In addition to both these factors, a crisis may occur that effects the child, the child's family, or someone who is significant to the child. These new stressors combine with the expected challenges of growing up and can prove overwhelming for many children. It is at this point a child may experience obstacles to his or her pace of development.

General Considerations for Child Mental Health

All children respond positively to an environment that acknowledges their own unique value. One in which they are not pushed to be someone else, "grow up faster", be smarter, or "act like your brother". This type of environment occurs with:

1. Physical and emotional safety for the child and all family members
2. Knowledge of typical developmental stages and acceptance of a difference in pacing within each stage (siblings are different)
3. Acceptance of feelings; it is OK to not like a rule, or a behavior, or a person. It is not OK to treat others disrespectfully because of those feelings.
4. Consistent structure; knowing what to expect and when to expect it
5. Recognition of individual and family strengths and use of those strengths to support family stability
6. A variety of sources for social and emotional support; develop a team of support for your child and your family (school personnel, church family, neighbors, organizations for children, pediatrician, etc.)
7. Fun times experienced with family members; it doesn't need to cost money

Developmental Milestones—Important Behaviors

These four key areas are important to monitor as a child develops. Crucial behaviors develop within each of these areas as the child matures. Behaviors/skills learned in these areas assist the child with managing the demands of "growing up" and are necessary for strong mental health. A child's lack of progress in one of these areas indicates a need for further assessment. Parents may benefit from information about how to help their child develop the skills in these areas. An obstacle may have presented itself in the child's life that is limiting his/her ability to develop these behaviors/skills. It is important to gain additional assessment sooner rather than later. Early intervention (often simple actions) can prevent problems from becoming more severe.

1. **Self-regulation.** This is the ability to recognize emotional distress and cope with it effectively. A child's environment teaches this skill. Preschoolers need to demonstrate some ability to calm themselves and control their impulsive behavior. This skill continues to develop as the child matures. Children learn this by observation and specific teaching (how to talk about feelings, different coping strategies).

2. **Relationships.** Children learn how to be in a relationship. Children learn about friendship—how to make and keep friends. They identify people they enjoy being with and feel safe with. They want to spend time with other people.

3. **Pretend vs. "Real Life."** Children learn to distinguish what is their imagination and what is actually occurring in their environment. A key skill is learning to deal with frustration and delay gratification.

4. **Communication.** This is the ability to express feelings and thoughts effectively and to convey empathy (understand the feelings of others). Children learn to face disappointment and competition and to manage without avoidance or overreaction.

What to Look For

Basic areas of a child's life provide information about whether or not the child is feeling good about him/herself and life in general. When considering if a child is having a problem, look for a pattern of behavior. Behaviors that arise once or twice over several months is not as significant as a consistent, ongoing change. For example, difficulty sleeping or decrease in appetite that occurs 2-3 time in 4-6 months, doesn't suggest the same significance as when it happens 2-3 times per week. *The exception to this is behaviors that put the child or others at risk, (suicidal gestures, self-harm, harm toward others/animals) require immediate assessment.*

Key areas to observe for changes in functioning

1. Sleep patterns
2. Eating patterns
3. Social patterns (withdrawing or isolating from people/situations that were previously enjoyable)
4. Emotions (anger, tearfulness, anxiety/worry, depressed mood)

5. Attitude about school or other organizational activities (successful engagement changes, strong negative feelings develop)
6. Behavior toward parents (that are new and problematic; i.e., disrespect, avoidance, clinginess)
7. Exposure to television, social media, computer (some children become overwhelmed with the content or the activity)

What Action to Take

1. Notice when and how often the change occurs; when did it start?
2. Don't assume you know what is going on—you might be correct, but don't assume
3. Use a calendar to take notes (relying on memory is not accurate); this will help when talking to a professional about the changes
4. Consider any change in the child's routine, or in your family's routine, regardless of whether or not it seems important to you
5. The important thing is to talk to your child: let them know you see a difference, you are concerned, you are there to help or to get help, not force them to talk. Ask what would help them be able to talk.
6. Recognize your child may not understand what is causing the change in his/her functioning and is not able to provide information.
7. Talk to key people in your child's life (teacher, babysitter, minister, family members, neighbor, etc.) and ask if they have noticed anything. Ask them to describe what they see, and don't assume it is the same as your observation.
8. If you are unable to understand what might be going on with your child or what might be contributing to the change in functioning, consult a professional. This might be the school nurse, school counselor, or a pediatrician. If you don't feel satisfied with one person's response, seek out another person.

What Experience Teaches Me

1. Trust your gut. Intuition can be wrong, and many times it is right. If something seems "off" to you about your child, pursue it until you get a satisfactory response.
2. Look for patterns of behavior, not a single occurrence.

3. Empower your child to work with you to find a solution. Say to him or her, "You are smart, you might not know the answer right now, let's open our minds to anything that might work for us. We will try it." Or, for older children, "If your best friend came to you for your idea with the same problem, what would you say to her?"
4. Take action soon, time passes too quickly during these years of significant development. These times of challenge for your child offer an opportunity for learning coping strategies exists. Don't wait for it to go away on its own.
5. Build in time to be together during simple activities (chores, cooking, reading, TV, walking) so that a relationship exists to support talking about the hard stuff when it occurs.

One of the most hopeful advances in treatment for young people experiencing their first episode of psychosis is Coordinated Specialty Care. There are four programs in NC, and even if a family is out of their area or they aren't taking referrals, the team can possibly consult with a young person and their family. The goal is to provide well-researched, coordinated services and medication management as early as possible in the young person's illness so that the course of the illness is changed and disability avoided.

Carrboro: https://www.med.unc.edu/psych/oasis

Wilmington: http://www.myrha.org/news/rha-behavioral-health-shore-program-opens-in-wilmington

Siblings

*I haven't spoken to my sister in 25 years.
All I wanted was a healthy relationship.*

I am the only one left to help my brother. Thank heavens he is in a group home. I could not cope with this schizophrenia.

I hate my brother.

One of the most difficult consequences of a child's mental illness is the impact it has on other children in the family. Parents dream of their children growing into adults who are friends who care for and support one another. They want them to get along and for family gatherings to be memorable and fun. Mental illness, when not well-managed, can make this impossible.

It is heartbreaking when a sibling decides that they must break off contact with their brother or sister. Some siblings do give up—often with good reason. Others try to get their brother or sister into treatment and feel defeated if they aren't successful. When one sibling has little conflict with their parents, a brother or sister with mental illness can perceive this as favoritism. They may become angry believing is responsible for their sibling's success or their own problems. Siblings may resent or be angry with a brother or sister with a mental illness feeling they get more attention, time, and concern. Many children, young and adult, worry about their parents, try to support them, and become defensive of them. They may blame their brother or sister for the pain or struggles they see their parents experience. Siblings may fear the day when their parents can no longer support their brother or sister if they will assume that responsibility. This can lead to fear, resentment, and anger.

When one child in a family develops a chronic illness or becomes disabled the other children are always affected. There are ways to help siblings cope—as children, adolescents, and as adults.

Bill and Amy had been close as children. Amy looked up to her older brother and enjoyed spending time with him. This began to change as Bill got older. He seemed to have trouble fitting in. Bill was often angry at his parents and at Amy. He was in therapy for a while and at one point threatened suicide. He struggled in college and could not seem to make the full transition to adulthood. Amy tried to support him. She worried about her parents who tried hard to support her brother. She did not feel she could talk about his problems with her friends. Amy just did not know what to do.

If Children Are Still Living at Home

First and foremost, make sure everyone who is living in the home feels safe.

- Sometimes those who are symptomatic are frightening to others because they seem unpredictable. Their actions and reactions may not make sense. Talk with your children about their fears—for and of their sibling. You can help them to understand mental illness and its symptoms. Knowing what symptoms are and how they affect people can help mediate any discomfort or fear they cause. Stress the importance of coming to you when they do not feel safe for any reason. Make sure they know you will always care for both them and their sibling.

- Your children should know what to do if they become afraid. Talk over situations that worry them or which you are concerned may occur. Develop a plan for what steps they can take.

- Younger children should know that any time they feel unsafe they are to go to an adult: their parents, or if their parents are not available, the closest adult who is.

- Adolescents should understand how and when to call 911 when an adult is not present. You can talk to them about what information they need to give the 911 operator.

- All families should have an emergency plan and information that is easily accessible to their children appropriate to their age. Keep this by the phone, or in central locations. Include addresses, key phone numbers, and the information that should be provided if help is needed.

- If there is a genuine concern for someone's safety, you should take action immediately.

Second, keep family life as stable as possible.

- Sometimes when a child has an illness, other children feel neglected or unimportant. This is natural. Caring for anyone, child, teen or adult, with mental illness is consuming. It is important to spend quality time with all of your children for their well-being and for yours.

- Make time for enjoyable activities one-on-one with all of your children. This not only provides an opportunity for them to speak privately with you if needed, but it also provides time with you which is not overshadowed by mental illness and its impact.
- Make sure that your family's home life is not dominated by illness. Siblings should be able to have friends over even when their brother or sister is symptomatic (take the sibling out to a movie or dinner, or to activities with other family members).

Third, attend to your children's emotional needs.

- Be an "askable" parent. Encourage questions. Talk about the illness. Parents can help children understand that mental illness is caused by something in the brain not working correctly. It is important they know that even though their sibling might behave in a difficult way, they are not able to control this and that with appropriate treatment symptoms can be managed.
- Involve children in family therapy sessions or find someone they can talk to. Many schools have groups for children with mental illness in their families. Talk to the school nurse, social worker or counselor at your child's school and find out what is available.
- Remind your children that they are not responsible for their sibling's problems. They cannot solve them, and they did not cause them.
- Ask for help. Sometimes other family members, friends, church members or neighbors can be valuable resources.
- Set limits. Get professional help in setting and enforcing limits—for your own safety and sanity—and that of your other family members.

When an Adult Child Has a Mental Illness

Jane was often difficult during family gatherings. Her illness made her controlling and angry. She would pace around the house, threaten to leave—and often would leave in a fit of anger only to return a few hours later. Her family, especially her sister, Martha was worn out by these visits. Everyone spent time walking on eggshells.

Mental illness can be exacerbated by the typical stress of family gatherings. It can make it difficult to plan holiday gatherings or vacations. Family members can feel caught in the middle as they try to keep everyone calm, happy, and make sure things go smoothly.

Some strategies that can help:

- Talk frankly and without judgment with family members about the symptoms and behavior that may result when someone has a mental illness.

- Encourage every family member to recognize the limits of what they can accept. Respect these limits. This may mean that traditional family gatherings change. Not everyone may be able to present every time or for the full gathering. Sometimes small changes can help avoid big problems. If there is something that tends to create conflict for your loved one or results in a negative response, consider ways to modify your time together.

- Keep gatherings brief or provide quiet spaces where someone needing downtime can go. As a family grows, gatherings will become larger and louder. They can be intense. A great deal of noise means confusion and over-stimulation. This can be especially difficult for someone who is symptomatic. Shortening the time everyone is together or having a place where someone can go that is quiet and soothing can help a great deal.

- Anticipate possible problems. Not every visit will go smoothly and families should talk about how situations can be handled if they arise. If people know what may happen and a plan is in place, everyone will be more relaxed and many problems can be minimized.

- Talk with everyone, including the family member who is symptomatic, about what would be disruptive and what can help. Have options for people if they become upset or over-stimulated and a place where your loved one can go to relax if things become overwhelming.

- If someone is good at supporting or helping your loved one they may be willing to be aware of how they are doing during the gathering. If your loved becomes agitated or over-stimulated, they can go for a walk or sit and talk quietly in another room until they are calmer. This will also allow everyone else to continue to enjoy the gathering without having to worry about their loved one.

- During family gatherings, members experiencing symptoms often have different or heightened needs. During times of crisis, they will face the additional burden of instability and uncertainty. Be prepared and have options available for providing a quiet, calming space. Sometimes the availability of a pet can be beneficial. Taking a dog for a walk, petting a cat or looking at an aquarium, can be relaxing and helpful in helping someone to regain control of their emotions.

- Allow for family gatherings that do not include everyone, or which may not include your loved one. This idea can be painful. Sometimes, those living with mental illnesses know a situation is beyond their comfort level. They may choose not to come. Sometimes experience has taught it is better for them not to be present. It is important for the health of the entire family—including the member who is ill—that there are moments not over-shadowed by illness. This can be done with love and with support for the person who is struggling.

Managing the challenges of mental illness may sound impossible. At times, it will be impossible for anyone to manage everything. It does not mean relationships must end. Even when your loved one is not able to participate in family events you and they can do things together at other times. You can do something simple, like baking cookies or going for a walk. You can do something more elaborate like visiting a museum. These simple acts can build on fragile relationships.

Make sure that you take care of yourself. And do not blame yourself. Continue to offer support and encourage treatment.

If Your Adult Child Lives at Home

- Be clear about your expectations. Must they be in treatment? Are there activities or behaviors that are expected or required? What will you do for them and what must they do for themselves? What would make it impossible for them to continue to live with you?
- Encourage as much independence as possible For example, encourage them to get a job, pay rent, carry out household chores, manage their own medications.
- Negotiate all of the things you would negotiate if they did not have an illness: hours for coming and going, rules about guests, cooking, etc
- Consider which of the strategies for managing family gatherings would be useful on a daily basis and in ensuring that other family members feel welcome and comfortable in your home.

If living with your adult child becomes so difficult that you cannot maintain your life you should help them to find alternative living arrangements. This may mean moving in with another family member or a friend. It may mean moving somewhere alone. It may mean finding a suitably-supported living environment or formal service.

If you decide your loved one needs to leave your home, they may refuse to leave or not find any alternative arrangement acceptable. You can have them legally removed. This is a difficult step to take—and one with uncertain consequences. Check with an attorney or your local police department before doing anything as there may be a procedure you must follow, such as filing for eviction. If having someone legally or forcibly removed may create an unsafe environment for you or for your loved one, you will want to explore other ways to separate from them.

> The pain that I feel on those occasions when I am enjoying myself, when our family is together for birthdays, holidays, dinners and Sarah is not there, is excruciating. I think of her sitting home—alone. I envision her by herself, apart from everyone. I look at her siblings' and cousins' faces and it breaks my heart knowing that she is not there having a good time with them. At the same moment, I also know there is nothing I can do to change this. This is the reality of where we are for today. She would certainly be miserable here.

Sibling Estrangement

Sometimes siblings will become estranged. You can be supportive and understanding but can't always prevent or repair estrangement. It is important to keep trying to maintain relationship with all of your children. Don't give up hope.

Be sensitive to the fact that family gatherings can emphasize the loss felt by the family member with mental illness. It can be very painful to observe the full, rewarding lives of others when your own life is such a struggle.

Estrangement

Joe goes off to college, drops out, comes home, goes back to college. He graduates with honors, but comes home and gets stuck again. He doesn't work, doesn't go out much. Later, he does not go out at all except when absolutely necessary. His parents talk to him about therapy. Joe goes sporadically, but his therapist says he is extremely resistant to therapy. His parents go into therapy. There has been so much worry. So much anger and guilt. And now after a troubled adolescence, a difficult college experience and a difficult 18 months at home, Joe's parents run out of patience. They give an ultimatum. They tell Joe he must move out.

Joe has many reasons why everything is his parents' fault. He refuses to cooperate. What else could they do? They call the police after telling him they would do that. Two officers come. He is told to leave. Which he does, without even taking a jacket. Designed to make his parents feel bad, which they do. They also believe that they truly had no alternative. They pay for an apartment for him. He eventually moves back home and then to another state. His illness prevents him from accepting treatment. He believes that everything that is wrong in his life is because of them. They continue to work with a therapist who helps them with their guilt. They come to understand what they could and could not control. The therapist helps them wade through the difficult emails and come up with supportive responses, helps them understand the nature of the illness Joe still cannot see. Helps them cope with family vacations and holidays which are always difficult. Helps them understand that sometimes the only thing to do is to maintain some sort of relationship—a relationship of hope if they can—but a relationship even when hope fails. And helps them understand that sometimes the illness pushes too hard and families have to take steps to save themselves. There have to be clear limits: "No, you can't visit right now. No, you can't always be included in every holiday. Sometimes other things take priority. But you will always be loved. Even if you don't believe it. Even though you believe the entire health care system is based on false research, bad intentions. Even when you are right about that, we cannot give up on the idea that there is help for you. Failing that, we will work to maintain a relationship—even when you say you want to sever ties. Even though you have said that, we never will."

Estrangement is difficult. It is painful. For those who think they would never reject someone in their family, it can be hard to understand. Families who deal with mental illness may have to deal with periods of estrangement. This can be physical if a loved one severs contact. It can be emotional, such as when a loved one becomes doubtful or suspicious of family members and limits their involvement with them.

There may be times when behavior becomes so destructive that family members cannot tolerate it any longer.

There are ways to cope if estrangement occurs:

- Repeat as often as you need to: I did not cause this illness and I cannot make it go away.
- Find a good therapist for yourself. This will provide you with needed support. A therapist can help you find ways to communicate better with your loved one. They can help you to set appropriate expectations and boundaries.
- Set boundaries as they are needed. Identify people whose judgment you trust in this. When you feel guilty, turn to them to for support.
- Find a few supportive friends who understand your situation and can talk with you about it.
- Try and "reach around" the illness in your family member and respond to what is healthy. This is not always possible. Respond to the emotions that they express rather than arguing about what you have done. Affirm your love and concern.
- Sometimes people can become very controlling. Be prepared to stand your ground. Be loving and remember you are not the cause of your loved one's problems.
- Clarify what you need to be well. Do what you need to do to secure those things. You cannot help your loved one if you and your life fall apart.
- Take care of your own health. Exercise, eat a healthy diet, try yoga or meditation.
- Maintain a balance between your loved one and other aspects of your life. Do things that bring pleasure. Do not let everything revolve around them and/or their illness.
- Don't give up. Keep trying to maintain contact.

The Elderly

Martha was watching television with her daughter at her assisted living facility She casually remarked that the people in the television set wanted her to change how she cooked her meals. She said they were talking to her.

Patsy was frightened. She lived alone and was unable to leave without assistance. She told her family that people were coming into her house. They moved her pictures. They brought clothes and put them in her closet. They had taken the train set she put out each Christmas. Most terrifying of all they projected pictures on the wall. Pictures of her house burning. Pictures of her dying in a car accident. Pictures of her and her husband's graves.

There are two situations to consider when facing the symptoms of mental illness in an elderly family member: those with a history of mental illness who are aging and those who first show signs of mental illness as they age.

In general, mental illnesses manifest early in life. Yes. There are times when a traumatic event or drug/alcohol use may cause someone who was not symptomatic to become so later in life. This is not the usual course of these illnesses, however.

There are many reasons why someone who is aging may begin to show symptoms that are associated with a mental illness. One common occurrence is the development of a cognitive disorder such as dementia or Alzheimer's. Sundowner's Syndrome is a condition which results in confusion "when the sun goes down." It may also cause hallucinations. Many medical conditions and medications can cause symptoms similar to those of mental illnesses. Medications affect the elderly differently, and they tend to need different doses than younger persons. As someone ages, even medications they have used for a long time can begin to affect them differently.

The bottom line is that if you have a family member who has had no history of mental illness and they begin to develop symptoms traditionally associated with these illnesses, you should look further. The first step is to find a physician who specializes in disorders associated with aging so that they can undergo a full and thorough evaluation. It is possible that at the end of the day they may be prescribed psychiatric medications to manage their symptoms. It is important, however, that you not start with the mental health field in determining your loved one's situation, but with a geriatric diagnostician.

It is often the case that those who do have a mental illness will find that their symptoms improve as they age. While less common, some find symptoms intensify. The fact is that our bodies change when we get older. Other illnesses may impact an existing mental illness. If your loved one experiences changes in the symptoms they experience because of their mental illness as they age, this should be addressed with an appropriate mental health professional. Medication changes may be needed. The dose may need to be lowered. New medications may be needed. A full geriatric evaluation can be of critical importance. There may be other conditions that are impacting their mental illness.

Anytime your loved one undergoes evaluation you should provide the evaluating physician with as much information and as many medical records as possible.

**Note: Pharmacists are an important part of managing the problems that an elderly person may encounter. Often those who are elderly will see a number of physicians who may or may not be aware of treatments provided by others. Their pharmacist knows all of the medications they are taking. They will be aware of lesser-known side-effects of medications which may contribute to symptoms or symptom management. They will be aware of drug interactions. They have expertise in medications and their use by older persons. Your loved one's pharmacist can be a great resource and an excellent place to start if they do start to develop problems, whether there is a history of mental illness or not.

Violence and Mental illness

Violent behavior is often expected of people who live with mental illnesses. This is a great disservice to the majority of those with mental illnesses who never become violent in any way. It causes isolation, deterioration of relationships, and can result in the loss of fundamental rights. Organizations whose advocacy is based on the violent consequences of untreated mental illness do exist and may skew statistics by distorting the actual incidence of violence due to mental illness. This creates a climate of fear within the community.

The overwhelming majority of those who develop a mental illness do not become violent. The likelihood that a person with mental illness will be violent is equal to or less than the likelihood anyone will. If a person did not use violence before they became ill, they are not likely to use it when symptomatic. They are more likely to be the victims of violence, however, than someone who does not have a mental illness. Research has shown that the most significant predictor of violence for anyone—those with a mental illness and those who do not live with this—is drug or alcohol use. If someone has a mental illness, non-compliance with treatment and delusions of grandeur can be indicators—but not predictors—of the potential for violence. If violence does occur, it is more likely to be directed at family members, especially mothers.

What often lies behind acts of violence is a delusional belief system. The person believes they are in danger or being threatened. In this context, violence makes sense. They are defending themselves, defending someone else, acting in response to a perceived threat.

It is important to listen to what someone says and to understand their perspective whether it makes sense or not. If you believe someone has the potential to be violent, you should avoid increasing the stress they feel or exacerbating their sense of risk or danger. Confrontations, shows of strength, demands, or anger only serve to heighten perceived threat. Never push someone into a corner physically or psychologically.

Individuals with mental illnesses can be frightening to others because their emotions and their reactions are often extreme or don't make sense. They may be unpredictable. Others don't understand the world as they do and don't know how they will respond. The expected doesn't apply. This can cause people to feel uncertain, disoriented, and afraid. The key thing to remember is that those who are not violent in the absence of symptoms or who do not typically use violence to deal with situations, do not often choose violence when symptomatic.

If you are concerned for your safety or for the potential of someone to become violent, you should always remove yourself from the person and situation. Warn others who you believe may be at risk.

Missing Persons

Sometimes people disappear. The reasons they choose to do this are as numerous as they are. When someone you love disappears, it can cut through your heart. Are they okay? Alive? If they are symptomatic you worry about what might happen if they encounter the police; if they encounter someone who will harm or take advantage of them. You worry about how they will eat, where they will sleep. You remember every tragic story that you have ever heard. What you imagine happening to them will inevitably be the stuff of your worse nightmares. There is no feeling more profoundly painful or torturous than not knowing where someone is and whether they are dead or alive. It can consume everything.

If someone you love has left AND they are not symptomatic, there are few things that can be done. Adults have the right to disappear, to leave everything and tell no one. If someone is actively symptomatic, however, they can be considered at-risk and this may give family members more leverage in seeking help to locate them. Here are some things that can be done:

1. Contact the police department in the area where they were last known to be. You must file a missing persons report with the police in that area—even if they did not live there. Each department will have its own guidelines as to how quickly after someone is known to be missing that a report can be filed. If you feel someone is at risk because of symptoms you should stress this—especially as it increases the importance of filing a report immediately. Do not let anyone tell you to wait.
   ***Due to concern for victims of abuse, law enforcement may resist locating a missing adult. Ask if the department has a Crisis Intervention Team (CIT). Ask to speak with a CIT officer. Clarify that you being told where they are is not as important as them being located and given medical assistance.
2. When you file a missing persons report, request (insist) that they also issue a BOLO. A BOLO is short-hand for Be-On-The-Lookout. This information is entered into a national database. Once a BOLO is issued if law enforcement anywhere encounters your loved one they will know they have been reported missing. They will then contact the police department that issued the BOLO.

3. In North Carolina, police are able to issue a Silver Alert. The Silver Alert system notifies the public and law enforcement that someone with a cognitive disorder that places them at risk is missing. Silver Alerts are actively broadcast where BOLO's are only system entries. Police departments across the state get notice of Silver Alerts and specifically try to locate someone. They would only know a BOLO exists if they check on a person they have already encountered.

4. Some police departments are more helpful than others when asked to issue a BOLO or Silver Alert. All too often, police departments discount family concerns when the loved one who is missing is an adult and not suffering from Alzheimer's or dementia. More adults than you realize choose to disappear for many reasons that have nothing to do with mental illness. If you encounter resistance, be polite, be firm, but insist. Explain why you believe your loved one is at risk. They may try to dissuade you. Insist.

5. There are non-profit organizations that help locate missing persons and/or maintain missing persons databases. Some provide templates you can use to develop a flyer. You can get information on these organizations by doing an online search under "Missing Persons." Register your loved one every place that you feel appropriate. If you choose, create a flyer using available templates—or use them as an example to develop your own. (Don't spend time reading over all the people who are posted on these sites as missing persons. It will break your heart.)

6. Create a flyer. This flyer should contain a recent picture or pictures and/or a written description of your loved one. It should include the phone number of the police department where you filed the report and, ideally, the name of the officer(s) that can be contacted and the case number. Detail when your loved one disappeared, from where, and any areas where they may be headed.

7. If you know where your loved one may be, or may be headed, you can look up the names, fax numbers, phone numbers, and even email addresses for every police jurisdiction (state police, sheriff, local police, etc.), every hospital, every mental health facility, and every shelter in that area, the surrounding area, or along the route they might travel. If you believe they are using the bus or train to travel, you can get information about each stop. Make a list.

8. Identify who on this list you feel you should specifically speak with and who you can contact in writing. Send your flyer to every single place on your list whether you plan to call them or not. You can both fax and email it if you have an email for a specific person- say the chief of police, or a contact person at the hospital. Along with the flyer include a brief note as to why you are sending the flyer, and why it is you are concerned about this person's well-being.

9. Begin calling the agencies and persons you have identified as worth calling. Let them know you have faxed, emailed them and/or will be.

10. If your loved one is traveling by train or bus you can also go personally to the local station and speak with someone there. You can ask the police in an area to meet a specific train or bus to see if your loved one is on it.

11. If you believe your loved one is in one specific area, you can also contact the media in that area—newspapers, TV—to ask if they will broadcast something.

12. Follow up on a regular basis with key places and people you identify.

There are a couple of points to consider:

- The squeaky wheel gets greased. The fact that someone is missing and believed to be at risk does not automatically get attention. You will need to be unrelenting, persevere, and a persistent thorn in people's sides. You do not have to be rude. You must be firm. You must be insistent. You must not back down. You must refuse to go away.

- Even when found, if someone does not appear to be in immediate danger the police do not have the authority to detain or hold them without a court order. It may not be sufficient to file a Missing Person's report. You may need to also obtain a Petition for Involuntary Commitment at the same time—and keep it current. (see **p. 267**)

- If your loved one is hospitalized, because of confidentiality, no one has to notify you. However, if a missing persons report has been filed and there is an active case number, they do have to notify the police. The police can tell you if your loved one is in the hospital.

- There is always a two-edged sword to consider when contacting the police. We have included a section in this manual with suggestions for working with the police. Ask each police department you contact if they have a CIT officer, and request the information you provide be given to that officer. Assess your loved one's risk of acting out if they come in contact with the police. You need to provide this honest assessment. If they have no history of aggression or violence make sure this is known. Especially if they may appear aggressive. If there are certain things which excite or calm, give this information to the police. If they do not have weapons—or if they do—this is important to communicate. Perhaps they have taken weapons only to protect themselves if needed but would not otherwise use them. If you believe this, make sure this distinction is clear so that police know to present a non-threatening posture should they encounter them. Give the police the best tools possible for dealing with this specific person: what you know.

> *When Joanne disappeared, all we knew for sure was that she was headed west. I had access to the debit card she was using and could see the general area she was in. I called the police in that area to let them know what was going on and to ask them to keep an eye out for her. When I was done, the officer that I spoke with commented that by asking them to keep an eye out for her, I might have caused something bad to happen. I was stunned. I felt a terror ripple through my core. Had I done the right thing? Reason reminded me that if they did not know what was going on and encountered her it was more likely to end badly. Now they knew she was sick. Now they knew why she was acting strangely. Now they knew what was going on.*

This is a hard, painful situation. Each day that someone is missing adds to the likelihood of a chronic crisis. What is described above is a full-court press. It is not something that can be sustained indefinitely. It will eat the life out of you. If you are looking for a missing person, please take care of yourself.

1. You must remember each and every day that you are not responsible for how this turns out. If there is an encounter with the police that goes badly, you did not cause that. Police are often the first point of contact when someone is in a mental health crisis. If your loved one is symptomatic, at risk, and in a strange place, sooner or later there will be an encounter with the police.

2. You must, as much as possible, live your life every single day. This does not mean you stop maintaining contact with the

police and others or figuring out new ways to search. It does mean that once you have made your initial push, you have to find a new healthy routine and live it. Maybe once every 3 days, or once a week you go back and follow up with key people and agencies. Perhaps you think of new places or people to contact, and then you do. But in the meantime, you must return to your life. Sometimes missing people are found quickly. Sometimes they are not. You can only live in this space but for so long.

3. The moment when you do begin to pick up your life and get back to some sort of normalcy can be one laden with guilt. How can you laugh? How can you get up every day and do normal things—go to work, to dinner, chat with someone on the phone—when someone you love is missing and may be in danger? The guilt you feel is normal, and it is not an indication that what you are doing is wrong. It's not. Know this. You are doing what you must and what you should do for yourself and for everyone else you love in a situation which is anything but normal or usual.

4. You need to care for yourself. Eat. You may not feel like it but make yourself do it. Sleep. If you can't, consider talking to your doctor to get something that will help you temporarily. Do things that do not revolve around this. Maybe you can read a book. Watch TV. Maybe you can go out to dinner or a movie. You may feel guilty (see #3) when you do. Consider this—*if you do not give yourself the food, sleep, and ability to decompress emotionally and move your mind elsewhere, you will quickly burn out and not be able to do what needs to be done. If you want to be able to keep searching, then you need to have moments in your life where you step away from the search altogether.*

5. If this becomes a long-term event, consider seeking outside support in the form of a counselor, or other professionals who can help you to deal with what you are going through.

It is devastating when someone you love disappears and you do not know what has happened. There is no closure. The potential for all things—good and bad—is an open-ended, daily possibility. Only you know what is best for yourself, for the person you love, and for all those who are involved in your situation. There is no way to find a perfect balance that feels good. What you seek is the best way possible to deal with an impossible situation.

Homelessness

Homelessness and mental illness are so linked in the public minds that it is almost cliché to speak of the homeless who are mentally ill. Untreated mental illness and chronic drug abuse or alcoholism are among the causes of homelessness—whether short-term or chronic. If someone you love is homeless, it can be painful and frightening. It can be guilt-inducing, too, especially if you are unable or unwilling to have them live with you.

There are times when a person's mental illness and their unwillingness to manage it become such a disruptive force that you are forced to make decisions about how much they can be a part of your life. You are forced to make decisions about how and when, and if, you will help or be involved with them. These kinds of decisions do not come easily. If, however, you have decided, for whatever reason it is not beneficial, healthy, or workable for your loved one to live with you or that you need to limit your involvement with them, you are not wrong.

There are times when those with untreated mental illnesses choose to leave their families or not to accept the help and support that they offer, even if it means being homeless.

If someone you love is homeless and you are still involved with them there are a few ways that you can offer support:

1. Do what you can to make sure they have food—whether this means periodically bringing them take-out or taking them for something to eat.
2. Do what you can to make sure that they have the proper clothing.
3. Help them to access local shelters and programs for the homeless. Many communities have programs where those who are homeless can get a meal, a bed, make phone calls, take a shower, wash clothes, and work with a case manager or social worker to access other services. They can be of assistance in helping people to get benefits they may be entitled to, find housing and get assistance with housing and utility costs.

** Local state and federal campgrounds may be a safe alternative to living in a shelter if your loved one is not disruptive. They are relatively inexpensive and afford a degree of privacy and shelter that they cannot find on the street. Additionally, many park rangers have experience with mental illness. Campgrounds are an option more individuals avail themselves of then you would imagine. They offer a degree of monitoring and knowledgeable response. State and Federal campgrounds generally limit the time anyone can stay at the facility to about 2 weeks out of any given month. This may give your loved one a break from the streets, or you may be able to help them move between campgrounds on a rotating basis until they are able to get on their feet.

Joblessness

Those who are dealing with a mental illness often go through periods without work. Someone may be unable to work due to symptoms. Lengthy breaks in their job history may make it difficult to find work when they are ready. Symptoms may be managed, but following a significant mental health crisis it can take up to a year to fully recover. During that time it may be impossible to manage the stress and demands of the workplace.

If someone you love is not working and is not able to work—because of symptoms or because they are recovering from a psychiatric crisis—they may be eligible for disability benefits. In addition to receiving a monthly payment, when they are ready to return to work, Social Security offers a number of programs that can help people in that process. Some programs will allow individuals to work a minimal number of hours without impacting SSDI payments. This allows those unable to work full time to participate in the workplace and maintain their sense of autonomy still. Another program will allow people to continue to receive/remain eligible for disability during the better part of the first work year. If they do have problems as they try to return to work, they will not have lost their disability status. Your loved one may be able to go to school or enter a training program and still be eligible for disability. The Ticket to Work program allows people to draw up a plan for getting back into the workforce—including going to school or undergoing training—and will provide additional help and financial support to carry out that plan.

Your loved one may also have the ability to access services through the Vocational Office of Rehabilitation. This is a government program whose sole purpose is to assist people in finding work. Vocational Rehab can offer training and support for school. They can provide job counselors and testing. They can provide assistance in finding employment. Not everyone is eligible for these services, but if your loved one could benefit from assistance, they should make an appointment and talk to a Vocational Rehab Specialist to determine what help they can provide.

At times people are not ready to return to work full-time, or they are unable to find a job. When their condition is well-managed not doing something can become mentally detrimental. One option is volunteer work. It is not necessary to identify volunteer work as "volunteer" on a resume. It is job experience. It also allows your loved one to work as much or as little as they are able without risking their health or their disability payments. If a volunteer position is not successful, it is easier to leave and there are fewer negative consequences. Volunteering is a great option on many levels and allows people to explore interests as they consider their path. Volunteering helps people to begin to pick up the pieces and reclaim parts of life that were put aside while focusing on their illness. It provides the opportunity to gradually adjust to the work setting and its stresses while discovering limitations. It affords flexibility in exploring how to handle limitations or problems imposed by their illness. It serves as an entryway back into community life and is an opportunity to meet and interact with others.

INTERACTING WITH THE POLICE

Guess Who's Coming to Dinner: When Police Respond to a Mental Health Emergency

Jim Huegerich, Former Director,
Chapel Hill Police Department Crisis Unit, Chapel Hill, NC

Mental illness can be the great divider, separating us from one another when we most need the support and safety net of community to both survive and thrive. To be honest, no one likes to think about law enforcement responding to our homes or workplaces. No one likes to be out of control. And for most of us, the arrival of law enforcement feels out of control and perhaps even a like failure on our part.

Our partnership with law enforcement in a time of crisis, however, is absolutely essential to survive and to thrive. This partnership can create a team that helps to provide a safety net for those experiencing mental health crises as well as supporting families, connecting the family (including the member in crisis) with the community supports (both natural and professional), defusing the situation, and jointly designing the next steps for stabilization.

Yet, these partnerships are not going to happen unless we are willing to recognize the need for them and understand what is necessary to make them happen and happen well. We must work hard to do our part.

Police are people just like you and me who sometimes experience extraordinary challenges. They do not like to be out of control, do not like to be surprised, and are no more comfortable dealing with chaos, confusion or crisis than anyone else. It is important we recognize that as family members we possess a great deal of information that can help responding officers do their job of defusing, stabilizing and connecting persons experiencing mental health crises.

What police should know about your family
Information to share with the police

Normal/History?
It is very important for the police officer called into your home to quickly understand what "normal" looks like for both the person in mental health crisis and the rest of your family, and also to know

how the family member has responded in the past. The best predictor of violence is not anger or even acting out, but rather what a person has done in the past given a similar scenario. It is important for law enforcement to know that when confronted with challenges whether your family member normally yells or scream, or silent and uncommunicative. Do they get aggressive or attempt to flee? In addition, in the past, what has helped the family member defuse or calm? What has worked to break the rhythm when the person is escalating emotionally and physically? Are there any triggers that make things worse, or conversely are there actions or soothers that work to calm the family member? Are there some things or places or people that make the family member feel safer or more threatened?

Danger/threats?

It is essential for the law enforcement personnel who respond to your family member to know if there has been a history of violence—assault, weapons, threats, or damage to property. If they are responding at a residence, they need to know the location of any weapons. Police are trained to avoid bedrooms, kitchens, and bathrooms because these are places where weapons are often kept or where "weapons of opportunity" can be found. Individuals in mental health crisis are no more dangerous than the general population; however, they can be more fragile during a crisis. They may perceive that the only way to protect themselves is blocked by the officer standing in their escape route. Officers are trained to not corner or block a person in crisis either physically or psychologically. We ourselves need to be aware of this when dealing with a family member in crisis. And we must be very careful not to touch an agitated person.

Supports/Resources?

Is your family member seeing a mental health professional? If so, does that person know what is going on right now, and what would they do or say if they knew? Are there family members or friends who either calm or escalate emotions with this family member? Police can find this information helpful in both defusing and stabilizing a crisis situation.

What families should know about police

"Well-being Checks"

Police offer "**Well-being** Checks" to family members, including home visits to check on a person's mental and physical condition. Is the person uncommunicative or unresponsive? Are they taking their medication? Do they pose a danger to themselves or others? Police also take missing person reports. It is helpful for responding officers to know the "normal/history" of the family member because you may not be present when police make contact with the family member. It is also important to know community supports for the person with whom the officer can communicate the conditions they discover.

Partnerships
Build relationships with police BEFORE a mental health crisis begins, sharing the "normal/history" information above. Police generally have no idea what is best for you, your family member, or the situation; they need you to help them understand.

Supports/resources
Keep support/resource information written on a piece of paper and handy for when police respond.

Remember, the partnership between law enforcement and the family is an essential part of a safety net for both the persons in mental health crisis and for family members. You can play a critical role in building and maintaining that partnership.

Our Family's Experience With the Police

By John Poetzsch

Writer Ron Powers has written a book titled *No One Cares About Crazy People* (Hachette Books, 2017). In the preface, he states "I hope you do not 'enjoy' this book. I hope you are wounded…wounded to act, to intervene." On January 6, 2013, my brother-in-law, Spencer Mims, died on his way to the hospital after being shot by the police. He was 55 years old. He was shot on his front porch, in front of his father. Spencer had a mental illness.

Since his death, I have had time to reflect on Spencer's life, the stigma that he faced, and how I had viewed him myself. There were times when Spencer's mental illness was disruptive. It was difficult not only for him but for his family. Spencer was also a good man. He was a loved and cherished part of his family. He was kind. We were good friends and I considered him my brother. He was godfather to both of my children. He was intelligent. He knew a lot about a multitude of subjects. He was outgoing, friendly, sensitive, and humorous. He was a loving son, brother, and very close to my children who never called him uncle. To them, he was "Ace." Spencer's family was involved in their church. He was in the youth group, sang in the choir, and played the trumpet. But like many other illnesses, his would periodically come back. Even when this did happen, never, once, was Spencer violent.

Spencer had been diagnosed in college. He suffered from bipolar disorder with periods of depression, anxiety, and at times excessive spending. He could be obsessive and he could act impulsively. Despite his mental illness, Spencer graduated from UNC-Chapel Hill and worked for the same company for over 25 years. He was a valued employee and he worked hard to maintain his mental health. Spencer's illness in no way defined who Spencer was.

Spencer's funeral was held at the same Methodist Church where he was baptized. Where he was a member of the youth program, sang in the choir, and played his trumpet alongside his brother as their father directed. At the visitation, friends and coworkers alike remembered times Spencer had helped them with both work and personal concerns. His mental illness had made him very aware of and sympathetic to the struggles of others. In some way, he had touched all of their lives. It was sad to realize how few knew of his problems until they read the headlines in the paper and saw his story on the evening news.

I did not make much of an attempt to learn more about Spencer's struggles in the 42 years that I knew him. I regret this. I regret that I did not understand better what he was struggling with. I know that we need to make this attempt—both as families and as a community. We fail the people we love when we do not understand what they are going through. That failure is complete when it leads to their death because of the ignorance and misunderstandings about mental illness by our police departments. We need to talk. We need to understand. We need to develop and to offer better ways of handling mental health crises. Police must be trained to deal with individuals in crises before they placed on duty.

On the night that he was killed Spencer became uncharacteristically upset with his father for no apparent reason. He cursed at him which he had never done. This was so unlike Spencer that his father, who he lived with, became concerned. My father-in-law decided to take a drive hoping that being alone would help Spencer to calm down. He came across a police officer and asked for assistance in dealing with his son who was in a crisis. With a plan to meet the police at home, my father-in-law returned there.

When the police arrived, they found Spencer sitting on the floor of the front porch. He had a box cutter at his throat. Spencer never made a verbal threat against himself, his father, or the officers. In fact, when an officer moved towards Spencer, he got up and moved away from the officer to the corner of the porch. Within seven minutes of their arrival and against all police procedures, the officers escalated the situation and in their panic shot Spencer three times. Spencer died on the way to the hospital.

Today, the reason that I share Spencer's story is that we do not want anyone else killed simply because they are in the midst of a crisis. We do not want any other family to go through what we now live with every single day. We do not want any other parent to witness their child being killed because they tried to get the care that they needed.

After over five years, the family obtained a rare jury double verdict of police negligence in the Wrongful Death of Spencer and the Negligent Infliction of Emotional Distress (NIED) on behalf of his father in witnessing the tragedy.

We can do better than this.

In memory of my brother-in-law, Spencer R. Mims, III, we should demand that all police officers receive the training required for handling citizens in crisis before being allowed on our streets.

Insights From Law Enforcement
Chris Blue, Chief, Chapel Hill Police Department, Chapel Hill, NC

No matter the type of call, the first priority of a law enforcement officer is the safety of all involved.

Officers increasingly find themselves interacting with individuals with mental illness or other developmental disability. So, it's critical that law enforcement agencies nationwide collaborate with mental health providers to appropriately respond to the unique challenges of individuals experiencing a mental health crisis. Initiatives such as Mental Health First Aid training, implementation of Crisis Intervention (CIT) Teams, and the use of mental health professionals within agencies can increase officers' knowledge and competence when responding to such calls. And, such tools help officers de-escalate and diffuse situations, and build ongoing partnerships with mental health providers in the community.

However, responding to a mental health crisis also requires a holistic approach that involves families. Families often wonder what actions they can take before, during, and after a crisis to help with a safe and successful law enforcement response.

For families with a member who is experiencing mental illness or another developmental disability and who may come into contact with law enforcement as a result, an important first step is to build a relationship with their local law enforcement partners. Taking the time to meet, connect, and engage with the local police agency can go a long way towards ensuring successful encounters if they do occur.

This interaction provides families and responding officers the opportunity to build rapport and trust with one another. Information can be exchanged that will help families understand the process of response, police tactics, areas of intervention, and possible outcomes. Additionally, officers gain information from families about their family members and important information that may be useful if a response is necessary.

When a crisis develops and it is decided that police assistance is needed, the first step is to call 911. The 911 operator will ask LOTS of questions to gather important information about the crisis which will then be shared with responding officers. Useful information to have handy when calling includes:

- the individual's name and the caller's relationship to them,
- any relevant presenting behaviors,

- safety-related concerns (access to weapons, history of self-harm or violence, or triggers that may escalate the situation),
- any medication use and reactions,
- use of drugs or alcohol, and
- physical descriptors of the individual in crisis (age, height, weight and current appearance) to help officers immediately identify them upon arrival

The caller can, and should, ask for a CIT officer to respond if one is available.

Callers should not be surprised if 2 or more officers respond. This is standard practice for the safety of all involved. The reporting person will, again, be asked to provide the information shared on the 911 call. It is also helpful for responding officers to know what precipitated the crisis, how the individual may react to officers, any changes that have occurred since the initial call, and if the individual cannot follow verbal instructions. When possible, it can also be helpful to have someone who is trusted and known to the individual in crisis to stay with them while the reporting person speaks with officers.

Once all of that important information has been shared, officers will consider a variety of interventions to include immediate de-escalation and diffusion of the crisis, outreach to additional resources such as a mobile crisis unit, an emergency (involuntary or voluntary) mental health commitment, or, rarely, an arrest and respond in the way that is most appropriate.

If there are any questions or concerns about the officer's response, you should share them. However, this is best done once the scene is under control and or the response is concluded. And, you if you ever feel that your concerns have not been adequately addressed, request to speak with a supervisor. It is their job to ensure the most appropriate, safe, and compassionate response is provided.

After any crisis response, following up with the department can be helpful and can inform any future response. You are encouraged to offer feedback, ask questions, and to seek clarification on the decisions and actions that were undertaken. Getting involved in local training and sharing experiences with other families, advocates, law enforcement agencies, policy makers and community partners can aid in future responses, community education and understanding, and can lead to systemic improvements. The perspectives of families and individuals touched by mental illness or other developmental disabilities are critically important and can have a lasting impact.

A PRACTICAL GUIDE TO SELF-CARE

1. Repeat as often as you need to: I did not cause this illness and I cannot make it go away.

2. If you cannot stop thinking about your loved one's problems try the following:
    - If you speak another language, even a little bit, try ruminating in that language instead of English. This stimulates another part of your brain and can help break the self-talk loop that can occur.
    - Think of a place where you are really happy and relaxed: the beach, mountains, a secluded lake, and visualize yourself there.
    - Write your feelings out.
    - Write a "letter" to your loved one, expressing your frustration, but don't send it.
    - Make a list of things you have done to support your loved one.
    - Play or listen to music.

3. Find a good therapist for yourself. This will provide you with needed support. A therapist can help you to find ways to communicate with your loved one. They can help you to set appropriate expectations and boundaries.

4. Keep a journal. This will help you understand your loved one's problem and your responses to it. Sometimes problems with mental illness recur and it can be helpful to see that you coped with a situation before.

5. Set boundaries as they are needed. Identify people whose judgment you trust in this. When you feel guilty, turn to them to for support.

6. Find supportive friends who understand your situation and can talk with you about it.

7. Try and "reach around" the illness in your family member and respond to what is healthy. This is not always possible. Respond to the emotions that they express rather than arguing about what you have done. Affirm your love and concern.

8. Be loving. Remember you are not the cause of your loved one's problems.

9. Clarify what you need to be well. Do what you need to do to secure those things. You cannot help your loved one if you and your life fall apart.
10. Take care of your own health. Exercise, eat a healthy diet, try yoga or meditation
11. Maintain a balance between your loved one and other aspects of your life. Do things that bring pleasure. Do not let everything revolve around them and/or their illness.
12. Don't give up. Keep trying to maintain contact.

CARING FOR YOUR MARRIAGE

When a family member develops mental illness, it can put an enormous strain on a marriage. There is no way to avoid this, but there are ways to support and nurture your relationship with your partner.

Recognize the problem: you are dealing with a chronic illness whose symptoms are challenging to cope with. Husbands and wives rarely see any problem through the same lens, let alone one as difficult as mental illness. Set aside time to talk about what is happening—just the two of you. Work to understand each other's point of view. One person may attempt to learn everything they can about the illness while another may be in complete denial. Neither is wrong. It often takes time to reach a mutual understanding of what the problem actually is.

Get help. This is critical. A good therapist, an understanding clergy, supportive and knowledgeable friends, your personal physician—all can be excellent resources.

Take the NAMI Family to Family class—together if possible. This 12-session program works to give families the insight needed to cope.

Learn all you can about how to deal with the symptoms your loved one has.

Avoid blame. This is easier said than done. It is easy to point fingers at one family or the other for a genetic predisposition. It is easy to blame parenting styles. These are fruitless and destructive lines of thought.
Be careful how you express anger. It is easy to be angry. You can be angry at the disease but not the person who has it. Try and use your anger to inspire action. Remember nothing you, your spouse, son or daughter did caused the illness.

Find someone other than your partner to whom you can vent your frustrations. It is important to have people outside of your family who understand your situation and will allow you to talk.

Do regular fun things together that don't revolve around your loved one's illness. Go out to dinner, for a walk, play with your dog, listen to music—something fun for both of you.

Continue your normal activities as much as you can. Continue to be involved with your faith community, if you have one. Avoid isolating yourselves.

Don't let your loved one play one of you against the other. Never allow bitter criticism of your partner. Your loved one—regardless of their age and place in the family—needs to know that you are a united pair and that you will work together to help them.

When life is difficult, take turns. One of you can address the problems for a time, and then the other one can take over.

When possible, plan how to handle situations that may arise in advance.

Accept that neither of you has control over how your loved one's illness progresses. An adult may refuse treatment. Some treatments are ineffective. Talk with each other about frustrations. Set appropriate and mutually acceptable boundaries. Respect one another's limits even when yours are different.

Sometimes one partner is resistant to seeking professional help. If this is the case, the other can go alone. You can share what you learn and the insights that it gives to you.

Recognize that you will both probably feel very sad. This is painful. This hurts. Help one another grieve. Remember, though, the process of grief is different for each person: the way someone grieves, when, and how this process unfolds. Honor these differences.

Most of all, be kind to one another. Be kind to one another. Be kind to one another. The more things you do to make this journey easier for one another the better it will be for you, your partner, your marriage, and for your family. And, be kind to yourself. Be kind to yourself. Be kind to yourself.

Step-parents and Marriage

A stepparent rarely has the same role as a natural parent—especially when both natural parents remain involved. This is especially true if a child is older when a stepparent joins the family. They may not take on or be given the authority of a natural parent. For example, their opinion about how to treat the illness, interact with the child or deal with problems may not carry weight. In spite of this, stepparents are often shoulder-to-shoulder with everyone else who is experiencing the impact of familial mental illness. This dissonance can be particularly pronounced if the stepparent does not have children of their own or when parenting styles differ.

Stepparents who do not have children may not understand the obligations or the urgency that a natural parent often feels—especially as children become adults. They may become frustrated with behaviors caused by symptoms and blame their partner for not imposing what would be natural consequences under other circumstances. They may not agree with allowing an adult child who is behaving badly to remain home. When a loved one is ill, their illness is causing prolonged chaos and disruption, everyone is under stress, parenting styles are different, and one partner does not have an equal voice in decisions, the marriage will suffer significant strain.

<u>If you are the natural parent</u>

Listen to what your partner thinks. This may not be their child. They may not be a parent in their own right. They do know you and your child. Their insights and ideas are valuable. The fact that they love you but are not involved as you may mean they see some things differently or more clearly.

Listen to your partner's feelings and take them into account in the decisions you make. This may not be their child but they are a part of this family and they are impacted. It is just as difficult for them though in a different way. They need to be heard and to feel that they matter—that someone sees how they are affected. When someone feels they have no control, it often means they do not feel heard—that their feelings and needs are not a consideration in the decisions made.

Allow your partner to be involved or not at the level they choose. Emotionally, they may not be able to be as involved as you must be. They may not accompany you on every trip to the hospital, or to visit your child. They may need to leave in the midst of a crisis when things get too intense. On the other hand, when they are willing, find ways to include them in the decisions that are made and in caring for your child.

Encourage your partner to set healthy and appropriate boundaries for themselves in their relationship with your child. They should not be subject to anger, abuse, rudeness, lack of respect, or other ill-treatment on an ongoing basis with no ability to respond. All too often this situation leads to a slow boil that can poison their relationship with your child and with you and can even finally erupt in aggression or violence.

Recognize that your partner may feel that they have even less control than you do in this situation. Find ways to help them exert control.

Seek counseling, both individually and as a couple, to help each of you deal with what is going on in your home and to learn to deal with it well as a couple.

Care for your partner. It may seem like a bit much to ask that you care for a sufficient adult in the midst of caring for a child who is ill. By this, we mean to be *aware* of your partner's feelings and needs. Take them into account as you are making decisions and juggling all that is on your plate. The more you each can do to make this journey easier for one another the better it will be for you, your partner, your marriage, and for your family.

If you are the step-parent

Learn about mental illness. Try to understand that this is an illness. It is not something your partner or their child can control. Remember that your step-child is more than his or her illness. Learn all you can about how to deal with the symptoms he or she is exhibiting. The more you learn, the more you will be able to see beyond the present circumstance and understand the potential for management of the illness and recovery.

Set appropriate boundaries with your step-child in ways that are appropriate for the illness and symptoms they have. The way we respond to someone who is symptomatic may be very different than the way we respond to the same behaviors in someone who is not. When we respond in ways that do not take the symptoms into account we can actually cause the situation (and symptoms) to worsen.

Listen to your partner. This is their child and they have known this child since birth. They understand how to best help this person. Try to understand why they make the decisions that they make, and what they believe will help their child through this illness.

Do not ask your partner to: give up on or end their relationship with their child; tell them that their child will never/can never get better; ask them to choose between you and their child; kick their child out of the home; or stop trying to help their child through this illness. In some situations parents do come to these conclusions. It is always a heart-wrenching process. The pain never goes away. If you pressure someone, more often than not it adds to the stress and anxiety that is present. No one will win in this situation.

Find someone other than your partner to whom you can vent. You need someone who is not emotionally involved, and who understands the obligations and responsibilities that both of you have. Someone who can provide a place for you to speak your frustration, anger, or fears.

Resist the temptation to blame the person who seems to have control—the natural parents. Recognize that neither your partner nor the child's other parent caused this illness and they cannot cure it. They may not be able to control how well the illness is managed. They cannot change their child's behavior merely by changing how they parent. They cannot make the mental health system provide the treatment their child needs.

Create spaces for yourself in your home. Have a place in the home you can go when you need to get away. Do things outside of the home that give you a sense of normalcy. Walk away for a while if you need to.

Spend time with your partner that does not revolve around their child's illness.

If you feel like you are going to explode: walk away.

Seek counseling—both individually and as a couple, to help each of you deal with what is going on and to learn to deal with it well as a couple.

Care for your partner. Your partner is under incredible stress and experiencing one of the most emotionally difficult experiences any parent can face—a potentially life-changing illness in their child. The single greatest gift you can give is to stand by your partner and to support them in the decisions they must make. This does not mean always agreeing with those decisions. You may disagree with your partner's decisions, with how they choose to support their child, or you may think their cause is hopeless. At the end of the day, what they need most from you is your support for each of these things—including the decision to keep trying. Practically, caring can mean that during a crisis you take on some of the things that your partner normally does: cooking, cleaning, bills, dealing with the details of everyday life. Emotionally, it means letting your partner know you believe in them—if nothing else—and you support their need to try to help their child. Ask yourself: if I do this, if I say this—will it make things harder for my partner or will it make it easier? The more things you each can do to make this journey easier for one another the better it will be for you, your partner, your marriage, and for your family.

Together

When possible, identify and agree in advance on how to handle situations that may arise.

Create illness-free zones in your time together and in your home. This is as important for you individually as it is for your marriage. When a child is living at home, you both need time and space that is not defined or ruled by your family member's illness. Whether your family member is at home or on their own, you need things in your lives *together* that do not revolve around them or any current crisis.

Remember that you both need to feel that your home belongs to each of you.

Most important: Be kind to one another. Be kind to one another. Be kind to one another.

The more you each can do to make this journey easier for one another the better it will be for you, your partner, your marriage, and for your family. And be kind to yourself, be kind to yourself, be kind to yourself.

PART THREE

THE MENTAL HEALTH SYSTEM

To My Service Provider

Oh how we love
in complexity, simplicity, honesty, even deceit
and without sense;
mucking our way through the requirements of a relationship
whose existence is fashioned of jello
(which having taken shape will inevitably lose it once again)
Do we seem
unskilled? Wrong?
Is it anger, disdain, disgust, rejection
desperation, confusion, loss that you see?
Do we complicate things?
It is all true
It is still illusion
In some fundamental and hidden place
amidst the apparent folly of holding
jello
Within the heated palm of a fist
remains who I was, she became, what he will be
looking for a miracle
wanting to believe
(there is a moment when something
solid forms)
It is so easy to get lost in the landscape of this gelatinous
mess,
to miss the hope, or turn away
as experience would predict jello doesn't hold form
And yet, this is how we come
Hoping
You can slow this melting away
 (will you give form to our beliefs
fears, desperations, desires, our pain,
what happens when we open this fist
And jello falls to your hand?)
Remember this,
This fist holds someone's child
perfect and full of all the possibility
that life promises
This fist is clenched in desperate love and fear
This fist loosens into your hand
with hope, trust
begging
that you will do what we can't
Find shape there

Donna Kay Smith

A Tale of Three Diseases

One

Jenny, aged 9, has a very sore throat and a fever of 101. Her mother, Jane, takes her to the doctor. A quick strep test is done; strep is diagnosed; antibiotics are prescribed and she recovers in a few days. Jane explained to her colleagues that Jenny had strep and she would be out for a few days.

Two

Jane finds a lump in her breast. She has a mammogram and then a biopsy and is diagnosed with breast cancer. There is a question as to the appropriate treatment: a lumpectomy, mastectomy, with or without chemotherapy and radiation. Her cancer will be assessed, and appropriate treatment will be determined. She may have to live with cancer or the possibility of cancer for the rest of her life. The treatments can vary but the diagnosis is based on specific clinical criteria. Jane's colleagues organize meals for her family and volunteer to help her with Jenny.

Three

Jenny has turned 20. She has been acting strangely. Her grades in college have fallen drastically, and Jenny cannot go to her classes. She has stopped seeing her friends. She talks about everyone being against her. Her parents are so worried they drive to her college to see what is wrong. They are terrified by what they find. They do not know what to do so they called their family doctor who offers to see Jenny. She refuses to talk to him. He suggests a psychiatrist. There is no clinical test to find out what is wrong. There is no roadmap for them to follow. No surgery, no antibiotic. Just the beginning of a long, arduous process of discovery.

INTRODUCTION

When we speak of the *mental health system,* we refer to the system a state implements for care. Funding is the basis for the distinction between the mental health system and private care. Most often, the primary system of care for mental illnesses is publicly funded. No *system* of care exists in the private sector. In the private sector, you must seek the individual professionals needed and work with each independent of any other professionals that may be involved. While this may be true to a lesser degree in other health care fields, the lines are more sharply drawn in providing treatment for mental illnesses.

While some services overlap, there is often a significant difference between services available to those with private insurance and those available to persons using Medicaid, Medicare, or state funds. Unexpectedly, those who rely on public funds may have access to a broader range of treatment options. Private insurance, with few exceptions, covers inpatient acute hospitalization, limited outpatient counseling, and outpatient drug/alcohol rehabilitation programs. Public funds cover inpatient programs as well as a range of supportive and medical outpatient programs and services.

In the 1960's, as mental illnesses were first known to be physical illnesses that could be treated with medication, the movement to provide services in a community setting gained significant traction. Before that there was little that could be done in the community for someone suffering the symptoms of mental illness. The norm was hospitalization—or institutionalization for long periods. For those with the most severe and difficult to treat symptoms institutionalization could last a lifetime.

Medication made it possible for many to leave the hospital. Those who would have otherwise spent their lives in an institution were able to return to the community. However, it quickly became evident that medication alone did not lead to recovery. The ability of a person to take medication as necessary—often while suffering unpleasant side effects that could also be debilitating—was far from the only problem. Dealing with the side effects of medication and the negative symptoms of these illnesses requires support. People recovering from a significant or severe mental health crisis are often not able to return to work immediately or in a full-time capacity. The lack of income, housing, and the inability to provide for basic needs places significant stress on someone who requires stress-free conditions to heal. The lack of appropriate and necessary supports all too often results in losing gains that have been made and ultimately in another mental health crisis.

In response to de-institutionalization, treatment providers worked to develop services that are called *community based*. These are out-patient services that enable someone to live in the community while they receive the care and support that they need. Often, these services are not covered by private insurance. Ironically, this means that someone who does not receive public funds may not be able to obtain the treatment that is needed to support them remaining at home.

This is frustrating for people trying not to let everything fall apart. The system requires that everything fall apart on almost every level before necessary care becomes available.

Private insurance most often authorizes medication for the treatment of symptoms. Medication is the most direct and cost-effective approach. The investment by insurance companies in pharmaceutical treatments spurs innovation and the development of better medications with fewer side effects. However, there is little impetus in the private sector for developing or providing other types of treatments that may lack such clear biological efficacy. Consequently, medication is often the only treatment considered essential for management of symptoms leading to a distorted treatment model. The burden for developing a full range of treatments addressing the broad range of needs present in recovering from and living with a mental illness falls on the poorly funded public sector. Ultimately, the promise of de-institutionalization and community-based services has never been fulfilled because the range and depth of the services needed have never received the financial support needed. And no one, not those with private insurance nor those with public funding, has easy access to the full range of care that is both possible and necessary for recovery.

North Carolina's publicly funded services have gone through many re-iterations or alternative structures since the 1970's. Today they are part of what is called a *Managed Care* system. The state selects a company to authorize treatment and disperse funds. These companies are called LME's/MCO's. An LME is a Local Management Entity. An MCO is a Managed Care Organization. North Carolina is divided into six different regions with LME/MCO's overseeing the services offered in their region. You can find a complete list of NC LME/MCO's on **page 5**. On **p. 145** you will find a full discussion of the role that LME/MCO's play in our mental health system.

There is no such thing as a seamless or integrated system of care. The onus for ensuring appropriate treatment often falls on the family as symptoms may make it difficult to care for one's self, and navigating a complex and inadequate system when you are sick feel impossible.

Make no mistake, navigating the system to access basic medical care is a difficult thing in North Carolina today. At times it may seem impossible. While our state provides a range of inpatient and community-based services gaps exist in the care continuum. Eligibility for services will depend on how someone is insured, the funding available, the number of people in need of that service, AND the area of the state they live in. You may have to research what is needed, what resources are available, and advocate on behalf of your loved one. You may end up putting together treatment plans and working with different providers to transition care as needs change. When the services needed simply do not exist you may find yourself piecing together the next best thing.

It is a fight in the best of situations and you should not expect it to be otherwise. If you are effective, you will not be winning most popular family member awards and you will often feel frustrated and blocked by the very system that is supposed to provide care. It is hard. It is stressful. It takes time. It takes perseverance and tenacity. You must believe in yourself and what you know is right. You must believe in the ability of the person you love to recover and do well with appropriate care. Advocacy is simply and unfortunately necessary to ensure the care that is needed to recover and thrive when one has a mental illness.

Robert's Story
Ruth

My son Robert was diagnosed with schizophrenia at the age of fourteen after years of turbulence, including learning disabilities and drug use. I know no other disorder that carries so much stigma or barriers to treatment. This is our story.

It was 1974, a time when mothers were deemed the cause of schizophrenia. Doctors even had a name for us—*schizophrenogenic!* When Robert was hospitalized the first time I was on a work assignment out of the country—which confirmed that diagnosis. His father panicked and called my office even though there was nothing I could do. I came home to find that everybody in my office knew and that Robert had become a non-person. No one ever asked me how he was doing. My sister blamed me because I was separating from my husband. My mother advised me to put a lock on my bedroom door. Robert's doctor predicted, "He will probably always be in the shadows, committing petty offenses."

I was blamed for Robert's disorder, and Robert was blamed for not getting well. Our social worker decided I was a "refrigerator mother." When I told her he was carried around a lot when he was a baby, she decided I was over-protective. Until I told her different people had carried him. I quickly learned that she believed, "however you raised him—that is why this happened." She advised me to get a job that didn't take me out of the country. Medical notes from that time describe me as having "abandoned" Robert. I had no other resources and NAMI did not exist. I found myself alone in charting a course for us.

Robert's first long-term hospitalization lasted almost a year during which the social worker "worked" on the parents. A successful session meant all the parents and children got together staff was able to get them fighting. When his father stopped going to the meetings, I went alone. Robert did not improve but was released. He lasted less than six months at home before he was hospitalized again for another year. Once again I was told, "I'm sorry, Mrs. Dennis, there is nothing more we can do."

After several more hospitalizations—none longer than three weeks—the doctors decided that Robert should not be living with his schizophrenogenic mother. For once, I was glad to have that label. I would finally get some rest. Robert roamed at night when he was psychotic. I dared not sleep until he did. Robert's father took him in on condition that he take his medications and not use street drugs. Mostly he complied.

I found an agency that provided casework services. They assigned a male caseworker to Robert. This reduced the number of crises he was having. One time I got a call from a ranger in the Shenandoah Mountains where Robert had been backpacking with a friend. He found Robert wandering alone and shoeless. The ranger was kind and kept him occupied until I got there. When I did, Robert greeted me with a bunch of wildflowers he had picked. He was perfectly calm but clearly psychotic.

When Robert's father died in 2000, I sold the family home. Robert was grieving and afraid. I bought a smaller home for him in a safe and familiar neighborhood so he would always have a place to live. His caseworker found him another psychiatrist and things went well until Robert ran out of medication. He became psychotic and trashed the house. He refused to let his caseworker or anyone in to make repairs. His caseworker began leaving food parcels on the front porch and we faced the next crisis. It became clear that Robert could not live independently. Robert, however, refused to even consider a group home.

Robert had never been violent but his case manager and I managed to provoke him into making a verbal threat and then convinced a magistrate that he was a danger. He was hospitalized and the caseworker was able to convince the psychiatrist to keep Robert longer so we could clear out his house and have it condemned. Because hospitals could not discharge a patient without a place to live, Robert was forced to go to the group home.

Robert rebelled against this placement. His caseworker found a therapeutic group home that provided a structured environment and a host of services, including medical, dental and psychosocial services, and room and board. Robert refused to consider that either. He decided he would "live on the streets." We took him at his word and set about preparing him to be homeless. We rented a storage unit for his belongings and got him a rolling suitcase and a cell phone. His caseworker took him to a soup kitchen and a shelter (which was full). I said my goodbyes and for the first time accepted the inevitable. Robert spent all his money on a hotel room before he got hungry enough to call me. He finally accepted his group home. It took him six months to settle down.

Robert is now 57 years old. He has turned the corner but I also know you never close the book on schizophrenia……nor on your child.

CONFIDENTIALITY

HIPPA, privacy laws and their impact on confidentiality are often misunderstood. Before we go farther into the mental health system, this merits attention.

The law requires that anyone over the age of 18 give permission before medical information about them is released. This includes 18-year olds in High School, living at home, and financially dependent on their parents. There are two exceptions. If someone is in imminent danger, professionals have a legal obligation to act. They are able to provide the police with relevant information and they must warn anyone who has been threatened with harm. Professionals may also share limited information with one another in specific circumstances to ensure that someone receives appropriate and necessary treatment.

Except for these situations—none of which involve family members—it is against the law for professionals to even acknowledge someone is receiving care without permission. This is also true when someone has been deemed incompetent, which can be a frustration for family when their loved one is experiencing a mental health crisis. Family and significant others are often the primary support and caregivers for those in crisis. If someone refuses to allow professionals to communicate with their family members, it complicates the family's ability to provide assistance and support.

When families are unable to share information that they have with professionals it may also impact the treatment their loved one receives. Professionals do not see what the family sees on a daily and intimate basis. They do not know the person and this can make identifying symptoms and their severity harder. Their observations take place in a controlled setting so it may not be clear how symptoms affect a person's ability to manage every day. Some people are able to control symptoms for a brief time or in certain circumstances and may not appear to be in crisis or in need of services. Emergency assessments, being brief and often conducted with little to no background or outside information, can fail. Despite this, over and again families who try to speak with the professionals caring for their loved one may be met with the response that no one can speak with them.

This is not an indictment of confidentiality and privacy laws. They exist with good reason. Even in the midst of a mental health crisis, they protect people at a time when staff are not able to gauge the relationship between family members or their motives. Privacy laws do not fail us in such moments. What fails is our understanding of how these laws function and what they actually allow.

The law does not allow professionals to speak to anyone without permission—even to acknowledge that someone is being seen for evaluation or treatment. What is not true, however, is the assumption that this means they cannot listen and/or receive information.

Privacy laws cover only what a professional may or may not do. They do not cover what a family member, significant other, or any non-professional person may say or may do. Families can provide any and all of the information that they feel is important to a professional treating their loved one. More so, it can be very important, essential even, that this information is available to those providing evaluation and treatment.

If your loved one is refusing to allow professionals providing their care to speak to you, what can you do?

1. You can ask the professional to listen, without response and/or even acknowledging that they know your loved one.
2. You can prepare the information that you want to share in writing and hand-deliver, mail, email, or fax it—this includes any medical records that you have.

In the coming pages, as we address different aspects of the mental health system, we will more specifically cover how confidentiality and sharing of information come into play. Remember, while confidentiality is required of professionals, they are the only ones bound by these laws. These laws cover the information they release. You are free to share whatever you think is necessary—and they are able to hear it.

> *Jan's son is good, very good, at being able to hide his symptoms for the 30 minutes that the assessing psychiatrist will speak to him. She can't remember how many times after he was seen someone would call her and ask "why is he here again?????" Sometimes, if he were really angry with her, he would not even allow that. Consequently, Jan became adept at writing it down. If he were in the Emergency Room she would call and get the fax number. She would tell them who she was and that she was sending information over*

on him for the psychiatrist to look at. She had a prepared history that listed all of the medications he had tried and how they affected him, a list of his hospitalizations and outcomes with names, addresses, phone numbers and the diagnosis he had been given, a his psychiatrist's name and current medications/dosages, and a family history. Each time he was hospitalized she would write up a brief outline about what was going on this time, put it together with all of this, and deliver it—fax it—whatever she needed to do to get it to them. Each and every time this helped the people working with him to place what was going on in context. It helped them to better identify what he was going through and to know what had worked and what hadn't worked before. Sometimes they could talk to her, sometimes they couldn't. She made sure she communicated with them though.

PROFESSIONALS: WHO ARE THEY AND WHAT DO THEY DO?

Case Manager

A Case Manager works with the client and his or her service providers to:
- see that the client's needs are met adequately and appropriately through securing the services and treatments needed;
- assist the client in accessing services, and;
- ensure coordination of treatment and the flow of information between providers.

Case Managers may come from several backgrounds with degrees in a human service-oriented field and may be certified or licensed. This is dependent on the criteria set by the individual business, service provider, LME/MCO and/or state.

Clinical Psychologist

A clinical psychologist has a Ph.D. in psychology and is licensed. They provide both specialized assessment services and counseling for a broad range of needs. They are not able to prescribe medication in the state of NC. They are able to diagnose mental illnesses.

Licensed Professional Counselor

Licensed Professional Counselor's or LPC's are individuals who have obtained a Master's degree in a mental health-related field and met the criteria for licensure. They are trained to work with individuals, families, and groups in treating mental, behavioral, and emotional problems and disorders. They provide counseling and use of psycho-educational techniques to individuals, couples, families, groups, and organizations.

Nurses in a psychiatric unit in a hospital

Psychiatric nurse-specialists work in a hospital or clinical settings. They are often the professional having the most contact with patients and their families. They are skilled in teaching families about the patient's condition and dealing with symptoms. They participate in developing and implementing treatment plans and, with social workers, can help plan for follow-up support.

Psychiatric Nurse Practitioner/ Mental Health Clinical Nurse Specialist (CNS)
> These advanced-practice nurse-specialists have graduate degrees in nursing and specialized psychiatric training. They may do many of the same things a psychiatrist does, including diagnosis of mental illness and development of treatment plans. In North Carolina, some Nurse Practitioners prescribe medicine under the supervision of a psychiatrist. Psychiatric Nurse Practitioners and clinical nurse specialists can also provide therapy helping patients with depression, anxiety and suicidal thoughts, and other conditions that can be remedied with counseling.

Psychiatrist
> A psychiatrist is a medical doctor who specializes in mental illness (just as an oncologist specializes in tumors, or a cardiologist specializes in illness of the heart) A psychiatrist is skilled in diagnosing mental illnesses. They prescribe medications and monitor its use. Some psychiatrists also provide therapy although many do not.

Rehabilitation Counselor
> A Rehabilitation Counselor provides counseling and other services focusing on disability and rehabilitation. This includes case management and vocational services including appropriate cognitive, and work-related testing, job assessment, and job placement services. Those with a Master's Degree are eligible for certification as a Certified Rehabilitation Counselor (CRC) or as a Licensed Professional Counselor (LPC: see above).

Social Worker
> Social Workers provide a variety of services including counseling, client advocacy, case management, and practical skills development with a focus on empowering those they work with. Some Social Workers have undertaken the training necessary to be licensed as counselors. They may have the following certifications or licenses in NC:
>> CSW: Certified Social Worker
>> LCSW: Licensed Clinical Social Worker (An LCSWA is someone who is working toward an LCSW and is licensed at the first level—an LCSW Associate)
>> LPC: Licensed Professional Counselor (see above)

When seeking professional help you want to check a professional's license or certification, their degree, and also their area of expertise. Most professionals will also indicate whether they have specialized training and any illnesses or disorders they focus on in their practice. Many times the exact training and license held by a professional is less important than the way they can work with your particular issue.

**Professionals may be able to specialize in a specific area or in providing a specific service without having actually undergone specialized training. If it is important, verify what training they have in providing a specific treatment or to a specific population.

Choosing a Professional

Unless you work in this field you are unlikely to have a list of qualified Mental Health professionals on your desk. How does someone choose whom to work with? Here are some guidelines:

1. Look for professionals who are qualified to provide the treatment. For example: if someone is trying to find out what is happening they want to see a qualified diagnostician. If they want someone to prescribe and oversee their use of medication, then they want to see a psychiatrist. If someone wants emotional support and/or counseling, then they want to see someone who is a trained therapist. You can review the descriptions of different professionals and what they do on **p. 124.**

2. Get information about any individual professional before making an appointment. There are several ways to do this:
   - Find out what credentials they have and their areas of specialty. Sometimes this information is in their advertising. If not, call their office and ask. Professionals often specialize in specific areas: one counselor may specialize in DBT therapy while another uses psychotherapy. One may work with those who have substance abuse issues while another specializes in bipolar disorder. ***Professionals may state that they have a specialty without specific training or credentials. If you are looking for someone who specializes, ask what specific training they have.
   - Ask others for referrals—both who they do and do not recommend. Ask them why.
   - There are internet sites where people rate professionals they have worked with. Typically people rate the professional in specific categories and add comments. While low or high ratings can be the result of a one-off situation, consistent ratings or many comments can give a fairly reliable idea of the professional's work. These sites may also help provide insight into areas that are of specific concern to your loved one.

3. Avoid professionals who:
   - Diagnose someone on the first visit or after a brief evaluation. Good diagnoses of mental illnesses take time, information, and require getting to know the individual. *This does not mean that treatment cannot begin during this process.

- Make medication changes when your loved one is not having problems with medication or asking for changes—especially the first time they see someone unless this was the reason for the appointment.
- Base medication recommendations solely on diagnosis. While diagnosis is important in prescribing medication (anti-depressants can send someone who has bipolar disorder into mania rather than alleviating depression, for example), medication effectiveness is very individual. It depends on the symptoms and the patient's response. Sometimes the most effective medication is one more commonly associated with other illnesses.
- Are not available outside of office hours. You want someone you can reach or has after-hours support in case there is a problem or a crisis, and who will be able to help you avoid seeking emergency room treatment if at all possible. If your loved one does have to go to the hospital, you want the evaluating physician to be able to reach your loved one's provider.

4. Choose professionals who:
   - Value your loved one's voice in the treatment process and listen to their unique concerns, needs, goals, what is difficult about treatment for them and what works for their life. The response to treatment is individualized, and many treatments will have both positive and negative impact. When your loved one has a voice they are more likely to follow treatment. A crucial factor in managing symptoms and finding hope is being engaged in the treatment process.
   - Believe that rehabilitation and a full life are possible.
   - Work to help your loved one learn how to manage their illness.
   - Treat your loved one with respect.
   - Recognize the importance of the family and significant others in treatment and recovery
   - Support a healthy, ongoing relationship between their patient and h/her family/loved ones.
   - Is someone your loved one trusts.
   - Will tell your loved one if they believe their treatment is not effective, they are at risk, and will hospitalize them if they are in need of intervention.

> One of the single most damaging aspects of our treatment system is that families are often thrust into the role of both managing their loved one's treatment and intervening when they become ill. This can create conflict between the person dealing with symptoms and their loved ones, especially when that person is an adult. When family members have to petition for involuntary commitment or are viewed as interfering it can undermine relationships and lead to estrangement. The best providers recognize this and the importance of a healthy family role in managing a mental illness. They will not only provide treatment, but set up structures to manage care and step in when interventions are required so the family does not have to. This supports the family acting as a source of love and support rather than being viewed as coercive, interfering, or controlling.

**Always keep in mind that a professional may not be the right match for your loved one. Sometimes we see someone who is very good only to realize they are not a good fit for us. If your loved one is not happy with, does not trust, or is not making progress with any person that they see, it is okay to find someone else. Unless the situation is very bad, they should find a new provider before leaving the current one. This way treatment will be ongoing, and someone is still available should they experience a crisis.

> The very first appointment lasted 15 minutes and she made a drastic medication change even though what he was taking worked well. We cancelled the next appointment, made sure our family doctor would continue to prescribe his medication in the interim, and started to look for someone else.

TREATMENT OPTIONS

Medication Management
Symptoms of mental illnesses are often managed through medications. Psychiatric medications are developed for symptoms specifically associated with given mental illnesses. Medications prescribed for other disorders, such as epilepsy, are also routinely used and very effective in treating some symptoms. The decision about medication is not based on diagnosis but on symptoms. A psychiatrist treats and manages symptoms with medication. While some psychiatrists also provide therapy, this is less common. Some family doctors, general practitioners, and mental health professionals who are licensed to prescribe medications may also prescribe and monitor medication use. Some medications require initial tests, such as blood tests, to ensure that dosages are properly adjusted. There are some medications which require regular and ongoing testing to ensure other physical disorders or problems do not develop. Anyone who uses medication to treat symptoms will need someone who oversees their use, is able to make changes if needed, and who can address side-effects or other problems that arise.

***Genetic testing has made it possible to determine what medications a person is most likely to respond well to and what medications may not work or will lead to an adverse reaction. This can make the choice of medication easier and more effective where the trial-and-error approach can take time. People often have to try several medications and experience problems that complicate their recovery before finding what works for them. Genetic testing has the potential to avoid these issues. It is not yet standard procedure, but you can request it or seek testing on your own.

Therapy or Counseling
Therapy is the use of counseling to deal with symptoms, adjustment to mental illness, and the management of symptoms or their impact. Counselors also assist in dealing with emotions, traumatic events, conflict or difficulty in relationships, in the workplace, etc. There is evidence that those learning to live with mental illness, especially more severe conditions, do best when they receive counseling in addition to other treatments. There are a number of counseling techniques which are used to address specific difficulties. Not all counselors are trained to practice all types of counseling and some have specialized areas of focus or expertise. When considering counseling, it is important to be clear

about what problems your loved one wants to address and their goals. It is possible to see more than one counselor if there are multiple needs—for example, work to address specific symptoms with one counselor and with another for family counseling. Some counseling types are:

Art Therapy
Art Therapy is the therapeutic use of a variety of art mediums within a professional relationship. Through creating and reflecting on the art products and processes, people can increase awareness of self and others, cope with symptoms, stress and traumatic experiences, enhance cognitive abilities, and enjoy the life-affirming pleasure of the creative process. Art therapy is based on the belief that the creative process helps people to resolve conflicts and problems, develop interpersonal skills, manage behavior, reduce stress, increase self-esteem and self-awareness, and achieve insight. Art therapy integrates the fields of human development, visual art (drawing, painting, sculpture, and other art forms), and the creative process with models of counseling and psychotherapy.[1]

Cognitive Behavioral Therapy (CBT)
Cognitive-Behavioral Therapy (CBT) is one of the most widely used therapies in treating those with mental illnesses. This therapy focuses on changing patterns in thinking as a means to develop coping skills. CBT alone can be effective in treating depression which is not severe, as well as anxiety and post-traumatic stress (PTSD), tics, substance abuse, eating disorders, and borderline personality disorder. It is often used in combination with medications and other types of treatment. CBT is recommended as the first line of treatment for a majority of psychological disorders in children and adolescents, including aggression and conduct disorder.

Dialectical Behavioral Therapy (DBT)
Dialectical Behavior Therapy (DBT) is used to treat personality disorders, mood disorders and to change behaviors such as self-harm, suicidal ideation, and substance abuse. DBT helps regulate emotions through identifying triggers and developing skills for coping with these events. This approach is underscored by giving people the skills that they need to counter their negative response to certain situations or events. DBT combines standard behavioral techniques for regulating emotions as well as developing tolerance to distress through mindful awareness and meditative practice.

---
1   American Art Therapy Association

Jungian Therapy
Jungian therapy is talk-centered and focuses on enabling the person to develop their full potential. The therapist and patient focus on the impact of past experiences and work to remove obstacles which may have resulted. This is especially relevant for persons who are experiencing difficulty related to a traumatic or painful life event or situation.

Person-Centered Therapy
Person-centered therapy uses a non-authoritative approach that allows clients to take more of a lead in discussions so that, in the process, they will discover their own solutions. The therapist acts as a compassionate facilitator, listening without judgment and acknowledging the client's experience without moving the conversation in another direction. The therapist is there to encourage and support the client and to guide the therapeutic process without interrupting or interfering with the client's process of self-discovery.

This is a link that you can use to explore a full range of therapies that are available:

https://www.goodtherapy.org/learn-about-therapy/types

You can also visit NAMI's website at:

https://www.nami.org/Learn-More/Treatment/Psychotherapy

Vocational Rehabilitation
Vocational rehabilitation is a process that enables people with functional, psychological, developmental, cognitive and emotional impairments, or health disabilities to overcome barriers to accessing, maintaining or returning to employment or other useful occupation. Vocational rehabilitation counselors use input from a range of healthcare professionals and non-medical disciplines such as disability employment advisers and career counselors. Techniques used can include:

- assessment, appraisal, job evaluation, and research.
- professional goal setting and development of work-site adaptions.
- provision of health advice and promotion, in support of returning to work.
- support for self-management of health conditions.

- making adjustments to the medical and psychological impact of a disability.
- case management, referral, and service coordination.
- psychosocial interventions.
- career counseling, job analysis, job development, and placement services.
- functional and work capacity evaluations.

Cognitive Rehabilitation
Cognitive rehabilitation is a program to help brain-injured or otherwise cognitively impaired individuals to restore normal functioning, or to compensate for cognitive deficits. It entails an individualized program of specific skills training and practice strategies that help increase self-awareness regarding problem-solving skills by learning how to monitor the effectiveness of these skills and self-correct when necessary. Cognitive rehabilitation addresses brain function using strategies involving memory, executive functions, activities planning and "follow through" (e.g., memory, task sequencing, lists).

Cognitive rehabilitation is an important tool for people with mental illnesses who experience negative symptoms—issues surrounding initiation, task sequencing, reasoning, judgment, and even impaired memory. A cognitive therapist can assess the presence and severity of negative symptoms and develop treatment to mediate their impact. This can significantly improve both the time it takes for someone to recover as well as the degree of function that they are able to recover.

Alternative Treatments

There are many treatments available that are considered "alternative." Some are well received by the professional community, for example, meditation or yoga. Some are not. What if your loved one has an interest in a treatment that is not mainstream and/or not well researched? Perhaps they would be willing to speak with a counselor—a Wiccan Counselor. They will use medications—if they can get them from a Chinese practitioner. How do you respond when someone wants to explore alternative ways to manage their symptoms?

Let's state the obvious: it is hard not to be concerned or even adamant when you believe a treatment may not work or may be harmful or life-threatening. Especially when your loved one disagrees. While there are some things worth fighting for, the key is to avoid turning this into a power struggle.

Mental illness can be devastating. The loss of control experienced by those living with these illnesses is particularly hard to cope with. Imagine being told that what you believe, what you experience, is not real. You cannot trust your senses. This is what happens to someone who experiences psychosis. Imagine if everything in your life *should* be good—you have a job, a good family, a home—yet every day you struggle just to get out of bed. No matter what you do. This can be what it is like to live with depression. When you live with an anxiety disorder, you may feel like you are dying every time you have to leave your house. You may be told you must take a medication whose side effects may be as debilitating as the symptoms it treats. You may have been committed to a hospital against your will. You may have lost your job and become dependent on others for money, food, and shelter. You may not be able to build the life you wanted. Imagine that one of the symptoms you experience is agnosia. You believe that you are well and yet everyone around you tells you that you are sick and you must be treated.

Anyone living with a chronic illness faces things that they do not control. This is especially true for those living with a mental illness. They experience first-hand the reality that we do not even, sometimes, control our own minds.

In addition to learning about the illness– what it means to live with this—how it impacts them—how others will react to them—what they can and cannot share openly—your loved one must discover what they control, what they do not, and they must make peace with that.

They must learn how to exercise the control they do have in a way that works for them.

Your loved one may explore different treatments as they try to figure out how to live their best life with this illness. This exploration may be part of controlling what they can. It may be something they do as they work to discover what they do have control over.

When treatment decisions become the subject of a power-struggle no one is going to win. You want the person you love to learn how to live with a mental illness: how to make good decisions about treatment and self-care. When you are no longer there you want them to have the tools needed to make necessary decisions: to be able to research and understand the treatments available; have an approach they can use in exploring treatment options; to be able to determine if a treatment is effective; to have guidelines to use in choosing the professionals they work with. You want them to accept treatment when it is needed.

Accepting the need for treatment is important. It means your loved one understands they are not doing well and have a desire to correct that. You want to support this. The main concern in trying alternative treatments is identical to that of trying mainstream treatments: are there good, appropriate safeguards in place in the event the treatment does not work or symptoms worsen? To this end, if someone you love wants to explore alternative treatments, you can:

1. Help them to do research. Find the best information available about different treatments and discover all the options available for any given treatment. If an option seems viable, even if alternative, find the most qualified people.
2. Encourage your loved one to use a multi-pronged approach to treatment. One treatment can often be more effective as part of a good treatment plan. Suggest they use a combination of treatments—both mainstream and alternative.
3. Encourage them to choose a professional to help them coordinate and monitor the effectiveness of all of the treatments they try. If they want to try a Chinese Practitioner, or a special diet they can also choose a psychiatrist, doctor, or counselor they trust to help them assess how effective this is and make changes as needed.**
4. Embrace the idea that just like finding the right kind of medication, most treatments should be approached on a trial basis. Help them to identify criteria to determine if a treatment is helping or not.

Remember, what works for any person is unique to that person. Even medications are most effective in combination with other treatments. The most significant concern, indeed the point, of this process is how well someone is able to function. Safeguards that will kick in if a new treatment does not work or a person's condition deteriorates are essential. If someone you love is interested in alternative treatments, you can build on this fact to support their recovery during this search. Many find a unique mix that works best for them. People may try many different things before they find that mix.

> **As much as possible, if your loved one is an adult, you want to encourage their working with a professional and not you, in deciding how to treat their symptoms. This will support the two of you having as healthy a relationship as possible as well as allowing you to be a supportive presence in their life rather than a potential source of conflict and frustration.

Examples of alternative treatments may be:

Meditation: Meditation is a precise technique for resting the mind and attaining a state of consciousness that is different from the normal waking state. Meditation is not a part of one religion. It is a science, which means that the process of meditation follows a particular order, has definite principles, and produces results that can be verified. Meditation is the practice of turning your attention to a single point of reference. It can involve focusing on the breath, on bodily sensations, or on a word or phrase known as a mantra. In other words, meditation teaches an individual turn their attention away from distracting thoughts and focusing on the present moment.

Mindfulness-Based Stress Reduction: Mindfulness-Based Stress Reduction or MBSR is a method of using meditation and yoga to cultivate awareness and reduce stress. It is based on the ancient practice of mindfulness, which is about waking up, being fully alive, and being present for the richness of each moment of our lives. Within this awakening, we gain access to our deepest inner resources for living, healing, and coping with stress. MBSR can help people who are coping with medical problems, job or family-related stress, and anxiety and depression. The majority of participants report lasting decreases in both physical and psychological symptoms. Pain levels improve and people learn to better cope with pain that may not go away. Most people also report an increased ability to relax, greater enthusiasm for life, improved self-esteem, and increased ability to cope more effectively with stressful situations.

Life Coach: Life Coaching is a profession that is profoundly different from consulting, mentoring, advice, therapy, or counseling. The coaching process addresses specific personal projects, business successes, general conditions and transitions in the client's personal life, relationships or profession by examining what is going on right now, discovering what their obstacles or challenges might be, and choosing a course of action to make their life be what they want it to be. Life Coaches may specialize in one or more of the following areas:

- Confidence, Self Worth & Self Esteem
- Loving Relationships
- Career Change
- The Mastery of Balance—Juggling a Life
- Self Care
- Managing Anger, Upsets, Frustration and Stress
- Managing Grief, Loss, Sadness and Change
- Parenting
- Food, Nutrition, & Optimal Health

Yoga: Yoga, as practiced in most places in the U.S. is a physical exercise which uses specific poses to increase physical strength, balance, and well being. The practice also has benefits in calming the mind and strengthening a person's sense of well-being.

Nutrition: Nutritional counselors and/or specific practices surrounding the foods we eat can help a person to address physical problems, concerns, or those surrounding a chosen lifestyle through developing a healthy diet.

Shaman: Shamanism uses ancient techniques of mind and spirit to deal with diseases and life problems. Shamans work to connect their clients with sources of wisdom and healing power in the spirit world, to remove spiritual energy intrusions and possessions, and help them recover personal power and emotional and physical well-being. Shamanic procedures take into account each person's unique situation, personality, and physical, mental, emotional and spiritual makeup and needs.

Evidence-Based Best Practice

As you seek services for your loved one you may run into the term: Evidence-Based Best Practice (EvBP) In theory, an Evidenced-Based Best Practice is one that has undergone rigorous scientific testing to determine its effectiveness. This testing has demonstrated that this treatment or service is significantly effective.

This designation is very reliable in most areas of medical care. Treatment and services for Mental Illnesses, however, are not always held to the same standard. Treatment providers may designate a service that they offer as Evidenced-Based without scientific proof. For this reason: buyer beware. You should not take the word of any provider or advertising as proof of the effectiveness of any treatment or service that is offered. Especially when the services offered are counter-intuitive. For example, Equine therapy as a significant treatment for drug addiction. Research is your best ally. Specifically, sources such as NAMI, DHHS, SAMHSA, IMH are particularly good resources for investigating the science behind the claims.

SERVICE DEFINITIONS

Inpatient/Residential Services

Detoxification: Detoxification is the process of physically weaning someone from a drug or alcohol when they are physically dependent. When physical dependence has occurred suddenly quitting can result in life-threatening withdrawal or even death. Covered by both private insurance and public programs.

- Many local hospitals have detox units.
- There are freestanding medical units which specialize in detoxification. Some psychiatric facilities may provide detox. Many Drug and Alcohol Rehabilitation facilities cannot provide detox, however, and require detoxification prior to admission.
- If someone is physically addicted detox facilities are not only a necessary first step in recovery they may be one of the best resources for gaining admission to a long-term rehabilitation program. Detox facilities often utilize case management staff who assist patients in determining the best and most appropriate step to deal with their addiction and can assist them in gaining admission to inpatient or outpatient services on discharge.
- If the primary mental illness is something other than addiction but addiction is present, detoxification may need to be undertaken in an Acute Inpatient setting because a Detox Facility may not be equipped to manage other symptoms.

Inpatient Drug and Alcohol Rehabilitation: Inpatient non-hospital programs of thirty to ninety days that assist someone to stop drugs or alcohol use. Covered by both private insurance and public programs.

- Many Rehabilitation facilities do not treat individuals with a dual diagnosis or co-occurring disorders. Additionally, they may not be licensed to administer medications that are prescribed. If this is a concern, you need to clarify whether a facility treats dual-diagnosis/co-occurring disorders and their criteria for medication use.

- Some Drug and Alcohol treatment philosophies adhere to the belief that a person cannot use any drugs, even those prescribed to them. This and other philosophies may be dangerous to or exacerbate other mental illnesses.
- Many facilities follow the AA 12-step approach; however, you should speak to the individual facility to clarify their philosophy.

Acute Inpatient Treatment: An Acute Inpatient treatment is appropriate for someone who is in crisis. Inpatient admissions often involve persons who are suicidal or a danger to others. Mental health crises also include those who are unable to care for themselves or whose symptoms place them at risk in any number of ways. Persons may admit themselves to an Acute Inpatient setting if they choose—and many do. The purpose of an Acute Inpatient setting is to stabilize symptoms and ensure that the person is no longer in crisis. The average stay in NC in an Acute Inpatient setting is 3-10 days. This is based on funding and a lack of beds rather then the time needed to achieve stability. Covered by both private insurance and public programs.

**Many, many localities do not have Acute Inpatient Facilities. Most Acute Inpatient Facilities have a significantly smaller number of beds than needed on a daily basis. Consequently, when inpatient admission is needed, one of several things may happen:

- A referral may be made to community-based services instead
- Admission may only be allowed for the minimal time needed to provide medications and attain minimal reduction of symptoms
- Admission may be made to a facility that is many hours from the person's residence because no beds are available in closer proximity
- Persons may find themselves spending days in the Emergency Room or Assessment Center while waiting for an open bed. ***This is especially true if the person for whom care is being sought is a child or adolescent as there is a severe shortage of facilities/beds that are equipped to handle children or youth.

Sub-acute Inpatient Treatment: Sub-acute Inpatient treatment is provided in the context of an inpatient hospitalization but geared to the needs of someone who has been stabilized and is need of more intensive supports before they will be able to maintain their gains and continue to make progress in the community. NC does not have specific sub-acute facilities. The closest approximation is the State Hospital system. It is extremely difficult to obtain a bed in this system. **The wait time can often be several months—which is often longer than the time that most persons would need Sub-acute care.** Those whose needs go beyond Sub-Acute care to long-term care are the persons most likely to receive services in these facilities. To get this specific type of care someone will have to go out of state. Another option is a psychiatric residential facility.

Psychiatric residential services: Psychiatric residential services provide a supportive environment with access to medication management and counseling services in a residential setting. Residents may stay in their own or shared rooms and their days will be structured. Treatment will focus on education and learning to manage their illness as well as vocational and other living needs. Residential facilities may offer a range of living situations and the freedom that residents have may change accordingly. Lengths of stay can vary widely. Residents may have either short-term, more intensely therapeutic stays or the facility may offer long-term residences with a stronger focus on re-building a normal day-to-day life. Supervision may be intensive or they may offer great autonomy. Cost and payment methods will vary according to the facility, the treatment that is offered, and the length of stay. You will need to do a significant amount of research before determining that a facility is appropriate and the best option.

Psychiatric residential facilities, while offering a comprehensive approach to treatment, are also difficult to access. Facilities are few and admission may require going out of state—often at a great distance. The treatment they provide is generally not covered by public funds and may not be covered by insurance. Cost is often prohibitive.

There are residential facilities for children and youth provided by the state of NC. The costs for these are covered through public funding. More information on these facilities can be found on **p. 75.

Group Homes: Group homes are structured, managed facilities that provide residence for those with mental illnesses who cannot sustain themselves on their own. Group homes generally DO NOT provide treatment. Their purpose is to provide a residence, 24-hour supervision, medication management, and meet s daily needs for food and hygiene. Group homes, while residential, are not therapeutic facilities.

Long-term Inpatient Facility/State Psychiatric Hospital: A long-term Inpatient facility is one that is able to provide treatment on an inpatient basis for as long as it is needed. The only long-term inpatient facilities in NC are State Psychiatric Hospitals. These facilities provide long-term intensive care for those whose symptoms are most severe AND which have not been able to be effectively treated or managed in an acute inpatient stay. The primary difference between a long-term inpatient facility and a sub-acute or a residential facility is the severity of symptoms and treatment needs which a person has.

There are 3 psychiatric Hospitals in NC: Cherry Hospital—Goldsboro, NC, Central Regional Hospital—Butner, NC, Broughton Hospital—Morganton, NC. These facilities provide comprehensive mental health services to adults and adolescents. Deaf Individuals may be served at Broughton Hospital. Children may be served at Central Regional Hospital.

Community Based/Outpatient Services

Assertive Community Treatment Team (ACT): Assertive Community Treatment Team is a community based intensive service that supports the treatment needs of individuals with significant symptoms of mental illness. This offers a team approach to provide the variety of services needed at the intensity that is required (including daily) to enable someone to remain in the community/at home through a coordinated effort. Teams will typically include: psychiatrist, nurse, therapist/counselor, case manager, vocational specialist, housing specialist, peer support specialist and will provide community assistance, medication management, assistance with daily activities, transportation, and work supports.

Club House: A Clubhouse is a peer-operated center offering opportunities for friendship, employment, housing, education and access to medical and psychiatric services in a single caring and safe environment—so people can recover and fully participate as valued and respected members of society.

Community Support Team: Community Support Team is for individuals who are more stable and able to function on their own with fewer supports. Key services include a focus on community and interpersonal skills, first responder interventions as needed, and assistance in linking with community services and resources.

Crisis Services: The nature of the crisis services available is dependent on the individual community. For specific information about what is available in your community:_____

- **Walk-in Clinic:** A freestanding clinic that provides walk-in/self-referred crisis assessment and intervention within the community. May have set hours or be open 24/7.
- **Mobile Crisis Unit:** A professional unit which can be asked to come to a person's location to provide emergency assessment/evaluation/assistance
- **CIT Officer:** A police officer who is specially trained to respond to situations involving persons suffering a mental health emergency
- **Emergency Room/Mental Health Assessment Center:** The emergency room at a local hospital or specifically designated cri-

sis assessment center which can affect an inpatient admission at an appropriate facility and to handle involuntary commitments.

> ***It is essential to be aware that many emergency rooms—especially in rural NC—do not have a mental health professional who sees or evaluates persons. Local facilities for evaluation may be hard to find or nonexistent. This is especially problematic if someone in crisis is brought against their will as there may not be an opportunity to get him or her to a location where an appropriate person can see them. If you find yourself in this situation you may have to advocate more strongly for your loved one to ensure that they receive adequate evaluation and care.*

- Tele-psychiatry: Many facilities, especially those in rural areas, are beginning to make use of tele-psychiatry. This is an assessment or crisis-intervention service which can be offered to people via the internet. Because this is a new and emerging field you should contact any given facility to determine if they offer this service.
- http://crisissolutionsnc.org/crisis-solutions-individuals-families/

Critical Time Intervention: Critical Time Intervention is designed to assist individuals who are in transition—particularly in transition from one service to another, such as from the hospital to home. This service provides additional supports in the absence of other services.

Individual Placement and Supports/Supported Employment (IPS/SE): This service provides assistance for those who want to return to or enter the workforce but need additional support in the work setting. Assistance can include both finding appropriate work as well as actual assistance in the workplace.

Outpatient Clinic: Site which is able to provide services which may be needed in a community setting including nursing, psychiatry, case management, medication management.

Outpatient Drug and Alcohol Rehabilitation: Outpatient drug and alcohol program for persons dealing with addiction that wish to or are able to remain in their home while receiving treatment.

Private Psychiatrist, Psychologist, Counselor: A trained professional who is able to offer assessment, evaluation, therapeutic counseling or therapy on either an outpatient or inpatient basis. On an outpatient basis can be accessed by self-referral or through the referral of another provider. Includes LSW, LPC, CRC, Psychiatric Nurse Practitioner.

INSURANCE AND FINANCES

The Department of Health and Human Services: DHHS

The Department of Health and Human Services, specifically the Division of Mental Health and Substance Abuse Services, is tasked with overseeing publicly funded services for people with mental health issues, as well as private providers who receive public funds. They also manage all public funds. On their website, they maintain information about these disorders, services offered and service providers. They directly oversee the LME/MCO's. They are a resource for determining what publicly funded services are available on every level and for obtaining assistance when you encounter problems in receiving services or have a problem with a service provider. DHHS also oversees Medicaid and Food Stamps as well as housing and other assistance programs.

The Department of Health and Human Services Mental Health, Developmental Disabilities, and Substance Abuse branch (DMHDDSAS) has a Customer Service and Community Rights Team. They work closely with the LME/MCO's to address complaints, concerns, and appeals. They additionally work to:

- Protect the rights of individuals served in their communities
- Respond to complaints or concerns
- Monitor community rights protection systems and customer service for quality
- Assist families and individuals to access public services
- Provide information about the DMHDDSAS System
- Collect and report complaint data

To contact the Customer Service and Community Rights Team, call 919-715-3197 or 855-262-1946. They can also be emailed at dmh.advocacy@dhhs.nc.gov.

Local Management Entity/Managed Care Organization: LME/MCO

North Carolina provides publicly funded services to those with mental health needs through a Managed Care System. What this means is that the state contracts with an organization specifically created by North Carolina state law to manage the funds allocated for these services: LME/MCO's.

An LME is a LOCAL MANAGEMENT ENTITY. An MCO is a MANAGED CARE ORGANIZATION. These are not-for-profit companies, but they're not a standard nonprofit either. LME/MCOs are quasi-governmental agencies contracted with the state. They may not make a profit from the management of state funds. Their employees are in the private sector but are still subject to specific public sector rules (such as CEO salary). LME/MCOs act like a health insurance company for NC Medicaid recipients who need mental health care, developmental disabilities services and/or substance abuse treatment. They also serve a similar role for certain segments of the uninsured and homeless population.

The state is divided into six regions, and each region is served by its own LME/MCO. DHHS determines the LME/MCO for each region. The LME/MCO answers to DHHS and is subject to both state law and federal managed care regulations. LME/MCOs authorize services and provide care coordination, provider network credentialing, and provider reimbursement. In return, the LME/MCO receives a set payment each month from the State for each person they serve. When the cost of services for any person exceeds the set payment, the LME/MCO loses money. If the LME/MCO provides services for less than the rate, they are allowed to keep the savings to use to pay for additional services.

The Difference between the traditional fee for service and managed care is this:

Traditional Medicaid or "Fee for Service":

- Providers bill the state Medicaid agency directly for reimbursement of a service.
- Any "willing and qualified" provider is permitted to provide services.
- Authorization for services is provided by a State contractor, other than the LME.
- Case management is a separate service provided by an independent, third-party provider.

Managed Care:

- LME/MCOs receive a fixed amount of money per consumer, per month (capitated rate).
- LME/MCOs can and do limit their provider network.

- Utilization management (UM) functions are internal functions of the MCO, and they decide whether to approve or deny requests for services.
- Care coordination has replaced third-party case management and is now an internal function of the LME/MCO.

There are many scenarios in which you would not interact with or even be conscious of your local LME/MCO. For example, when a loved one is admitted to a hospital, voluntarily or through involuntary commitment, the hospital might work with the LME/MCO while you may not be involved. Likewise, if on discharge they are referred to community services the LME/MCO may be involved but you may not be aware of their role or ever speak to them.

If you are seeking services, want information on what is available in your area, or need assistance paying for services, you can start with your LME/MCO. Because they manage publicly funded services, they won't refer you to a private provider unless they work with them. However, they have a great deal of information about available resources and can be of assistance to you in navigating the system and finding services. They can also help to find needed funding.

** All LME/MCO's have a complaint/grievance process. If there is a concern about a provider, call the LME/MCO and ask to make a complaint. The LME/MCO will ask what you want to see happen, investigate, and then follow-up with you.

A full list of North Carolina's LME/MCO's and the regions they serve along with contact information is found on the first page of this manual.

Medicaid (MA)

Medicaid is a jointly funded, Federal-State health insurance program for low-income and needy people. It covers children, the aged, blind, and/or disabled and others who may be eligible. At this time, Medicaid is the primary source of payment in NC for public MH services. Some private professionals are able to receive Medicaid payments. There are several things to be aware of:

- Those who are eligible for Medicaid are also automatically eligible for Food Stamps
- In determining eligibility for Medicaid, the total income of all persons in the household is taken into account. This is true for

adults who are over the age of 18, disabled, and still living at home UNLESS they pay rent to reside in the home.
- The income eligibility for Medicaid is very low.
- You will not be eligible for Medicaid if you have savings
- There are several types of Medicaid. Someone who does not qualify for medical coverage may still be eligible for the type of Medicaid that pays Medicare premiums. The income eligibility for this type of Medicaid is higher than for medical coverage through Medicaid.
- You must apply for Medicaid unless you receive SSI. If you are approved for SSI, you are automatically eligible for Medicaid and will be automatically enrolled.

State Funding

The state of North Carolina directly funds some services when an individual is not eligible for Medicaid and is need of assistance. These funds are managed by Local Management Entities/Managed Care Organizations (LME/MCOs). At one time, state-funded services were called "IPRS dollars," which stood for Integrated Payment and Reporting System. IPRS was the mechanism through which the state (via the Local Management Entities and the Division of Mental Health, Developmental Disabilities and Substance Abuse Services) tracked how state services dollars were being used. The LME/MCO authorizes the state-funded services and providers of state-funded services provide services to individuals. State-funded services are typically used for individuals who have no other resources to pay for services and supports. State funding may cover inpatient services and some outpatient services. State-funded services are not considered an entitlement and are dependent on the availability of funding from the legislature. These funds have been drastically reduced in the past couple of years.

Medicare

Adults 18 and older who have been determined by Social Security to be disabled for two (2) or more years (i.e., have received SSI or SSDI for 2 or more continuous years) are eligible for Medicare. Medicare has several different options which include inpatient coverage or hospitalization, some outpatient services, and medication coverage. Medication coverage is provided by Medicare but through a 3rd party provider who manages the funds.
- There is a premium for Medicare, but it is very low.

- Individuals with very low incomes may be eligible for Medicaid payment of their Medicare premiums even if they are not eligible for full Medicaid.
- Outpatient public treatment providers generally do not accept, nor are they covered by Medicare.
- Some private outpatient providers—such as psychiatrists or counselors and doctors accept Medicare.
- Medicare covers inpatient hospitalizations
- An adult who has been disabled since childhood becomes eligible for Medicare at age 22.

Private Insurance

We will assume that you have a basic understanding of what private insurance is and are familiar with the plan you may have. A couple of notes, however:

- Because NC did not accept expanded Medicaid under the Affordable Care Act, some individuals earn or receive too much money to qualify for Medicaid, but do not receive enough money to be eligible for a subsidy which would allow them to purchase private insurance through the Marketplace. If your loved one is in this situation, then the most likely place where they can receive monies to cover medical costs is through the State Funding described above. You will need to work through an LME/MCO to determine this.
- Most community based public services do not accept private insurance. This is because the system is a public one that is funded through public funds—Medicaid and State Funds. This does not mean you cannot get care with a private provider. It does mean that you may not have access to comprehensive services such as ACTT, and you may need to build your own system of care.

Questions to Ask Your Insurance Carrier

1. What types of care does your coverage include: length of inpatient stays, types of facilities? What is required to document ongoing need?
2. Are they able and willing to approve payment for services not normally covered in specific instances?

3. What is your liability if someone is taken for assessment and not admitted as an inpatient? Do they cover assessment facilities as well as traditional emergency rooms?

4. What outpatient services are covered? (i.e., psychiatry, counseling, case management) What degree or certification is required of any given provider?

5. Will they be willing to work with you to develop an individualized treatment plan if the need and benefit can be demonstrated?

6. What medications do they cover? More importantly perhaps, what medications do they not cover?

7. Will they allow an adult child who is disabled, not working, and not attending school to remain on your policy or to be put on your policy? What criteria do they have for deciding this?

8. Do they utilize case managers or teams to follow your loved one's needs and work with you or them in obtaining care as needed?

9. Will they advocate for your loved one with service providers?

10. Do they use network providers? What is the additional cost of you go out of network? Is there an additional cost if they do not have an in-network provider in the area that is needed?

SSI/SSDI

Individuals who qualify as disabled and unable to work OR when working, meet the minimum income guidelines due to disability, may be eligible for monthly disability payments from the government. Your inability to work due to disability must be such that you will not be able to work for at least one (1) year, or longer. Disability payments are made through one or both of two (2) programs: SSI—Supplemental Security Income—and/or—SSDI: Social Security Disability Income.

There are a couple of things it is important to understand when considering SSI and/or SSDI.

For the purposes of these programs, disability is defined by your ability to work—not the fact that you have a disability or any of the other ways that a disability may impact you and your life. For example: Being blind or deaf is considered a disabling condition. However, the government does not consider that being blind or deaf in and of itself means that someone cannot work. There must be some demonstrated impact from being blind or deaf which interferes with or makes an individual's ability to work impossible for them to receive SSI or SSDI.

Mental Illnesses are considered disabling conditions. However, for someone with a mental illness to receive SSI or SSDI the impact of their illness must be such that they either cannot work or, if working, cannot work enough to earn the minimum income levels set by the Social Security Administration. (Because this amount changes you will need to find out what it is at the time you apply to determine if your loved is eligible for assistance).

While SS says that someone must be disabled for a year or more, you do not need to wait a year after someone becomes disabled, or develops symptoms to apply. You will need to show, however, that the nature of their disability is such that they cannot be expected to improve or work due to their condition for at least a year from the date of onset.

SSDI: Social Security Disability Insurance
SSDI is paid to individuals who have worked.

When you work you pay into the SSDI system. Think of it as government disability insurance—like AFLAC, or other disability private insurance which you or your employer may purchase. In this case, though, payment is automatically taken out and paid with their income tax for every working person. A person who has worked must have worked long enough and paid in enough to qualify to receive disability payments. They must have a specified number of something called **work credits.** The number of work credits that an individual is required to have depends on their age.

- In 2017 a work credit was defined as $1300. The average adult will need 20 work credits earned in the last 10 years.
- Younger workers—those who cannot have worked 10 years—can qualify for disability benefits with fewer work credits. If you become disabled before age 24, you must have earned 6 credits in the three years prior to the onset of your disability. If you become disabled between age 24 and 31, you need 16 credits.
- You will also need to have worked recently to qualify for Social Security disability benefits. I.E., someone who worked 10 years ago and then left the workforce to raise children would not be eligible. Generally, an individual must have worked any 5 of the past 10 years.
- If you have worked intermittently, but have earned income within the past couple of years, you may be eligible for Social Security disability benefits.

- The amount that you are eligible to get is determined by how much you have paid into the system. An 18-year-old who worked part-time while in school will necessarily be eligible for a lower payment than someone who is 32 and has worked 10 years full time. A 30-year-old who has earned $60,000/year will qualify for more than a 30-year-old who has earned $24,000.
- You can work while receiving SSDI. If you do, you will continue to receive SSDI payments—to a point. SS sets a limit as to how much you can earn in any month and still continue to receive SSDI.
- SSDI and the amount you may receive is not based on the income of anyone else in your family or your dependency on someone else. If you have dependents, your dependents may also be eligible to receive SSDI while dependent on you.

<u>SSI: Supplemental Security Income</u>
SSI is paid to individuals who have never worked, and to those who have worked but do not have enough work credits or who have an SSDI payment which is less than the minimum income level set by the Social Security Administration

- If you have never worked, or if the amount of money you receive from SSDI is so low that you fall beneath the minimum income level set by SS, and you are found to be disabled, you may receive SSI payments.
- If you have dependents, they will not also receive SSI, but your minimum income level will be adjusted to reflect your dependents.
- The amount of your SSI payment will be the amount that is required to ensure that you receive the minimum income level set by SS.
- If you are eligible for SSI, you are automatically eligible for Medicaid.

The SSI/SSDI system is intimidating for most of us. On the one hand, there is a misconception that many people who are not genuinely disabled receive SSI or SSDI. On the other, it is widely known how hard it is to get approved for either. A prime example is the number of attorneys who solicit representation of those who have been turned down. The process can also be complicated and a long, arduous one.

The primary reason why people get turned down for SSI or SSDI is a failure to successfully make a case for how their disability impairs their ability to work enough to support themselves. The overwhelming majority of people who receive SSI or SSDI, however, are individuals who are disabled by mental illness. Social Security well understands the disabling impact of these illnesses.

> **If your loved one is 18 or older, one of the harder decisions you may face is whether they need to become established as financially independent adults to obtain the services and benefits that they need. An 18-year-old who is still a dependent of their parents may not receive Medicaid and consequently may not be able to access community-based services. An 18-year-old who is not dependent may be eligible for the full range of public funds AND the services that are provided with these monies.
>
> This is an especially difficult decision if your loved one is unable to work or care for themselves due to their symptoms. The course can be tricky to navigate. For example: if you give your loved one money to help them make ends meet this may be counted as income for the purposes of some funds. That can make them ineligible. You will need to weigh what your loved one needs and what their situation must be for them to receive this. The balance you arrive at may be imperfect.
>
> Your best recourse is to make an appointment with the appropriate agencies—Medicaid, your local LME/MCO, your Social Security office—and have an intensive fact-gathering discussion. Find out everything you can about what your loved one is eligible for and what things would impact that eligibility. Determine how these things will benefit them and what they may lose without them. And then, you will need to be creative. If you cannot give someone money to buy food, you can still buy them food. You can buy them clothes. You can formally charge them rent to separate their finances from yours while enabling them to live at home. The key is to find ways to support your loved one in the areas where you can while opening the doors for them to receive the treatment and care that they need in the places you cannot.

AN IDEAL CARE SYSTEM

We noted that a continuum of care, per se, does not really exist in NC. It may be helpful, however, in understanding how mental illness is treated, and in determining where to begin to seek care for your loved one to provide a diagram of what an ideal system might look like.

Condition	Services
Distress—changes in behavior, mood, ability to care for self, relationships	Outpatient providers in order of professional training: • LCSW, LPC, CRC, Psychiatric Nurse Practitioner • Psychologist • Psychiatrist Purpose: evaluation, support, assessment and/or referral for additional services as needed, counseling, therapy, medication. Self-referral or referral by other professional
Crisis—danger to self or others including inability to meet basic needs	Emergency Room, Crisis Intervention services including police, mobile crisis unit, crisis assessment center Purpose: evaluation and referral/linkage to appropriate services. Self-referral, walk in, involuntary commitment papers taken, police intervention, assistance of professionals above.
Significant distress which does not respond within 4-6 weeks of treatment or where someone is yet unable to function at basic levels	Inpatient Hospitalization—Acute Assessment, initiation of treatment, stabilization Self-admission, parental admission for minors, involuntary commitment
Significant distress, inability to function, inability to provide self-care or meet basic needs, danger to self or others, symptoms which significantly interfere with function	Long-term Psychiatric Facility Intensive long-term treatment and supports Referral
Symptoms present but no danger to self or others, in need of supports to maintain gains and continue to make gains. May require assistance with medication management and daily activities	Providers listed in order of support provided: • Inpatient Hospitalization—sub-acute • Residential Services • Assertive Community Treatment Team Provide high-level and broad range of supportive services that are able to quickly adapt to meet changing needs. Referral, some self-admission/parental admission for minors
Stable and/or controlled symptoms with concurrent functional ability	Outpatient providers in appropriate combination: • LCSW, LPC, CRC, Psychiatric Nurse Practitioner • Psychologist • Psychiatrist • Community Support Services Provide moderate level supportive services to maintain stability

TREATMENT MANAGEMENT

Putting a Treatment Plan Together

When someone you love has a mental illness, you may find it difficult to obtain the treatment needed. Someone who is hospitalized may be quickly discharged with a stack of paperwork, names, phone numbers, and little else. Referrals may be given without consideration of your loved one's unique needs and wishes. No one may ask what matters to your loved one in choosing a provider or if there is someone they want to work with. You may be told that certain services simply do not exist in the area where you live. That may or may not be true.

A case manager will develop a treatment plan based on professional recommendations, a person's willingness to receive treatment, AND their treatment goals. Using the information gathered, the case manager researches available treatments and where they are provided. The case manager determines how service providers are paid—whether they are private or public providers, accept insurance or public funds, and are able to adjust rates for those who are paying privately. The case manager has an understanding of the individual's financial situation and what benefits they may receive that can assist them in meeting medical costs. The case manager will also gather information about individual providers and how they provide services to determine if they are a good match with the individual. Having all of this information in hand, a case manager will then put together a treatment plan. The goal of this plan is to provide the person with the care that meets their needs based on their unique preferences, goals, and financial situation AND with providers they are likely to trust and work well with.

Once a person has begun treatment, the case manager will continue to follow the person to monitor how well they are working with any given provider, how well treatment is working, assess when other treatments are needed or whether a treatment is no longer needed, resolve any problems that may arise, and ensure that information is disseminated among different providers so that they can work with the person most effectively. If a particular provider is not working, the case manager will help find and transfer care to another. If a service is no longer needed the case manager will help to determine what services are needed next, and assist in transferring to those services.

Case Managers may also talk with funding sources to ensure that needed care is covered and that the need for care is properly communicated. They may work to get approval for treatments that are not a part of standard coverage, demonstrating how this will benefit the individual and be cost-effective for the payor. They may advocate on behalf of the individual with the LME/MCO, insurance company, doctors, counselors, community service providers, private providers—anyone involved in providing care—to ensure that the person receives the care that is needed in the way that it is needed.

In NC today, the role of case manager most often falls on the shoulders of the family. Time and again it has been shown that treating a mental illness requires more than medication alone. Those who are most successful at dealing with these illnesses have access to a range of treatments throughout recovery and in managing their illness long-term. As treatment needs and life-situation change, different types of providers may be needed. Recovery from a mental illness, rehabilitation, and successful ongoing management require an array of services and supports.

While this may seem daunting, it is possible. Be clear and concrete with your loved one so they understand what you can and cannot do. Listen to them and let them know their concerns and desires are part of every consideration—even if it is not possible to develop a plan that is exactly what they might want. Explain the challenges that funding and lack of services can create. You can do this!

- Determine what needs your loved one has and their goals for treatment and recovery.
- Assess their non-medical needs. Do not think only in terms of your loved one's symptoms. They may need vocational assistance. They may need transportation assistance. Assistance getting to appointments. Getting food. Finding housing.
- Familiarize yourself with the range of treatments that are available. Get information on the services available for non-medical needs. As you begin this process do not consider what is available in your community. Learn everything you can about how mental illnesses are treated. Consider both therapeutic and non-therapeutic services: counselors and vocational specialists, for example, as well as private providers and community-based services: cognitive rehabilitation and ACTT.

- For each need identify the service or form of treatment that would ideally address that need.
- Note any special concerns or preferences: what does your loved one want in a doctor or counselor; is there a specific type of therapy that they want or which would suit their unique needs; are they interested in specific alternative treatments.
- Lay out the ideal treatment plan—in a perfect world, what would your loved one receive and how would they receive it? Who would they receive it from?
- If a service is not available, identify what will best meet the need from those which can be accessed.
- Assess their financial situation.
- Determine what financial resources are available on federal, state, and local levels that may help meet these needs.
- Assist them in applying for any benefits they may be eligible for.
- If they have insurance find out what is covered and talk with the insurance company to see if they will approve treatments or services not covered.
- Determine what providers and systems are in place for these services where your loved one lives. Research these providers. Find out what they provide. What others who have received services say about them.
- Find out what type of payment is required by these providers. Talk to individual providers, DHHS, your local LME/MCO, Medicaid office, to find out how payment might be managed.
- Put together a treatment plan that covers the range of needs, goals, interests, and preferences that your loved one has and assist them in connecting with the appropriate providers and services.
- If possible, obtain releases of information that will allow providers to share information with you and work to make sure that the information you receive is shared as needed with all providers. Make sure providers are aware of and have contact information for any other providers your loved one is working with.
- Advocate for your loved one when it is needed: help fill out paperwork, go with them to visit agencies they may be seeking assistance from. Keep records for them. Help them to navigate the maze of forms and requirements that providers and service agencies may have. Add your voice to theirs when they are not treated well or have a grievance.

- Think outside the box:
    - If a specific service or treatment is not available is there something which is a close approximation or which can substitute? Is there another way to get that service?
    - Consider things which might not traditionally be considered treatment to add to your plan: yoga classes, a gym membership, local classes of interest to your loved one that will help them to get back into the community, interacting with others, living a life which is not encompassed by their illness.
    - Consider faith-based services such as pastoral counseling. These are often provided free of charge or at a minimal charge.
    - If a community service does not provide the full range of services desired, or if their counselor is not providing the type of therapy your loved one needs or wants, find another provider that they can see at the same time (some community services will require that your loved one work with their staff while receiving that service. For example, ACTT clients must see the ACTT psychiatrist. They may see an ACTT therapist or vocational specialist. Your loved one, in this instance, may not be able to see another psychiatrist but they can see a therapist on their own as well as the ACTT counselor)
    - Are there alternative ways of paying for a service?
    - If a particular provider is not working for your loved one, help them to find a new provider and to transition care safely and effectively.

> As much as possible, at all times possible, encourage your loved one to work with their providers. Encourage providers to take responsibility for your loved one's care. Your ideal role is that of a supportive, loving presence. Much of the stress and conflict between those living with mental illnesses and their family arises because families members all too often must take on the role of managing their loved one's recovery. The best role for you as a case manager is that of a supportive resource. You hear or help identify the need. You get the information. You help establish connections. Then you let the professionals do their job, and you support your loved one on their path.

***See the section on Medical Records on **p. 168**. This may be of tremendous help for you as you work to navigate the system and in managing your loved one's care.

Treatment Walls and How to Get Around Them

We wish it were possible to identify every wall or difficulty that you may encounter in seeking basic care and services. And that there was a solution for each. It is not possible, and there is not always an answer. Our treatment system is flawed. Whether your loved one receives care through community providers and public funding or has private insurance, there will be gaps in care. The care that is received may not be provided in the way it ideally should be. There will be walls, and there will be doors.

The single greatest assets that you have are your persistence and your voice. There is truth to the axiom: the squeaky wheel gets greased.

> *I have often felt that the mental health system is like a big, limp puppet. It just sits there. When my child becomes ill, I become the puppet master. I have to get in and make it work the way its supposed to. I jerk at this leg and move that arm. I push this unwieldy and unresponsive piece of wood in the directions that it needs to go in. Again and again. Each and every time.*

Below are some typical walls or difficulties that people encounter that have not been covered more specifically elsewhere in this manual. Hopefully, these examples will give you ideas as to how to respond when you encounter others.

1. **An individual who has been hospitalized is quickly discharged although not stable enough to maintain the gains they have made.**

    Hospitals are safe, supportive environments. By 'supportive,' we do not necessarily mean that they are warm and cozy. Hospitals see that people's needs are met. They are kept safe at times when their judgment, their emotions, their reasoning may put them at risk. While it is not fun to be in the hospital, it is also not stressful in the way day-to-day life can be. This is important when someone has experienced a medical crisis because stress is often the single most significant impediment to improving. When someone is discharged before they are ready, this can interfere with their ability to recover.

    We do not provide hospitalization for the time that it is needed in many instances. If you feel someone is going to be discharged and that this places them at risk, you need to be vocal. You will need to present your concerns in a very specific way. It will not be sufficient to point out that they are still depressed, are delusional, or even that they are psychotic. You need to make a case as to why this places them at risk. And you will need to take all of the factors in their life into account. One person may be discharged to an apartment and live on their own. Another may live with family who can provide some support. One person may stop medication as soon as they are no longer supervised. Another may take medication religiously. One person may be eligible for ACTT or other community services where another cannot receive any of these supports.

   a. First review the section on Involuntary Commitments—specifically the information about how to how to complete the petition on **p. 175**. You will need to express your concerns in the way this section describes.

   b. Identify in concrete functional terms the symptoms your loved one is experiencing, how this impacts their ability to function, how this places them at risk and of what, AND why continued hospitalization is needed and how not receiving this may lead them to get worse and/or go into crisis again. Be very specific.

   c. Put your concerns in writing and provide this to any and everyone at the facility who has any ability to speak to your loved one's status. This includes the psychiatrist, case managers or social workers, counselors, even the facility CEO if necessary. Contact your state representative(s) to express your concerns. They actually can be quite responsive and do have the ability to work on your loved one's behalf. Contact DHHS and/or your local LME/MCO. (Note: your local LME/MCO, if they oversee funding for your loved one's stay, have a conflict of interest in advocating for them. The money that is not used for your loved one is money that they can apply elsewhere. They have a vested interest in minimizing the care that any one person receives.) If your loved one is covered by private insurance, contact your insurance company, voice your concerns *and follow up with them in writing also.* Above all—do not stop speaking, writing, documenting, and expressing your concerns up until the moment your loved one walks out the door.

2. **Your loved one is unable to afford the medication or other treatments that they need.**

    As noted elsewhere, NC does not participate in expanded Medicaid under the AFCA. What this means is that individuals who receive too much money each month—whether from work, disability, or because they live with others who are working—are not eligible for Medicaid. Yet, they earn too little to qualify to purchase subsidized insurance through the Marketplace. If they do not receive Medicare and are not able to be covered by a family member's insurance, they may quite literally have no coverage for prescriptions or other treatment forms that they need. The average psychiatrist appointment can be more than $100 for a 15 minute visit. Counselors regularly charge this or more for an hour. Many community services are only available to those who qualify for Medicaid. Prescriptions can cost over $1000/month. What are they to do?

    a. Find a pharmacy with programs that assist people without insurance. You can also contact the company that produces the medication your loved one is prescribed. Many pharmaceutical companies have programs to assist those who cannot afford medications. Research prescription-only plans. A pharmacist can be a great resource in helping you to find a way to cover prescription costs.

    b. Find professionals and service providers who offer sliding-scale fees and/or who will accept payment plans. Consider alternative providers for some services—such as clergy, who may provide counseling free of charge.

    c. Contact your local LME/MCO and/or DHHS to find out what resources they know of. Your loved one may be eligible for State Funding even if they cannot receive Medicaid. The LME/MCO may know of providers who will be able to work with your loved one on cost.

3. **Your insurance company does not cover the treatment that is needed.**

    It is little known, but insurance companies have latitude in approving care that is not covered by their policy. True—the primary motivation in doing this is cost. Unlike public funding sources, however, insurance companies have a vested interest in keeping costs down over the long-haul. They take a big-picture view of treatment for chronic illnesses. Where public funding sources often react to what saves money today, or in this fiscal year/under the current budget, insurance companies want to minimize costs over a lifetime. If a treatment that your loved one needs is not covered by your policy, but you can show how this treatment will help the insurance company minimize the cost of your loved one's care in the long-term, you may be able to get them to approve it.

An example would be: covering ACTT services and keeping your loved one stable in the community may be cheaper than hospitalization every 3 months. Some ACT Teams may be able to work with your insurance company even though they are typically funded by the state. Another example: Being able to work with a counselor over the course of the year (instead of the 10 allowed visits) may help your loved one adhere to their medication or keep them working, instead of being repeatedly hospitalized. Ask for a case manager if your insurance company uses them. This is someone who will be individually and personally assigned to your loved one and who can be of assistance in getting treatment approved and thinking outside of the policy when it comes to care.

4. **The care your loved one needs is not available in their area.**

    This is a difficult situation. If your loved one does not live in or near an urban area of North Carolina the services and professionals which are available will likely not meet the full range of needs they have. Furthermore, because these areas of the state do not have the professionals needed, those who practice there are stretched very thin.

    a. Consider alternative ways of obtaining the treatment. If your loved one does not have access to counselors are there others, such as clergy, who are trained and able to provide counseling? If they need assistance or supervision in taking medication on a daily basis is there a local nursing agency who would be able to stop out and give them medication? Is there someone who is able and qualified to provide a similar service and can make some adaptions to help your loved one?

    b. You will also want to do research as to where the closest providers and professionals are? Is it possible to arrange transportation so your loved one can reach these services in a nearby community?

Advanced Psychiatric Directive, Guardianship, and Power of Attorney

Advanced Psychiatric Directives

An Advanced Psychiatric Directive (also known as Mental Health Advanced Directive) is a document which describes what someone wants to happen if and when specific circumstances arise. These documents can be legally binding or not depending on how they are designed and executed. In the instance of a psychiatric directive an individual is able to lay out their preferences and desires for their loved ones and treating professionals should they become ill. They can designate a legal representative who is able to authorize care on their behalf.

There are a variety of ways to prepare an advanced directive depending on the individual's plan for its use. Samples of advanced directive forms can be found in the Appendix on pages 235 and 243. Some of the things that an individual can address are preferences in treatments or treatment facilities; medications that have been useful to them; actions that they want family members to take should certain situations arise, and; name persons who are legally able to manage their affairs and/or make medical decisions for them.

The benefits of having an advanced directive are immense. Often, when a person is in crisis, they are not able to clearly express their wishes or preferences. Families may be left scrambling to do the right thing but not knowing what that is. It is not uncommon for individuals to be angry with family members and the decisions that they have made during a time of crisis. When an Advanced Psychiatric Directive has been completed the family can act with some assurance that they are following their loved one's wishes. Your loved one is able to have a voice in their care even when they are no longer in a position to act effectively. An advanced directive helps providers to incorporate the knowledge and desires of the person they are treating. If your loved needs to be involuntarily hospitalized, an advanced directive giving legal authority to make medical decisions for them can facilitate this process.

Crises, by definition, are intense and often emotional. They place us in a position of chaos and uncertainty. They contain the potential for conflict and inadvertent error. Advanced planning—considering the situations that may arise and how we will act if they do occur—reduces the chaos. It lessens the severity and intensity of the emotion which occurs.

Additional information can be found at NAMI's (National Alliance on Mental Illness) website — https://www.nami.org/Learn-More/Mental-Health-Public-Policy/Psychiatric-Advance-Directives-(PAD) — and SAMSHA (Substance Abuse and Mental Health Services Administration) https://www.samhsa.gov/section-223/governance-oversight/directives-behavioral-health

<u>Guardianship</u>

Guardianship, either temporary or permanent, is a court order giving a person or agency legal authority over an individual who has been determined not to be competent to manage their own affairs and/or care for themselves. There are different levels of guardianship. The appropriate level will depend on any person's unique situation. Obtaining guardianship is, rightly, not an easy process. Some families have found it necessary. Generally, guardianship is considered when treatments have not been effective at managing symptoms, AND a loved one is chronically resistant to treatment AND unable to care for themselves, or a chronic danger to themselves or others. Additionally, there may be situations in which temporary guardianship is needed because the path to recovery will be long and an individual is not expected to function well for a significant period of time.

Hospitals prefer adults with severe and chronic mental illnesses to have a guardian as this can make providing treatment exponentially easier. The question which must be considered, however, is the impact on the individual living with a mental illness. Does obtaining guardianship communicate to them that they will never be able to manage their condition or that they are incapable? When a family member seeks guardianship how does this affect the relationship with their loved one? Does it create conflict, schism, or estrangement? Is it prudent to consider a public agency or non-related designee when guardianship becomes a consideration? What does this do for the family's ability to advocate for their loved one or be a part of their care?

There are no easy answers as to when seeking guardianship is best. The process is not easy, and it can be costly. This is a significant step to take and before you consider the option, it should be clear that your loved one's needs are so high and the risk to them so significant for an extended period of time that the failure to intercede will likely result in harm.

Power of Attorney

A Power of Attorney (POA) is a document which allows one adult to act on behalf of another in a legal capacity. There are many types of POA. One kind of POA allows someone to handle an individual's financial and legal affairs when they are unable to act on their own behalf. This can include managing finances, bank accounts, leases, and other legal obligations. Another allows a designated person to make medical decisions when an individual has been determined unable. There are other options in addition to these. An attorney can best answer questions you or your loved one may have as to which POA is most appropriate.

There may be a number of benefits to having a POA. An individual must designate their POA and what rights they give to the person and under what circumstances those rights should be exercised. This must be done when your loved one is competent and their symptoms managed. It cannot always be done during a crisis. Exploring and deciding upon a POA is something that is best done during a period of calm and before the need arises.

Advocacy

Advocacy literally means to support or argue for, to plead in favor of. When we speak of advocating for someone with a mental illness, it means to speak or act on behalf of the person for whom we are an advocate. This can mean many things. As has been seen throughout this manual, it can mean to help someone receive the services and/or treatment that they need in the way that they need it. It can mean advocating for their rights—with a provider, in a treatment setting, in the community. It may mean working to enable them to receive the benefits and assistance that they need. It can also mean to ensure that the person we are advocating for has a voice in all of these places and that their voice is heard.

While advocacy has been covered in other sections, the last point bears some special consideration. Because those whose lives are impacted by mental illnesses often experience symptoms that may skew their perceptions, impact their judgment, or affect their cognitive process, their voices and perceptions are all too easily discounted. There are few other illnesses which cause providers to discount the opinion, perspective, or preferences of the person they are treating. Rarely are those living with mental illnesses seen as experts on themselves and/or their lives. Rarely are they seen as rich resources for what they need to manage their illness.

The fact that someone has a mental illness, or is experiencing symptoms, does not mean that they cease to perceive or interact with the world around them. It does not mean that every perception, reaction, or emotion that they have is a product of their illness. You know the old saying: *just because you are paranoid it doesn't mean that someone isn't watching you.* Many professionals in the system only see people when they are in crisis or symptomatic. Our system is structured to address crises, not prevent them. It is all too easy for individuals to be acted on rather than engaged as partners in the treatment process. Adults may find themselves treated like children who have no preferences that matter, or no valid insights into themselves or their condition and its treatment. Professionals who are stretched thin may find themselves telling clients or patients what they will do instead of talking to them about their options. Individuals who are delusional or psychotic may find that everything they say is discounted as a product of their illness. Even when symptoms are controlled, the very fact that someone is diagnosed as having a mental illness may cause those working with them to perceive them as less than capable.

Mental Illnesses can be managed. They are not a measure of capability. When symptoms are effectively controlled, patients are able to live full lives. They are also illnesses which are difficult to adjust to, difficult to manage, and pose ongoing challenges for many. When someone is a participant in their treatment—when they are viewed as a partner in their recovery—the ways symptoms are managed are ways that the individual owns for him or herself. Participants in treatment have a voice in deciding how symptoms are managed and in developing ways to manage their illness which work for them and support their goals. Participants in recovery develop a sense of ability and skill at living with mental illness and meeting its challenges and become capable adults who also happen to have a mental illness. All of these things are not only tremendous assets in effectively treating a mental illness but often necessary achievements for those who learn to manage their illness well and live lives that are meaningful and functional. Key to each of these is your loved one feeling that they are heard, that their voice matters, and that they have valuable insights into what they need to manage this illness well.

Your role as a family member is to always see and advocate on behalf of your family member when they have legitimate concerns that are not being heard or given weight. It is important to support their role as a participant in managing their illness. As their advocate, you make sure that their voice is heard and what they say valued. You listen to them, ask their opinion, clarify what their goals are. This does not mean that they can have everything that they want. However, when they have legitimate concerns, desires, preferences, choices and they are not being heard, you can bring these things to the attention of the professionals working with them. You can insist that they are heard. You can lobby on their behalf.

As your loved one's advocate, requiring that they have a voice in their life, that they be treated with respect, and their voice valued, may be the one thing for which there is no compromise or alternative. You may not always be successful. There may be times when your loved one blames you for the failures of others. Advocacy is a marathon. Don't give up and don't lose hope.

Medical Records

We have mentioned medical records and their use in ensuring proper treatment for your loved one several times.

Our mental health system often results in fragmented care: someone may receive treatment from a number of providers who have no connection to or communication with one another. When this happens, each provider essentially must start from the beginning in determining what illness your loved one has and what treatment(s) may be best. This creates roadblocks and slows down both treatment and recovery.

Because family and loved ones are likely to be the single constant in anyone's life, you are key to facilitating care and ensuring providers have the information they need to build on your loved one's treatment history. There are several things you can prepare on your own, without access to your loved one's treatment records. There are records you may be able to obtain.

Let's begin with the records. Each time your loved one is seen, the person who provides evaluation and/or treatment must generate a written record of that contact. Records from an inpatient hospitalization can include nursing, social work or case management notes, therapeutic notes, psychiatric notes, records of evaluations, any tests performed, and pharmacy records. Records from community-based service providers such as ACTT can include assessments by each person meeting with your loved one, and summaries of every contact. These records are invaluable. At times of crisis, they provide background, including what has precipitated or occurred during prior crisis periods—and just as importantly, what worked to resolve the crisis—and what did not work. When someone is seeking new treatment, these records provide history a practitioner can use.

If your loved one is under the age of 18 and you are their parent or legal guardian you can request and receive any records without their permission. You may be required to pay copying and/or processing fees for records.

If your loved one is 18 or older and gives permission, signs a Release of Information (a sample ROI is found on **p. 269** of the appendix), you can likewise request any medical records related to their treatment. You may be required to pay copying and/or processing fees for records.

Your loved one may not be willing to give you permission to request their records, but they may be open to you keeping copies of these records for them. In this case, he or she can request the records and give them to you.

If you obtain records, you should put these in a binder where they are kept in chronological order.

Even if you do not have access to formal medical records/provider information, there are records that you can create which will be helpful in assessing your loved one and determining the best course of treatment.

Facilities and providers may share treatment information with one another without permission to provide care in very specific circumstances. Your ability to provide the names and contact information of anyone who has treated your loved one to someone who is providing care to them today may facilitate information being shared between providers. Create a cover sheet that lists each provider, hospitalization, and the period when your loved one was seen by this person or treated at this facility. Include names, addresses, and phone numbers where possible.

You can also create a sheet listing any medications your loved one was prescribed, the period when the medications were taken, and the results of using that medication—why it continues to be prescribed or was discontinued. This will help providers to avoid medications that are already known not to work or to cause problematic side effects and to focus on medications that are known to be effective.

Another significant document you can prepare is a Family/Psycho-Social History. This is a written narrative that provides biographical information about someone and highlights key points and relationships in their life. On a basic level, because mental illnesses have a genetic component, understanding a patient's familial mental health history can help to shed light on what is going on with this individual. Family/Psycho-Social Histories also provide important information about family dynamics and relationships and important events in a person's life. All of these may have contributed to the development of symptoms, and the course that the illness has taken. There is a sample family history at the end of this section.

You may find the following outline helpful in preparing a Family/Psycho-Social History. There is no right way or wrong way to do this. Your purpose is to provide as much information as possible to help the person treating your loved one.

1. Describe the person's family and childhood: When were they born? Do they have siblings? Where are they in the pecking order? How would you describe them as a child? What was the family's relationship like? What was their relationship with their parents, with their siblings? Were there any significant family events: did they move a lot? Were the parents divorced? How did that impact them? Did the family experience any trauma? Likewise, what strengths did the family have? How did this person do in school? Did they have friendships? What were their interests? Did their relationships with family, siblings, or friends change as they grew—for better or worse? Because of any specific event or reason? What was the family's support? Did they go to church? Was the extended family close? This is just the start of a list of the type of things you want to consider discussing. Not all may apply. There may be other things that you feel are important to cover. Your goal is to give the person reading this both a sense of the person they are evaluating—who they were, how they became who they are—and a sense of the world they grew up in.

2. You will want to bring this history as closely as possible to current time. What are the relationships that parents/siblings/friends have with the person now? Where do people live in relation to one another? How involved are they in one another's lives? Is this involvement positive or negative? Supportive or stressful? You should include as full a school and work history for this person as possible.

3. Note any other family members who have been diagnosed or believed to have a mental illness. Provide a diagnosis if one is available, how they were treated (even medications if you are aware of them), and the success of any treatment. Discuss any significant illnesses that the person you love or other family members have had.

4. You will want to specifically address how any suspected mental illness began to emerge and what has happened since symptoms first appeared. What were the first signs that something was wrong? How did your loved one respond? How did those close to your loved one respond? What was the impact on school, on work, on relationships? Has any treatment been sought? If so, when, what has the outcome been? Have there been any hospitalizations—how did your love one react to this? What was the outcome? What worked? What made things worse?

In addition to the above, you can include any of the following:

- Parents: What sort of people are/were they? What kind of relationship did/does the person have with them? What kind of work did/do they do? How often does the person see them? If they are dead, when did they die? How?
- Siblings: Ages, gender, personalities, and circumstances: the nature of their work, marriages, children. What sort of relationship does the person have with them?
- Religion: What religion? Role of religion in family life/in the person's life.
- School: Did they like school? How did they do in school? Did they do well academically? Did they make friends? Do they still have friends?
- Dating: At what age did they start dating. Sexual experiences? Did/do they have good intimate relationships? Are they involved with someone now? Is that relationship good?
- Drug and alcohol experimentation and/or use: At what age did they first use? What have they experimented with? Do they currently use? How often?
- Medical History: Any illnesses, hospitalizations, operations? Outcomes.
- Emotional history: Any history of abuse or other trauma.
- Symptoms: An account of when symptoms began and how they progressed.

Many dedicated, passionate, and deeply caring people provide treatment to those living with mental illnesses. When meeting your loved one, however, they have no context in which to place him or her. They do not know them—certainly how they function when they are well. They do not see them in the context of their family and their larger community of extended family and friends. They do not know the life they have been a part of and the world they inhabit. What they see and know is the symptomatic person in front of them who may not be functioning well, if at all. When you provide this history, it not only provides the professional with a great deal of significant information, it shows them the person behind the symptoms they are treating. It helps them to differentiate between the person and the symptoms. It points an arrow to how they got where they are today and to where they may go. The best care is grounded in your loved one being a complex, multi-dimensional person—someone who has a life and relationships which encompasses more than their mental illness.

This is not a quick, easy, or necessarily brief document to create. It is also not an objective document—because you—being emotionally involved with this person and part of the history you describe—are creating it. That is understood, and it is okay. Once you have created this, however, you will be able to provide each professional with a wealth of invaluable information that will assist them in assessing and treating your loved one. At most, you may need to revisit it from time to time to provide updates as circumstances suggest. Once you have completed this history, it should become part of your binder of records.

To summarize, create a binder that contains relevant medical information for your loved one. Maintain records in chronological order. When your loved one is admitted to a facility for any reason, or begins treatment with a new provider, you can provide any or all of these records to assist the provider in determining the best course of treatment. This binder should include as much of the following as possible:

1. *A summary sheet with dates of hospitalizations, the reason for hospitalization, condition on discharge, and hospital contact information. Note any diagnoses made.*
2. *A summary sheet which lists service providers, service provided, dates of service, and contact information. Note any diagnoses made.*
3. *A summary sheet which lists medications, dates of use and impact of medication—especially any side effects, allergies, or problems.*
4. *Medical records obtained from any service providers, inpatient hospitalizations, outpatients treatment programs, or community-based services filed in chronological order.*
5. *Family/psycho-social history*

Sample Excerpt: Family/Psycho-Social History

NAME: _____
DOB: _____

- Mother: NAME, CONTACT INFO (Representative Payee)
- Father: NAME, CONTACT INFO
- INSURANCE INFO
- Diagnosis: Depends on who you talk to: Bi-polar with Psychotic features, schizoaffective, Schizophrenia
- Age of onset of psychosis: 18 year 18 months.
- First hospitalization: 18 years 11 months of age
- Medications causing severe adverse reactions: Abilify, Geodon, Depakote
- Best Medications in resolving symptoms: Zyprexa *30 mg. Klonopin 1 mg Lithium (this combination has been the silver bullet for him)

Hospitals he has been in: List names, locations, length of stay

Community Service Providers:

Family History

Alan is an only child. His parents divorced when he was 3 years old. He spent a great deal of time with both parents, who were actively involved in his life. He had no significant childhood illnesses or injuries. No behavioral problems. He exhibited no signs of mental illness.

He was in the higher percentile for his age group in height and weight. He tested in the higher percentile for intelligence and was in honors or expedited classes. He graduated from High School in 2002 and was accepted to a state university.

In essence, he was a very easy child to raise and to get along with. He had good relationships with both parents, residing primarily with his mother. He did well in school. He was not difficult and did not get into trouble. He was bright, slow to anger, laid back and easy going. He had many friendships and activities that he enjoyed. He began work at the age of 14. He purchased his own car and paid for the insurance, gas, and repairs. He was responsible, reliable, honest, warm, intelligent, self-possessed, friendly, outgoing.

Psychiatric History

He first began to exhibit psychotic symptoms about a year after graduating from HS. He was involuntarily committed about 3 months later. He was an inpatient for 7 weeks. After discharge, he returned to his mother's home and in January started school. At this time he immediately stopped his medications. He was again committed in April of that year.

Over the first two years following diagnosis and initial hospitalization he went off his medication or had adverse medication reactions and was hospitalized a total of 7 times. On one occasion he left on foot and disappeared. He was found 6 weeks later homeless on the streets of another state.

Approximately ten years ago following an 8-week hospitalization, he began adhering to his medications. He was able to work full time, get off of SSDI, support himself and begin school. He went off his medications again, was hospitalized for 8 weeks and while his adherence was not strict he did not need to be hospitalized again for 4 years. At that time he was hospitalized for 8 weeks again and was able to continue to live independently with 6 years of no hospitalizations.

INVOLUNTARY COMMITMENT
Not Just Suicidal or Homicidal

The Involuntary Commitment process is one of the most difficult things that anyone goes through. It also can be one of the most confusing and misunderstood.

Involuntary Commitment is the process whereby someone is forced into treatment—inpatient, acute hospitalization—because there is (1) imminent risk of harm to self or to someone else if no intervention occurs, and (2) they are refusing treatment. Both of these criteria must be present. Most often when we refer to Involuntary Commitment, we are thinking of the initial phase of this process. The process is complex with several phases, each guided by defined criteria and rules. It can play out over a considerable period of time—sometimes weeks or even months.

The process of asking that someone you care for be involuntarily committed is fraught with uncertainty and emotion. It is never an easy decision—and it should not be. At its most basic when someone is involuntarily committed their basic right of autonomy is nullified, even if temporarily. The only other time in our society when someone is held against their will is when they are incarcerated. Is it any wonder then that this process is viewed negatively?

If you are in this situation you may experience at least some of the following:

- Turmoil as to whether someone needs to be committed. You may wonder if their condition is bad enough to warrant this step. You may doubt yourself; question your judgment over and again. Rarely is the decision clear-cut.
- You may be concerned that once seen for evaluation they will not be admitted or if admitted, that they will not be kept for sufficient time to improve. You will have initiated a traumatic experience to no end.
- You may fear creating or worsening a crisis.
- You may fear damaging your relationship with your loved one. You may fear their anger—especially if there is concern that they may be a danger to you or to others. You may fear alienating them.
- You may feel guilt about doing something you know is going to be painful and difficult. You may worry your loved one will feel betrayed or believe you do not care.

- You may face opposition or criticism from other family or friends. They may not agree there is imminent danger. They may be concerned about hurting your loved one. They may feel strongly about taking away someone's personal rights.

- You may feel intimidated by the process. Professionals may discourage you when they tell you how hard or difficult it is to get someone approved for commitment. They may agree that your loved one is at risk and needs hospitalizations but dissuade you from trying because of how hard it is.

- You may be told, "it isn't against the law to be crazy and being out of touch with reality is not sufficient reason to hospitalize someone."

- You may find yourself frustrated with a system that fails to act until harm has already occurred. You may feel panic, overwhelmed, frightened, or at a loss for how to proceed if there is no alternative available.

It is not always clear whether seeking an Involuntary Commitment is appropriate. You may spend days or even weeks watching someone you love deteriorate, unable to step in and stop it. This is a fearful, painful process. You may move through each day knowing that if you act too soon he or she will not be admitted while believing if you act too late real harm will result. You may find yourself walking a fine and difficult line where the moment to take action is never clear. Walking this line is walking in hell.

> You should know that while the decision to seek Involuntarily Commitment for someone you love is one of the hardest decisions you will ever make—and it may be one of the most gut-wrenching—if you believe that this person is in genuine danger—because they cannot care for themselves, they place themselves at risk, they may harm themselves, or because they may harm someone else—taking this step is the right thing to do. There are times when the only thing that has importance is life itself. Whatever the ramifications on your relationship with this person, there is no relationship if they die. Even if there is not death, the damage which an untreated mental illness can wreak on a person's life—the pain that comes with it—is a deep and bottomless pit. There comes a time when these things carry greater weight than any voice in your ear on the other side—when this step is the right thing because it chooses life.

In the state of NC, when discussing Involuntary Commitments with professionals you may hear over and again that Involuntary Commitments are for two situations: 1) danger to self (suicide), or; 2) danger to others (violence toward others). This is incorrect. It speaks volumes to the state of our mental health system that many of the same professionals involved in this process do not understand it. You may need to educate them. This should also prepare you for the fights you may face in obtaining the basic care your loved one needs.

The NC statute reads as follows:

NCGS 122C-3(11)a and b

"Dangerous to himself or others" means:
- a. "Dangerous to himself" means that within the relevant past:
    1. The individual has acted in such a way as to show:
        - I. That he would be unable, without care, supervision, and the continued assistance of others not otherwise available, to exercise self-control, judgment, and discretion in the conduct of his daily responsibilities and social relations, or to satisfy his need for nourishment, personal or medical care, shelter, or self-protection and safety; and
        - II. That there is a reasonable probability of his suffering serious physical debilitation within the near future unless adequate treatment is given pursuant to this Chapter. A showing of behavior that is grossly irrational, of actions that the individual is unable to control, of behavior that is grossly inappropriate to the situation, or of other evidence of severely impaired insight and judgment shall create a prima facie inference that the individual is unable to care for himself; or
    2. The individual has attempted suicide or threatened suicide and that there is a reasonable probability of suicide unless adequate treatment is given pursuant to this Chapter; or

3. The individual has mutilated himself or attempted to mutilate himself and that there is a reasonable probability of serious self-mutilation unless adequate treatment is given pursuant to this Chapter.

Previous episodes of dangerousness to self, when applicable, may be considered when determining reasonable probability of physical debilitation, suicide, or self-mutilation.

b. "Dangerous to others" means that within the relevant past, the individual has inflicted or attempted to inflict or threatened to inflict serious bodily harm on another, or has acted in such a way as to create a substantial risk of serious bodily harm to another, or has engaged in extreme destruction of property; and that there is a reasonable probability that this conduct will be repeated. Previous episodes of dangerousness to others, when applicable, may be considered when determining reasonable probability of future dangerous conduct. Clear, cogent, and convincing evidence that an individual has committed a homicide in the relevant past is prima facie evidence of dangerousness to others.

This statute says that <u>in addition to</u> the risk created by suicidal intention/ideology or physical aggression, a person is at risk sufficient to need intervention when they are unable to care for them self. This can be when they are unable to attend to their basic daily needs (food, sleep, shelter, medical care, and safety) and/or they are unable to exercise the reasoning or judgment needed to maintain their physical safety, and/or their behavior is so grossly irrational or uncontrolled that physical neglect, harm, or other debilitation may result.
The statute speaks to a person's ability to function. This criterion—the ability to function and how it impacts life—forms the basis for each clause. Your challenge will be to explain how your loved one's ability to function—or lack of—places them at risk.

Seeking to Involuntarily Commit someone is and should always be the step of last resort or the only option available in an emergency. It should be undertaken only to protect life and never only to force someone into care who is not willing. It is the nuclear option—and with good reason.

> If police respond to a crisis and determine that someone is in immediate risk of injury or death, they can take them immediately into custody without having an Involuntary Commitment order in hand. The police can ONLY do this if the danger is immediate and waiting to act may result in injury or death—as in cases of suicide or violence to others. When this happens, a magistrate must still be contacted to obtain the appropriate paperwork.
>
> You cannot and should not call the police in an attempt not to have to go through a magistrate. Call 911 ONLY when there is an emergency.

Involuntary Commitment: Step 1—The Petition

In NC, the involuntary commitment process begins when a magistrate issues an order instructing the police to pick someone up and take them for evaluation. Anyone can request, or *petition,* a magistrate to issue this order if they have first-hand and recent knowledge of the person's behavior/condition. Not every request is granted.

If you have decided to seek an Involuntary Commitment the first thing you must do is speak to a magistrate. At this time, you will explain why you are requesting this order and you will complete a written petition. <u>You will need to go to a magistrate in the county where **your loved one** is or is believed to be.</u>

> ****To find out where a magistrate is available you can call the local police department NON-EMERGENCY number in the area where an order must be requested. Magistrates are available 24/7. In some counties, the magistrate may have to be called in to review your request and you may have to wait for them to arrive. Other counties have a magistrate in the office at all hours. In either case, this may be a lengthy process.*

When you meet with the magistrate, you will be given the petition to complete. A copy of this petition can be found in the appendix on **p. 267**. You can see that the petition asks for several types of information about *"The Respondent."* The Respondent is the person you want to be evaluated. Do not worry if you are unable to provide all of the information requested. Things such as date of birth or social security number will not impact the magistrate's willingness to grant your petition. An address is not even essential (although desirable) as long as the police have a way to try to locate the person. Provide as much information as possible. You want to be able to give them the information they need to be able to locate the person, and then to be sure that they have located the right person.

The most crucial information that you will provide will be the reason(s) why this person should be evaluated. This is also the place where most requests for evaluation fail.

***If the petition is granted the information that you provide here is also the information that is provided to the person conducting the psychiatric evaluation. It is essential, therefore, that you be as specific and complete as possible about why you believe commitment is necessary.

<u>How to complete the Petition</u>

The portion of the petition where you explain why you feel this person is at risk reads as follows ***(You may use as many additional pieces of paper as needed to explain your concerns):

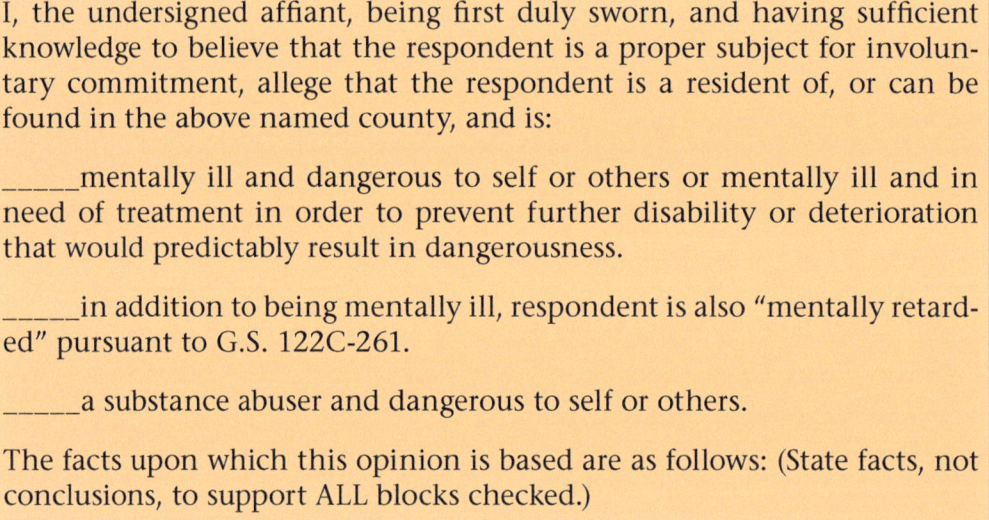

I, the undersigned affiant, being first duly sworn, and having sufficient knowledge to believe that the respondent is a proper subject for involuntary commitment, allege that the respondent is a resident of, or can be found in the above named county, and is:

_____mentally ill and dangerous to self or others or mentally ill and in need of treatment in order to prevent further disability or deterioration that would predictably result in dangerousness.

_____in addition to being mentally ill, respondent is also "mentally retarded" pursuant to G.S. 122C-261.

_____a substance abuser and dangerous to self or others.

The facts upon which this opinion is based are as follows: (State facts, not conclusions, to support ALL blocks checked.)

The first thing to note is that you are asked for facts, not conclusions. You want to describe what is happening: not your opinion about what is happening and not your feelings about what is happening. You don't want to project into the future—what you think will happen or what you believe may happen. For example, the fact that someone may be in danger in the future is not sufficient to force treatment today. They must be at risk right now.

For the magistrate and the person conducting the evaluation to understand why someone is at risk, you must <u>explain **HOW** their behavior puts them at risk.</u> The fact that someone has delusions, or that they hallucinate, or has any other symptom, does not alone mean that they are at risk. How these things impact their behavior and/or their health is what is important. You must explain concretely how their condition impairs their *self-control, judgment, and discretion in the conduct of their daily responsibilities and social relations, or to satisfy their need for nourishment, personal or medical care, shelter, or self-protection and safety; and (explain why) there is a reasonable probability of their suffering serious physical debilitation within the near future unless adequate treatment is given.*

Examples

Don't write: *Troy talks crazy and it makes me afraid.* This is subjective and vague. What do you mean by crazy? What is it that Troy says or does that leads to you being afraid? What are you afraid of?
Do write: *Troy says that I am not his mother. He tells me that I am an alien who has taken over his mother's body. Troy says that I want to hurt him. He has told me that he will kill me in order to protect himself if he needs to.*

Don't write: *Melissa is delusional and believes things that are not true.* What does Melissa say that is delusional? How are her delusions impacting her ability to function or her well-being?
Do write: *Melissa believes that her food is being poisoned and has stopped eating. She has lost 15 pounds in the last 2 weeks.*

Don't write: *Alex puts himself in bad situations and he is going to get killed.* Many people put themselves in bad situations. How is this related to symptoms? How do his symptoms lead him to do things he would not do otherwise? Why are the things he does dangerous?
Do write: *Alex believes that God will protect him no matter what he does and he should act without regard for his safety. He left home with no money and traveled 10 hours to Manhattan where he slept on street. He said he wanted to bring God's love to the people there. He told us that if someone tried to hurt him God would protect him. When we told him he could get killed, he told us that if someone killed him then God had decided it was time for him to die and it was ok.*

Don't write: *Erin doesn't get along with anyone anymore. She yells at people and spends all of her time alone.*
Do write: *Erin will begin yelling at strangers on the street. Sometimes people get angry with her but this doesn't stop her. Yesterday someone punched her because she yelled at them and she has a bad cut on her head. This morning when I took her to the store she still yelled at a man in the parking lot because she thought he looked at her strangely.*

Don't write: *Luke sits and stares into space. He tells me he is going to help me in the yard and I know he wants to but he will just sit and wait for me to tell him what to do. He is dirty and wears the same clothes all the time.*

> **Do write:** *Luke is having difficulty when he tries to do things: he seems to not be able to think through the steps he needs to take. He wants to help me in the yard—but when he tries he gets confused/overwhelmed. He will just stand there not knowing how to start. This spills over into everything he does—he cannot cook. He doesn't bathe or change his clothes.*
>
> It may seem obvious to you that if someone is delusional or hallucinating they are not functioning well or they are at risk. Neither the magistrate nor the person who is conducting the evaluation knows your loved one or their situation. The only information they have is what you tell them. An Involuntary Commitment is a legal decision about a medical condition whose symptoms and impact can vary widely from person to person, and for any given person at different times. Your task is to explain what the situation is now, for this person, and how it is that he or she is at risk due to this.

- Provide background: does this person have a history of mental illness? How long have they had a mental illness? What kind of mental illness do they have? Have they been committed involuntarily before? Are they taking medication? Do they take it as prescribed? Does the medication work? If they have never been ill, it is equally important to report this along with some description of how their behavior has changed and when.
    - **You are answering the question: what has led to the current situation?**
- Identify behaviors and/or symptoms as thoroughly and concretely as possible. What specific signs indicate to you that this person is not well and that they are at risk? <u>For each sign that you report, describe the impact that this is having.</u>
    - **You are answering the questions: how is this person not functioning or not functioning well, and what is the impact of that?**
    - Describe symptoms and give concrete examples of each symptom you describe—including linking symptoms to behavior.
    - Explain what the person says they believe. Explain how their thinking is flawed or how they are not functioning well cognitively. Explain how this impacts their behavior and/or their ability to do things.
    - Describe specific behaviors—what someone does and/or does not do. Tie behaviors to their consequences and/or explain <u>how their behavior places them at risk.</u>

You can also bring in past history of risk. If someone has done things in the past that were risky or have been harmed due to actions taken while symptomatic, describe what they did and what happened—*especially in instances where what has happened in the past is similar to what is currently happening.*

As much as possible, make sure that for everything you describe you answer the question: *How does this place this person at risk?* If the answer to that question is not clear—if you can still ask that question for any point you make—then you have not provided enough information or the information you have provided is not concrete enough.

> **Substance Abuse and Involuntary Commitments**
>
> You may have noticed that the petition allows for—*a substance abuser and dangerous to self or others*—as meeting the criteria for involuntary commitment.
>
> Generally, we don't think of substance abuse when we consider the reasons that someone may be involuntarily committed. It is possible, however, to seek an Involuntary Commitment for someone on the basis of substance abuse when that substance abuse places the person's life in imminent danger. In this instance you would complete the petition as you would for any other mental illness. You would describe their condition and the behavior that they are engaging in terms of how this places them at imminent risk.

Involuntary Commitment: Step 2—The evaluation

Once you complete the petition and review the information with the magistrate, the magistrate will decide whether or not to grant the petition. If the petition is not granted, the process stops here. This does not mean you cannot come back and try again—even as soon as the next day—and especially <u>at any point</u> if anything in the person's condition or situation changes.

If the petition is granted, **it is valid for 24 hours.** This means that the person must be picked up within 24 hours. If they are not, and if you believe that they are still at risk, you will need to return to the magistrate and begin again at Step 1.

Once a petition is granted an order is given to either the sheriff or a local police department. They must then locate the person and take them into custody. Once in custody, the person is taken to an appropriate facility where they will be seen for preliminary evaluation.

The purpose will be to determine if there is sufficient concern to keep them for further evaluation and/or treatment.

The NC Statute states that a person must be evaluated within 24 hours of being taken into custody. It is entirely likely that they may wait at the facility for many hours before being seen. Evaluation generally includes a nursing and non-psychiatric, physical evaluation as well as the psychiatric evaluation. If someone is emotionally unstable, they may be given sedating medications. If they are physically aggressive they will be forcibly restrained. A police officer—either from the department which brought them to the facility or a facility officer—will remain with them throughout the evaluation process. The reason for this is that once an officer has served the order for evaluation, they are in police custody until that evaluation is completed and they are admitted to the hospital or released.

When the person has been evaluated a determination will be made as to whether they should be admitted or released. If they are to be admitted the assessing facility will assume custody and begin to try to find a bed at an appropriate inpatient facility. If the person completing the evaluation decides that they do not meet the criteria for an involuntary commitment, then they will be released.

***The statute requires that the person who initiated the petition be notified within 24 hours of transfer of the individual to an inpatient facility.

THIS IS NOT THE END OF THE PROCESS

WHAT YOU NEED TO KNOW

- Once a petition has been authorized and an order issued to the police, you cannot walk it back or take it back. It is possible for a person who knows that an order has been taken out for them to go to the hospital, appropriate facility, or police department on his or her own. Once an order has been taken out it must be served and they must be evaluated.
- In serving an order, the police are authorized to take someone against their will. The police will try to get a person to go willingly for evaluation. If they refuse, however, the police may use physical force to restrain and take them to the appropriate facility.
- Someone taken into custody by the police **may** be transported in handcuffs. This is hard. It seems cruel. It is hard to imagine any other medical emergency where someone

would be handcuffed and taken in the back of a police car to receive medical care. This is done for the safety of both the police officers and that of the person being transported. It does not make it easier or less traumatic.

- You can provide the person completing the evaluation with any information that you feel is important to assist them in their exam. To this end, you can fax or hand deliver written materials to the facility and request that they are given to the person doing the evaluation. You can ask to speak to the person by phone or in person. They may cite confidentiality at which time you should make clear that you are not asking them to share information with you, you are seeking to share information with them without any acknowledgment on their part.

- It is important that if you are able to speak with the person conducting the evaluation, you do so. This is your best opportunity to express why you took this step and what your concerns are. Evaluators may do an excellent job but they can only assess what is before them. The person who is being evaluated may have a vested interest in not speaking honestly and accurately—and even those who are very sick can often mask the depth and range of their symptoms for brief periods and in certain situations. The information that you provide enables the person doing the evaluation to place the person and their presence before them in context and can point them in the direction of specific assessment areas.

- In addition to the information that you provided on the petition, if your loved one is receiving treatment from a professional—psychiatrist, therapist, community service provider—you want to make sure that the person doing the evaluation has their contact information. Let your loved one's providers know that you are doing this and ask if they would be available to talk to the doctor doing the evaluation.

- There are many areas of NC—especially rural areas that do not have access to an urban center—where persons under an order to be evaluated are seen in an emergency room that does not have access to a mental health professional. In these instances, the psychiatric evaluation may be done by a medical doctor or a nurse with no expertise in psychiatric conditions. This creates a difficult situation for all involved. If this is the case, then it becomes all the more important that you provide the evaluating professional with as much information as you can about your concerns. It is also important to provide contact information for any mental health professionals who can speak to your loved one's condition.

Involuntary Commitment: Step 3—Admission and Initial Treatment

Once it has been determined that someone requires hospitalization the next step is to transfer them to an appropriate facility for further evaluation and to begin treatment. This is an acute hospitalization. The goal of a voluntary acute hospitalization is to bring symptoms under control and achieve minimal stability. However, the goal of acute hospitalization when someone has been involuntarily committed is less than this. It is to bring symptoms under sufficient control that the person is no longer at imminent risk. You cannot and should not expect that someone will remain hospitalized until their symptoms are controlled or until they are even fully stable in NC—especially if they remain resistant to treatment.

You should be aware:

The average length of stay for someone hospitalized following an order for evaluation is 3-10 days. The reason for this is 3-fold: 1) inadequate financial coverage for hospitalization, 2) a shortage of acute care beds, and 3) the law requires that a second hearing be held, this time in front of a judge if someone is to be involuntarily hospitalized for more than 10 days. Because of these factors, hospitals move patients through quickly. Very quickly. The day someone is admitted hospitals will begin work to link people with services in the community so that they can be discharged.

- It is somewhat easier to work with private insurance or Medicare in ensuring adequate inpatient treatment. This is because private insurance allows for a length of stay that is not contingent on a person's danger or risk but encompasses their overall condition. It is possible to call and speak to someone at a private insurance company in a way that is not as easily accomplished with Medicaid. This only applies, however, if your loved one agrees to admission. Without this agreement, there is still the requirement for a second hearing and the hospitals tend to avoid this if at all possible.

Because of the shortage in beds, people may spend days at the assessment facility before being transferred. In some rural areas, the entire inpatient stay can be spent in the emergency room without someone ever seeing a mental health professional. They are not ever transferred to an appropriate hospital but discharged.

- This is obviously problematic because the emergency room and/or assessment facility setting is not the place to treat someone having a mental health crisis. Often hospitals are unable to separate those suffering mental health emergencies from other medical emergencies. This can be quite distressing to a person in crisis. This is a noisy, chaotic, stressful environment. In an emergency room, patients may be unable to leave their bed or cubicle and generally will not have even the few amenities offered on a regular hospital ward. They may not receive any treatment other than medication.

Likewise, the shortage in needed beds places pressure on the hospital to move people through as quickly as possible as there is always someone else who is in great need of that bed.

- This places the emphasis in treatment not on stability but on a strict measure of risk. Just as professionals often limit criteria for involuntary commitment to suicide and homicide, they will as often limit their criteria for a person's stay to these same situations even if your loved one agrees to the admission when given the opportunity. This is especially true for those patients who do have a support system in the community because there is some assurance that on discharge there is someone who is monitoring their condition and will work to meet their basic needs even when the person cannot.

> TIP: Your most essential role at this time is advocating for your loved one. Sometimes that means getting on the phone and calling hospitals yourself to find a bed. Sometimes it means actively expressing concerns to the staff about the person's condition and their readiness to be in the community. Sometimes it means demanding a qualified professional see them. *Do not be afraid to push back.* Do not be afraid to be annoying. (But also, as much as you must be persistent and firm—be polite and courteous.) You will need to be as specific and concrete as you were in completing the petition for evaluation. It sounds harsh, but the best thing you can do if you have concerns is to put everything in writing to the facility—even and especially following conversations with them. What you are doing is documenting your concerns and ensuring that they are aware those concerns are recorded and can be brought to bear if something terrible should happen following discharge. In documenting everything, you are holding them accountable.

On admission to an appropriate facility, the doctor will often attempt to get the person to agree to the hospitalization. If they agree to admit themselves, they are no longer under an involuntary commitment order and regain control of their admission and treatment. It is not necessary for an involuntary commitment hearing to be held (see Step 4).

- There are pros and cons to this. Obviously, if someone agrees to treatment the doctor on some level is able to engage him or her in the treatment process. The patient participates in their care and recovery. This changes the tenor of their stay and supports their making gains. It circumvents the adversarial relationship that the commitment process sets up and enables the physician to build up trust with the patient. The facility may be able to keep them for a more extended period than they would under an involuntary commitment order. This is good.

- On the con-side, once someone has agreed to admit himself or herself, they are then free to discharge themselves whether or not the doctor agrees with their decision. This means that someone who is no longer at imminent risk, but still not capable of caring properly for themselves without supports, can leave the hospital. Even if their doctor believes they should stay. When this happens, all too often, people cannot and do not maintain the gains that they had begun to make. Their symptoms re-intensify. They end up having to be hospitalized again. A vicious cycle commences with no resolution. This is bad.

TIP: If someone has agreed to treatment and then decides that they want to be discharged and you believe they are still at risk, you can push the facility to reinstate the commitment process. Doctors do not like to do this. Understandably. It can create an adversarial dynamic between the patient and themselves. It erodes the trust that is necessary for the treatment process. However, you can state your concerns and how it is that you feel this person is at risk, to the facility. You are the one who understands best what this person will face on discharge. This means you are in the best position to know how their current condition will impact their safety when they are no longer in a supportive environment. The information and insights that you have are invaluable in staff decisions toward someone who wants to be discharged.

This is the period where families are most often shut out of the treatment process. Even someone who is involuntarily committed retains the right to determine whom their information is shared with and what information is shared. Perhaps they are angry at what has happened. They shut their family out because this is one way they can exercise any control at all over what is happening to them. They shut their family out because they do not want them to be able to say anything further to the doctor, potentially influencing the decisions that are made about them.

Even in those situations where a patient allows the facility to share information with their family, the facility may be poor at communicating. They may not involve the family in the treatment process. They may not provide updates as to assessments, treatment plans, concerns, or plans for discharge.

> TIP: If the facility is not allowed to share information with you, remember, you can still share information with them. Review the section on Confidentiality on **p. 121**, the section on Medical records, **p. 168** and start faxing. Once someone is admitted, their history and a review of what led to this hospitalization will be invaluable to hospital staff. Knowing what treatment a person has had—what has worked and what happens—is essential to choosing an effective treatment plan today. The doctor and treatment team do not need to start over at square 1.
>
> If the staff is allowed to communicate with you, don't wait for them to call you. You can call and speak to the patient's nurse and request updates and share concerns. You should communicate to them anything that you note—good and bad—during your interactions with your loved one. Make sure that they are aware of what the situation will be when the person is discharged—who will they live with, what kind of support will they have. What they will need. This information will be essential to discharge plans and referrals to services. You can ask to sit in on team meetings—some facilities will allow this. Establish a good relationship with your loved one's Social Worker or Case Manager. If you have questions, need assistance in knowing how to support and/or interact with your loved one—ask for it.

Involuntary Commitment: Step 4—Second Examination and Treatment Pending Hearing

Within 24 hours of transfer to an appropriate facility, the physician there must complete a new assessment. If the physician determines that a person does not meet the criteria for an involuntary commitment, they may be discharged at that time. Likewise at this time, the person can agree to voluntary admission.

If, however, the evaluation determines that the person meets the criteria for Involuntary Commitment and they do not agree to admit themselves, the Clerk of Superior Court in the facility's region must be notified. It is then the responsibility of the Clerk to set a formal hearing date.

- The hearing must be held within 10 days of the time when the police take the person into custody, and it may not be continued more than 5 days from that date.
- The petitioner—you—are to be notified of the hearing—date and time—no less than 72 hours prior to the hearing date.
- If at any time before the hearing the physician determines that the person is no longer in need of treatment, the physician may discharge the person. The hearing would be canceled.
- The hearing is before a District Court judge. The purpose is for the judge to make a determination as to whether to continue the involuntary commitment and if so, for how long. The reason that this goes before a judge is that an involuntary commitment is a legal act—not a medical decision—which temporarily removes a person's right to decide for themselves whether or not they are hospitalized, whether or not they treat their condition, and how.
- The person who is hospitalized may retain their own attorney, or they will receive an attorney appointed by the court to represent their interests and to ensure that their rights are not violated. An attorney representing the State may or may not be present.
- Certified copies of reports and findings of physicians and psychologists and previous and current medical records are admissible in evidence, but the respondent has the right to confront and cross-examine witnesses.
- As the petitioner, you may be present at the hearing and you may speak. The judge and/or attorneys can also request the presence and testimony of anyone they believe has relevant information to offer.
- The judge can end the commitment or continue it. If the judge decides that commitment should be continued they will set a time frame which can span a week up to 180 days. At that the end of that time frame another hearing would be required to continue the commitment.
- The hearing may be held at the facility where your loved one is hospitalized, or it may be at another location.

It is not common to make it to this stage of the Involuntary Commitment process. As noted earlier, many people are discharged within 3-10 days. The doctor will make every attempt to work with the patient so that he or she agrees to admit him or herself on arrival at the facility. At that time the petition for Involuntary Commitment would be dropped.

If, however, you arrive at this point you should know that often no doctor will come to the hearing or testify. The facility may have staff present. They may or may not speak. Your loved one has a right to be present at the hearing, but he or she may also choose to not be present. The judge will control who speaks and what information is to be shared. You may be allowed to sit in on the entire hearing or only that portion of it when you speak.

Our system is flawed. Because doctors are not required to be present at these hearings the judge may have difficulty determining whether your loved one's condition meets the criteria set forth in the statute. It also may be difficult for the judge to know what treatment is recommended and how long the commitment will be needed. The judge is not a doctor or even necessarily trained in mental health concerns. If the medical system treating your loved one fails to provide the appropriate and necessary information, then the judge must rely on what is available.

Remember, this is not a hearing to determine whether your loved one is sick, or symptomatic. It is not even to determine if they are very sick. If commitment is denied this not proof that they are not in need of care or able to adequately care for themselves. The hearing is strictly to determine if their current condition makes it reasonable to believe that if they were discharged they would be harmed—and how long this may be the case with appropriate treatment. The statute itself gives broad definition to these criteria. However, in NC the tendency has been to interpret it narrowly. If you are allowed to speak, you should focus on the same things that led you to petition the court: what is going on and how does this place the person you love at risk.

VOLUNTARY ASSESSMENT AND/OR INPATIENT ADMISSIONS

We have spent quite a bit of time covering Involuntary Commitments because they are complex. Not all admissions to an inpatient facility are involuntary. Many of the things that you can do to support your loved one and the care that they receive during an involuntary commitment are equally applicable at times when they admit themselves, or when, as a parent you admit them.

Admitting a Minor

To begin, please read the section on Special Populations: Children, for more information on the unique situation and concerns parents with minor children face. This is located on **p. 71**.

If you are the parent of a minor—someone under the age of 18—and/or their legal guardian, you can admit them for care. You do not have to obtain Involuntary Commitment paperwork to obtain an evaluation for your child if they are in crisis or in need of hospitalization. Admission to the hospital, however, does require an evaluation. The exception to this would be if your child is seeing a professional who has admitting rights at the facility your child is admitted to. That professional may admit your child without this assessment. In any other instance, your child will have to go through the same initial evaluation as a person who is considered for Involuntary Commitment.

If you believe that your child requires hospitalization you need to take your child to the emergency room or assessment center in your area. There, they will be assessed and a determination will be made as to whether inpatient hospitalization is needed and recommended. If this is deemed appropriate, then the next step is to find a bed in an appropriate facility.

As noted, there is a significant shortage of psychiatric beds in the state of North Carolina. This includes both public and privately funded facilities. As bad as it is for those 18 and older, it is even worse for children. There are very few facilities that treat children on an inpatient basis. This means:

- You may find yourself and your child sitting in the emergency room or in the assessment facility for days. Some children and their families have spent up to two weeks or more in this situation waiting for an available bed.

- If you live in an area where there is no treatment facility and you must go to an emergency room, the emergency room may or may not have a specific emergency area reserved for minors. They may not have access to a mental health professional to assess your child, much less one specializing in pediatric or adolescent psychiatry.

- When a bed is located it may be several hours or more from your home—which can significantly impact your ability to be in contact with your child and involved in their treatment.

- You may feel that once admitted, you have little voice in your child's care: that the hospital and staff fail to communicate well with you; that decisions are made about your child's care without your input and/or permission.

- If your child still poses a risk to others and/or is not able to be safely managed at home after they are ready for discharge they may be recommended for temporary placement in a residential care home. If your child is transferred to a residential home, this may not be located near you or other family members.

What you can do:

- Prepare the packet of information outlined in the Medical Records section on **p. 168**. Keep this update. When you take your child for evaluation, bring a copy of the packet with you. Review the guidelines for preparing a petition for an Involuntary Commitment on **p. 175**. You will need to present the reasons why you feel your child needs to be hospitalized in the same way.

- Prepare for the fact that your child may be in the facility where they are being assessed for a significant period of time. To this end, you will want to make arrangements as needed for other children, work, and you or someone you designate should be with your child at all times.

- You can call facilities that offer care to children to try to locate a bed. You can let the assessment facility know where beds are available and that you have spoken with the facility.

- When your child is admitted for treatment, make sure that you are in contact with the facility on a daily basis even if you cannot visit. You have the right to not only speak to nursing staff, social workers or case managers, but also to your child's doctor. You want the facility to know that you are involved and that you want to be involved in treatment decisions whether you are able to visit daily or not. Visit as often as you can.
- Provide the facility with your Medical Records packet.
- Ask questions about the results of evaluations. Find out about treatment plans and what is being done. Ask questions about how your child is responding. Ask to be present at team meetings.
- Ask what your child will need when they are discharged. Participate in setting up a discharge plan. If you do not have outpatient service providers that you like and/or trust—talk to people—find out what providers are recommended—who are not.
- Contact providers that you are interested in having your child work with and talk with them about your child's situation and transfer of care. Make sure the facility has the names and contact information of any providers you want working with your child after discharge.
- Express any and all concerns you have to your child's staff and doctors. Report to them what you are seeing as treatment progresses—is it helping, not helping? How is the medication your child receiving impacting him or her?
- Ask questions about medications; what are their side effects? Have they been tested on children? Are other medications with fewer side effects available? Research the medications your child has been prescribed on your own. Speak with your family physician or pharmacist to get more information if you have concerns.
- If you feel your child may need support additional to that set up by the facility on discharge, research the services you are interested in and make appointments.
- If you feel your child is not ready for discharge, speak up. Tell the staff and his or her doctor in clear terms why you are concerned (review the guidelines for preparing a petition for an Involuntary Commitment on **p. 175**). Advocate for your child to receive the care they need. Follow up with any conversations in writing so that you document what you have told the facility.
- After discharge request a copy of all of your child's medical records.

Adult Voluntary Assessment and/or Admissions

Adults (of at least 18 years or older) may themselves seek assessment at an assessment facility or emergency room. They may ask for a referral to an appropriate service provider or ask to be admitted to the hospital.

When someone presents for a Mental Health evaluation, professionals will assess the care needed. This is a twofold process. If someone is not in need of hospital admission the assessment facility will determine what treatment is necessary to address their immediate situation, and what services they should be referred for. When someone is assessed for an Involuntary Commitment, the primary concern is the degree of risk they present. When an adult asks to be admitted, while risk is evaluated, the primary concern is the distress they are experiencing and how best to treat that.

After assessment, some people may receive immediate or short-term treatment and are then referred to an appropriate outpatient provider. Some may be recommended for admission. If you are supporting someone who is in crisis, it is important to stress that the purpose of evaluation/assessment is not only a prelude to hospitalization, nor is it strictly to determine if they are at risk. It is to determine their condition and what needs to be done to help them. This may mean hospitalization, but it may not. Hospitalization may be recommended but as long as they are not at risk, they have the ability to refuse and ask for a referral to outpatient services.

**Be aware that if someone voluntarily presents for evaluation and is found to be at risk but decides they do not want to be admitted, staff may petition for Involuntary Commitment at that point.

Points to Keep in Mind

- Assessment is not for the purpose of admission alone. People who are in crisis do not always need or want to be admitted to a facility. There may be measures that can be taken at the time of assessment to ease the symptoms and/or distress that someone is experiencing. That person can then be referred to an appropriate community provider for follow up and additional care.
- If your loved one is receiving services and their provider agrees that they need more intensive care, consider enlisting their provider's assistance in this process. Their provider may be able to provide help or supports which will facilitate the process

and increase the odds of them receiving appropriate care. They may have contacts or even admitting privileges at an appropriate facility. If your loved one is in crisis and working with a provider they trust, contact that provider for assistance.

- If your loved one is willing to seek assistance, even admission to a facility, they have greater choices in facilities. Have they been admitted to or received services before at a facility they like and would like to be treated at again? Likewise, is there a facility that they do not want to go to? Is there a facility that is close to home that may be appropriate? Do they know if they will be seen by a Mental Health professional at their local emergency room, or is one not available? Because they are seeking assessment and/or admission themselves, you or they can call facilities in advance to determine where beds are available. You or they can travel to an assessment facility where you can be sure someone with the appropriate qualifications will see them.

- If your loved one would like to be admitted to a specific facility, speaking directly to that facility before assessment will help you to both determine whether an appropriate bed is available and the best place to go for assessment. You can then provide the assessor with the details of your conversation.

- Seeking treatment or admission voluntarily also increases the number of facilities that may be available for care. Some facilities are not equipped or able to work with those Involuntarily Committed. These same facilities will be options for persons seeking to admit themselves.

- While risk and the degree of risk is the primary determining factor for admission when someone is Involuntarily Committed the criteria are different when someone is asking for treatment. There is much greater latitude in determining the best way to meet their needs because they are seeking care themselves.

- The average length of a hospital stay for mental health crisis is 3-10 days. The reason for this is 2-fold if the admission is voluntary: 1) inadequate financial coverage for hospitalization, 2) a shortage of acute care beds. Because of these factors, hospitals move patients through quickly. Very quickly. The day someone is admitted hospitals will begin work to link people with services in the community so that they can be discharged.

- It is somewhat easier to work with private insurance or Medicare in ensuring adequate inpatient treatment. This is because private insurance allows for a length of stay that is not contingent on a person's danger or risk but encompasses their overall condition. It is possible to call and speak to someone at a private insurance company in a way that is not as easily accomplished with Medicaid.

> *Michael's son had been discharged from the hospital 3 weeks earlier. Since that time his condition had not improved. In some respects, he was worse. He was agitated and could not get comfortable. He was having difficulty sleeping. He continued to experience delusions.*
>
> *Michael was growing more concerned. His son was covered by his insurance policy. A week earlier the family had gone to the beach for a long-anticipated two-week vacation with out-of-town family members. Michael had spent much of every day of that vacation on the phone with his son's psychiatrist and the insurance company. The insurance company was unwilling to approve a second hospital admission so soon after discharge. Finally, in frustration, Michael told the case manager that he did not care what they authorized. His son needed care, and they would be responsible for what happened.*
>
> *The insurance company approved admission. During this time Michael had also been contacting hospitals. He wanted to find one equipped to handle his son's needs. Michael had chosen a facility that was 4 hours away from where they were staying, but 30" from their home. He did not want to put his son through the stress of the drive and evaluation if he could not be admitted though. He asked his insurance company to call the hospital and confirm there was a bed available. He also had them tell the facility in advance that they had approved admission. He followed up with the facility himself and let them know he was bringing his son for admission.*
>
> *Assured that there was a bed and that insurance had approved admission, Michael left his family and relatives and drove his son to the hospital. After evaluating his son, they told Michael his son did need to be admitted. They were not going to admit him there, however, but planned to transfer him to the State Hospital an hour and a half away from their home. They were aware his son had been involuntarily committed in the past and preferred not to admit him in light of this.*
>
> *Frustrated, Michael stood his ground. He told the facility that he knew that they had a bed available. His insurance company had spoken to them and approved the bed. His son was not in imminent risk and was voluntarily admitting himself. Michael was adamant that if they refused to admit his son he was not going to allow him to be transferred to the state hospital. He would take him home and find another facility.*
>
> *Michael's son was admitted to that facility. They were able to determine that he was having an adverse reaction to the medication he had been put on. They kept him in the hospital while transitioning him safely off of that medication and on to a new one. This allowed him to gain the stability that he needed to return home and continue to make gains while ensuring that the new medication did not cause further problems for him.*

A Letter to My Family
Anonymous

When I go into the hospital, it affects every part of my life. Imagine if you got sick and not only did you have to go into the hospital, but when you were ready to leave—and usually not completely well and on your feet—you had maybe lost your job, or the place where you live. Maybe you no longer have your friends. You had to drop out of school. You have bills that have not been paid and no money to pay them because you have not been working or you stopped getting disability payments because you were in the mental ward. Now imagine what it would be like if even the things you owned had gotten broken, lost, or discarded in some way because you were gone and could not take care of them. When I get sick, I am taken out of my life. When I am ready to go back and I discover that everything has been lost this becomes a new trauma all on its own.

It is usually up to you, my family, to take care of my affairs when I cannot. When you are in the middle of a crisis, remember—I am too. For you, though, the crisis begins to end when I go into the hospital. That's the moment you think—this is going to get better. When I leave the hospital to a world that has fallen apart, though, an entirely new crisis begins for me. Instead of things getting better—everything has just gotten worse. The single greatest thing you can do for me when my world falls apart is to hold as much of it together as possible until I can pick it up again. But I need for you to do this in a certain way. I need for you to see and to treat the things that make up my world just as carefully and with as much importance as you treat the things that are yours.

I know you care and are trying to help, but you haven't always cared for my affairs properly because you are focused on other things. The mistake you make is thinking that these things are least important at the moment. They are not. I know you cannot keep my job, or attend my classes. Maybe you cannot pay the bills. You can keep the things that belong to me safe and secure. It is easy in the moment of crisis to forget just how important these things can be to someone who has lost everything else. Having just my pots and pans and clothes and books and memories—these little pieces of my life—when I have lost everything else, helps me believe I still have a life. They give me some ground under my feet to build from. Something to come home to.

To help me:

- *If you ask someone to take care of my things because you cannot, be careful who you choose: sometimes people are not reliable or trustworthy—even in our family. They are willing to help, but they do not think these things are important. They approach dealing with my stuff like the task of disposing of the belongings of someone who has died. They assume that because I am sick, I don't care about what I have, that I will not need them any longer. They sell things. Give them away. Throw them out. Remember, these are my things. It is not up to someone else to decide what I want or what I need, what I choose to keep or to throw away. Consider this and select someone who can be trusted to understand that their task is to care for my things—not to take possession of them and make them their things; not to sort through them and discard them.*

- *If you are the person taking care of my things be careful with them: Don't store them in ways that will break them or where they will get lost or ruined. Keep the pieces together—even when you don't know what together is. There will come a time when I can and I want to sort all those pieces out. I know it is tedious to clean up someone's life. I know that you are under stress. If you find you cannot do this, ask someone else. Everything I have means something and has a purpose for me. As you care for these things, consider how you would feel if they were all you would have in the world when you got out the other end of a long, deep tunnel. Understand that when this happens, they are the most precious things in the world.*

- *Listen to me when I tell you what I need and what I want: Even though I am sick, I can still be right about what needs to be done and who I know can't do it. Not everything I think is because of my being sick. Let me make the decisions I can make. I can tell you what is important to me. I can tell you how to take care of what is important to me.*

I need you to realize the state I am in and what I will need and not let everything else in my life fall apart further. I need you to hold it together for me so when I am released, I do not have to worry about starting over with nothing left at all. When I leave a mental ward the best thing I can find is that all of the things I need to take care of myself, all of my property, are still there and in one piece. When you can do this for me, it makes all the difference in the world.

THE MOLE
by John Haines

Sometimes I envy them
who spring like great black-
and-gold butterflies
before the crowded feet
of summer—
              brief, intense,
like pieces of the sun,
they are remembered and celebrated
long after night has fallen.

But I believe also in one
who in the dead of winter
clinging darkness,
nosing the soil of old gardens.

He lives unnoticed, but
deep within him there is a dream
of the surface one day
breaking and crumbing:

and a small, brown-furred
figure stands there,
blinking at the sky,
as the rising sun slowly dries
his strange, unruly wings.

APPENDIX

Types of Mental Illnesses

It is not the purpose of this guide to detail all the types of mental illnesses that a person can experience. There are many excellent references available should you wish to gain greater insight into or knowledge about mental illnesses and mental health or any specific condition and we have listed some in this appendix. There are a few terms, however, which may be helpful to understand:

Attention Deficit Disorder/Attention Deficit Hyperactivity Disorder (ADD/ADHD)

ADHD was formerly called ADD, or attention deficit disorder. Symptoms may include inattentiveness, impulsivity, and hyperactivity and can differ from person to person. Both children and adults can have ADHD, but symptoms begin in childhood. Adults with ADHD may have trouble managing time, being organized, setting goals, and holding down a job.

Anxiety Disorder

Anxiety disorders are characterized by significant feelings of anxiety and fear. Anxiety is extreme and painful worry about events that may or may not happen or about current or potential problems. Fear is a reaction to specific current events. When experiencing anxiety or fear the person may not understand why they feel as they do. These feelings may cause physical symptoms, such as a fast heart rate and shakiness. There are a number of anxiety disorders: including generalized anxiety disorder, specific phobia, social anxiety disorder, separation anxiety disorder, agoraphobia, and panic disorder. A person may have more than one anxiety disorder.

Co-occurring Condition

Most often the term co-occurring conditions is used when referring to someone who has a mental illness other than Drug and Alcohol Addiction AND abuses or is addicted to a drug or alcohol. Treatment for someone who is experiencing both addiction and another mental illness is more complex and may be different in key ways from someone who is experiencing just one illness. This term can also be used anytime combinations of mental illnesses are present.

Mood Disorders
Mood Disorders are mental illnesses, which affect an individual's ability to regulate their moods. People with Mood Disorders may also experience emotions that are not consistent with their situation. Bipolar disorder (sometimes called manic-depression) and clinical depression are the best known. Bipolar disorder is characterized by periods of depression and periods of mania—or hyperactivity. It is often the case that women experience greater depression and men experience mania.

- Depression is low, or deflated mood which is independent of anything that the individual is experiencing in their life situation. Depression can also be experienced as anger, irritability, agitation, and inability to focus or concentrate, to complete tasks or work, or to begin tasks or work.
- Mood Disorders may or may not be accompanied by psychosis. The degree of intensity and the type of mood are unique in every person.

Obsessive Compulsive Disorder (OCD)
OCD is a mental disorder where people feel a need to repeatedly and/or obsessively engage in a behavior or specific thoughts or sentences which go through their mind in an unending fashion. People with OCD are unable to control either the thoughts or the activities for more than a short period of time. Typical activities include hand washing, counting of things, and checking to see if a door is locked. Some may have difficulty throwing things out. An example of a ritual is when someone must open and shut a door a certain number of times before leaving. Someone may need to walk through a door a certain way, or touch certain objects as they begin or end an activity. These activities often occur to such a degree that the person's daily life is negatively affected. Often they take up more than an hour a day. Most adults realize that the behaviors do not make sense. The condition is associated with tics, anxiety disorder, and an increased risk of suicide.

Personality Disorder
A personality disorder is defined as a rigid and unhealthy pattern of thinking, functioning and behaving. A person with a personality disorder has trouble perceiving and relating to situations and people. This causes significant problems and limitations in relationships, social activities, work, and school.

Because personality disorders are not well understood, treatment can be difficult.

Schizoaffective Disorder

Schizo-affective disorder is a condition in which a person experiences a combination of the symptoms of schizophrenia, such as hallucinations or delusions, and those of a mood disorder, such as depression or mania. The two types of schizoaffective disorder—both of which include some symptoms of schizophrenia—are:

- Bipolar type, which includes episodes of mania and sometimes major depression
- Depressive type, which includes only major depressive episodes

Schizoaffective disorder may run a unique course in each affected person, so it's not as well understood or well defined as other mental health conditions.

Schizophrenia

Schizophrenia is not the same as split personality while commonly associated with that disorder. Schizophrenia is a mental disorder involving a breakdown in the relation between thought, emotion, and behavior, leading to faulty perception, inappropriate actions and feelings, withdrawal from reality and personal relationships into fantasy and delusion, and a sense of mental fragmentation.

Autism, IDD (Intellectual/Developmental Disability) and LD (Learning Disability) are NOT mental illnesses. However, those having these conditions do also develop mental illnesses. Diagnosis is often difficult due to both communication problems and the fact that many of the behaviors associated with these conditions appear as symptoms of different mental illnesses: impulsivity, poor judgment and reasoning, perseveration, flat affect, outbursts of anger or aggression, and compulsive actions. Diagnosis is best made by a professional well versed in both these conditions and in mental illnesses.

Symptoms: Terms To Know

Addiction
Physical addiction occurs when the body has come to depend on the substance. When this happens and the substance is taken away, physical withdrawal results and can be life-threatening. Psychological addiction occurs when mentally a person relies on a substance for coping or pleasure and is unable to stop using, even when negative consequences occur.

Agnosia
A person experiencing the symptoms of mental illness is often unable to see that they are having a problem. They cannot understand that hallucinations are not real. They cannot see the flaws or problems with delusional thoughts. They cannot see the way that symptoms are negatively impacting their life, or the problems they have in functioning. They may not be able to recognize any of the behaviors that others see as symptoms or recognize them as problematic. Agnosia is in and of itself a symptom and not something that is within a person's ability to control.

Anxiety
Anxiety is a feeling of worry, nervousness, or unease, typically about an imminent event or something with an uncertain outcome. As a symptom of mental illness, anxiety is often extreme or even incapacitating. It may not be linked to anything objectively present in the environment.

Apathy
Someone is experiencing apathy when they have a generalized lack of interest, enthusiasm, or concern.

Delusion
A Delusion is an idiosyncratic belief or impression that is firmly maintained despite being contradicted by what is generally accepted as reality or rational argument. Delusions are present in spite of evidence and reason to the contrary. Delusions often take a form that is not logical but they may also be logically structured despite their connection to reality.

Depression
Depressed mood, which is not associated with what is occurring in the environment and which lasts over a period of time without relief. Often depression is expressed as fatigue, apathy, irritability, or lack of motivation.

Detachment
Feeling of being disconnected from other people and events, frequently accompanied by a generalized lack of emotion toward these things.

Disjointed or Disorganized Speech
This is speech in which words and phrases are disconnected from other words and phrases in the same sentences and which do not make logical sense. It is an inability to speak coherently or in a way that can be understood.

Disorganized Thought
These are thoughts, which are random, unrelated to one another or to occurrences in the environment and result in the inability of a person to make sense of their own impressions or ideas. Often results in generalized confusion.

Emotional Lability
Someone is emotional labile when they experience emotions that change rapidly and are often present in extreme form. For example, a person may rapidly move from crying to laughing and joyful to anger. May or may not be connected to events in the environment.

Flat Affect
Affect is said to be flat when emotions are not present or expressed. A person with a flat affect may appear disconnected or robotic in demeanor.

Hallucination
A hallucination is the perception or experience of stimuli in the environment, which are not present. Involves the senses and may be auditory (hearing voices), visual, tactile (bodily sensations), olfactory (smells).

Impulsivity
Impulsivity is a tendency to act on a whim, displaying behavior characterized by little or no forethought, reflection, or consideration of the consequences.

Mania
Mania is an emotional state which is generally not related to any occurrence in the environment that is characterized by great excitement, euphoria, delusions, and over-activity, racing thoughts, inability to sleep, impulsivity, lack of judgment, rapid speech.

Negative Symptoms
Negative Symptoms are symptoms that interfere with the way that the brain processes information or functions. Some examples of negative symptoms include a decline in self-initiation, task sequencing, short-term memory, judgment, reasoning skills. The severity of a psychiatric incident often determines how long negative symptoms take to resolve. It can take up to a year of stability.

Paranoia
Paranoia is a state when delusions take the form of persecution, fear, unwarranted jealousy, or exaggerated self-importance, typically elaborated into an organized system.

Perseveration
Perseveration occurs when thoughts, words, ideas, phrases are repeated over and over and either expressed verbally or occupy the mind.

Phobia
A Phobia is an intense fear.

Positive Symptoms
Positive symptoms are symptoms such as delusions or hallucinations, depression or mania. Medication may begin to resolve positive symptoms quickly—sometimes within a month or even in just a week.

Psychosis
Psychosis is the presence of delusions or hallucinations.

Self-Initiation
Self-Initiation is the ability to begin a task on one's own.

Task Sequencing
Task Sequencing is the ability to follow the steps, which are required to complete a task in the correct order.

Tardive Dyskinesia
Tardive Dyskinesia is involuntary, repetitive movements caused by medication.

Tardive Dystonia
Tardive Dystonia is a form of tardive dyskinesia. It is a movement disorder characterized by involuntary muscle contractions caused primarily by taking dopamine receptor blockers like antipsychotic medications. Examples include: a "dragging leg," cramping of the foot, involuntary pulling of the neck, uncontrollable blinking, speech difficulties.

> **Take care when utilizing resources on the Internet or which do not come recommended by professionals. There is a lot of disinformation available. In addition, there are many diverse opinions as to how mental illnesses are best treated. In the beginning, it is best to stick with people and resources that you know are good and are trusted.

Useful Documents

The following two documents are reproduced with permission from Rethink Mental Illness, a UK-based service. Some information may be different or non-relevant for those living in the United States.

Suicidal thoughts

How to support someone

Suicide is when someone purposely ends their own life. This factsheet looks at why someone might think about suicide and how you can help them.

- People might think about suicide for different reasons.
- If you are worried that someone may be thinking about suicide, talk to them. Ask them about how they are feeling and offer to help.
- Talking to someone about their suicidal thoughts does not make them more likely to end their life.
- You can help someone who is feeling suicidal by listening to them without judging them and trying to help them think about other options.
- You may need to get crisis help from mental health services or the emergency services.
- Helping someone with suicidal thoughts is likely to have a big impact on you. Find out what support is available to you.
- If someone does try to end their life, this is not your fault.

This factsheet covers:

1. What makes someone think of suicide?
2. What are the warning signs that someone feels suicidal?
3. How can I help someone who is feeling suicidal?
4. What services can help someone who is feeling suicidal?
5. Are people with mental illness more likely to feel suicidal?
6. Are self-harm and suicide linked?
7. How can I get support?

1. What makes someone think of suicide?

There is rarely a single thing that makes someone want to end their own life. Experts believe that a number of complex issues can make someone feel this way.[1]

If someone is thinking about suicide, they often feel nothing will help with the problems that are making them feel suicidal.

Certain things can make someone more likely to think about suicide. These might include:

- difficult life events – such as having a traumatic childhood or experiencing physical or emotional abuse,[2]
- something upsetting or life-changing happening such as a relationship ending or a loved one dying,[3]
- misusing drugs or alcohol,
- living alone or having little social contact with other people,
- having a mental health condition such as depression, schizophrenia or personality disorder,[4]
- having a physical health condition, especially if this causes pain or serious disability,
- problems with work or money.[5]

Why do people choose to end their lives?

A person may choose to end their lives to:

- escape what they feels is an impossible situation,
- relieve unbearable thoughts or feelings,
- relieve physical pain or incapacity.

What kind of thoughts might someone have?

When someone feels suicidal, they may have some of the thoughts listed below.

- I have let myself and other people down.
- What is the point in living?
- I will never find a way out of my problem.
- I have lost everything.
- Things will never get better for me.
- Nobody cares about me.

Some people might feel confused why they want to take their own life. Some people may definitely want to die while some people may not care if they live or die.

Some people feel guilty for thinking about suicide if they have people who care about them.

2. What are the warning signs?

A change in someone's personality and behaviour might be a sign that they are having suicidal thoughts. You may be the best judge of when someone you know is behaving differently.

Changes can include:

- becoming anxious, irritable or confrontational.
- having mood swings.
- acting recklessly.
- sleeping too much or too little.
- preferring not to be around other people.
- having more problems with work or studies.
- saying negative things about themselves.

There are some signs that suggest someone is more likely to try suicide. These include:[6]

- threatening to hurt or kill themselves,
- talking or writing about death, dying or suicide, or
- actively looking for ways to end their life, such as stockpiling medication.

It is rare for someone to be certain that they want to end their own life. Most people will be undecided about suicide, seeing some 'pros' and 'cons' of living and dying.

A lot of people try to seek help before attempting suicide by telling other people about their feelings or by self-harming to show people that they are in emotional pain.

3. How can I help someone who is feeling suicidal?

If you think that someone may be feeling suicidal, encourage them to talk about how they are feeling.

Remember that you don't need to find an answer, or even to completely understand why they feel the way they do. Listening to what they have to say will at least let them know you care.

It might help to:

- let the person know that you care about them and that they are not alone,
- make sure someone is with them if they are in immediate danger,
- try to get professional help for the person feeling suicidal and support for yourself.

You could reassure the person that they will not feel this way forever and that they can get help, including help from a doctor.

If you are not sure that someone is feeling suicidal, you could ask:

- "Are you thinking about suicide?" or
- "Are you having thoughts of ending your life?"

These questions might seem direct but it is better to address the person's feelings directly than to skirt around the issue. Most people do not have this sort of conversation every day and so you may feel uncomfortable and unsure of what to say. This is entirely normal and understandable. However, you can help by being calm, supportive and non-judgemental.

Try to see the world as the person sees it. Try to do this without judging, criticising or blaming them.

What won't help someone who is feeling suicidal?

When someone tells you that they are feeling suicidal you may feel like trying to cheer the person up or telling them that they have no reason to feel like that. These are understandable responses but may not help that much.

Someone who wants to end their life will not want:

- to feel rejected by friends, family or colleagues,
- people to change the subject when they are talking about how they feel,
- to be told that they are wrong or silly,
- to be patronised, criticised or analysed,
- to be told to cheer up or 'snap out of it',[7]
- to be told that they should be grateful for having such a good life.

Reassurance, respect and support can help a person recover at this difficult time.

What if someone is saying they want to end their life now?

Talking about suicide can be a plea for help. Don't assume that because someone has talked about suicide they won't try to take their own life. You should always take this seriously.

If you talk to someone about their feelings and it seems as though they want to end their life soon, try to keep them safe in the short term. It is unlikely that you will be able to make their feelings go away, but you can help by making them see that there are some things worth living for.

It might help to:[8]

- be supportive and accept what they are telling you,
- ask whether they are thinking about ending their life now or soon,
- try and get a better understanding of why,
- ask about their reasons for living and dying and listen to their answers. Try to explore their reasons for living in more detail,
- ask whether they have tried to kill themselves before,
- ask if they have a plan for how they would do it in the future,
- try to make them safe and be open to making reasonable steps to help them,
- follow up any commitments that you agree to.

If you live with the person, you could also try to remove things from the house that they could use to take their own life. The kind of thing you could try to remove depends on the person's immediate plan for taking their own life. They could include sharp objects and knives, cleaning products, medicines and belts. If the person is in crisis, do not leave them alone.

Section 4 goes into more detail about how to get professional help for someone.

You can find out more about how to get someone help in the following factsheets:

- Worried about someone's mental health?
- Getting help in a crisis

4. What services can help someone who is feeling suicidal?

Crisis and home treatment teams

Crisis teams are sometimes also called home treatment teams. They are part of mental health services. They are help people who are having a mental health crisis. They should be available 24 hours a day, seven days a week and are an alternative to going into hospital.

How someone gets help from a crisis team varies between different areas of the country. You may be able to contact them as a friend or family member. GPs, Accident and Emergency departments (A & E) and the police can also ask them to see someone.

You can get more information in our '**Crisis Teams**' factsheet available from www.rethink.org.

Accident and Emergency department

If someone is feeling suicidal, you could try and them to a local hospital that has an Accident and Emergency department (A&E). Staff can speak to them about how they are feeling and 'triage staff' will decide if they need to be admitted to hospital or not.

You can give A&E staff as much information as possible so they can make the right decision.

Emergency services

If you think that someone is in urgent danger, is going to try and take their life immediately or has already tried, call 911.

Other services

- Crisis houses help people in crisis and are an alternative to going into hospital. Usually people only stay in a crisis house from a couple of days up to a month. The NHS, charities and other services run them. They are not available in every area of the country but you can check what there is locally through the local crisis team or doing a search online.

- Emotional support services help by listening to someone's concerns and giving them space and time to talk through how they feel. Details of emotional support services are at the end of this factsheet.

What happens next?

Hospital

When someone is feeling suicidal and has tried to take their own life or plans to, usually they will be taken to hospital. Sometimes they might be treated at home or visited regularly by the crisis or home treatment team.

After someone has been in hospital, going back home can be difficult and someone may still need a lot of support.

Links between services

There should be good links between Accident and Emergency departments (A&E) and mental health services. However, these links are not always good enough.[9]

A&E do not always pass details onto the local crisis team. If they don't, then you can contact the crisis team instead.

Letting someone who is suicidal leave hospital

Doctors should carry out a risk assessment when thinking about discharging someone from hospital. This might look at whether someone is feeling suicidal and is thinking about ending their life. Carers should also be part of this decision if possible.

Getting more help from mental health services

Some people get passed back to their GP with no other support.

If this happens, the GP should think about asking for help from the local mental health services such as the Community Mental Health Team (CMHT). This sort of team can give more specialist help.

The person you are supporting could get help under the 'Care Programme Approach' (CPA) if they meet the criteria. CPA is used to organise many people's care who are under mental health services and who have complex needs.

You can find more information about CMHTs and CPA at www.rethink.org.

5. Are people with mental illnesses at greater risk of suicide?

People with mental illnesses are generally more likely to feel suicidal and try to take their own lives than people who do not have mental illnesses.[10] Research also shows that a person could be more likely to try to end their own life if they have recently been discharged from a mental health hospital or unit.[11] At this time, it is important someone gets the right support.

Making sure that someone attends appointments with health services and has a care plan in place is important to keep someone well and prevent them feeling suicidal.

6. Self-harm and suicide

Self-harm is when someone deliberately tries to harm or injure themselves. Someone may do this more than once.

There are different views on whether someone trying to take their own life is the same as self-harm.

People do not normally self-harm to take their own life. Instead, people can self harm to deal with emotional pain, punish themselves or express distress to other people.[12]

If the person you care for self-harms, they may do this privately and may not want to talk openly about it. You can try to talk to them about why they do it. Let them know that you do not judge them and are there to talk if they need to. If they refuse to stop self-harming then you may be able to persuade them to do it safely, or to try safer alternative methods. It is unlikely that they will stop altogether just because you have asked them to.

You can get more information in our 'Self-harm' factsheet which you can download at www.rethink.org.

7. How can I get support?

If you know someone who talks about or has tried suicide, you might feel upset, frustrated, confused or scared. These are all normal responses.

Supporting a person who is suicidal is likely to be a stressful time in your life, and a time when you are likely to need support yourself. You could:

- talk to friends and family,
- talk to someone on an emotional support helpline (see our useful contacts),
- talk to your own doctor,
- join a support group for carers, friends and family,
- take some time out to concentrate on yourself.

REFERENCES

[1] NHS Choices. *Suicide – Causes*. 2016]

[2] World Health Organisation. *Preventing Suicide: A global imperative*. 2014. http://apps.who.int/iris/bitstream/10665/131056/1/9789241564779_eng.pdf [Accessed March 2016]

[3] As note 1

[4] Arsenault-Lapierre et al. Psychiatric diagnoses in 3275 suicides: a meta-analysis. *BMC Psychiatry*. 2004; 4: 37. Published online 2004 Nov 4. Available online at http://www.ncbi.nlm.nih.gov/pmc/articles/PMC534107/ [Accessed February 2016]

[5] World Health Organisation. *Preventing suicide: A resource for general physicians*. 2000:P8-10. www.who.int/mental_health/media/en/56.pdf [Accessed March 2016]

[6] NHS Choices. *Suicide Warning signs*. www.nhs.uk/Conditions/Suicide/Pages/warning-signs.aspx [Accessed February 2016]

[7] World Health Organisation. *Preventing suicide: A resource at work*. 2006: pg19 http://apps.who.int/iris/bitstream/10665/43502/1/9241594381_eng.pdf [Accessed February 2016]

[8] Ramsey, R.F. *Suicide Intervention Handbook 10th Ed*. Calgary :Living Works; 2004, pgs 63-70.

[9] The College of Emergency Medicine. *Mental health in emergency departments*. (2013) pg 11-12 www.rcpsych.ac.uk/pdf/CEM6883-Mental-Health-in-EDs---toolkit-(FINAL-FEB-2013)-rev1.pdf]Accessed February 2016]

[10] See references 1 and 4

[11] Crawford, M.J. Suicide following discharge from inpatient psychiatric care. *Advances in psychiatric treatment,* 2004:10; 434-438. Available from http://apt.rcpsych.org/content/10/6/434.full.pdf+html [Accessed February 2016]

[12] Royal College of Psychiatrists. Self-harm, Suicide and Risk: helping people who self-harm. London: RCPsych; 2010 pg 22-23.

FACTSHEET

Dealing with unusual thoughts and behaviour

This factsheet is aimed at families, friends and carers of people with a mental illness such as schizophrenia or bipolar disorder. There are suggestions for dealing with common symptoms associated with these conditions such as delusions, withdrawing from other people and risky behaviour.

We use the term 'your relative' for the person you know with unusual thoughts and behaviours, though we do understand that you may not be related.

- Unusual thoughts and behaviour are often two of the hardest aspects of mental illness for many friends, families and carers to understand, accept and cope with.
- Common problems you may encounter include unusual or paranoid beliefs, hearing voices, problems with thinking and speech, loss of motivation, withdrawing from other people, aggression, risky behaviour or becoming over-dependent
- The following pages deal with each of these behaviours and attempts to explain them, how you can cope with them and how you can help a person with a mental illness to cope with them.
- Examples are informed by professional advice, from people with mental illness, and from friends, family and carers.

This fact sheet covers:

1. Delusions and paranoia
2. Lack of motivation and loss of interest and/or pleasure in things
3. Withdrawing from other people
4. Problems with thinking and speech
5. Aggression
6. Risky behaviour
7. Becoming over-dependent
8. Further reading

221

1. Delusions and paranoia

Delusions are false beliefs or thoughts with no basis in reality. For example, some individuals may believe that they are being targeted by law enforcement agencies or that their thoughts are being influenced by external forces. Delusions are a psychotic symptom which can be experienced as part of a number of mental illnesses. You can find more information about psychosis and psychotic symptoms in our factsheet **'Psychosis'**.

If your relative is experiencing delusions for the first time you should encourage them to seek medical advice as early as possible. Understanding how to communicate effectively with them about their delusions may help you to do this. You can find more information about how to access help for someone who may be experiencing mental illness in our factsheet **'Are you worried about someone's mental health?'**.

Even if your relative is receiving treatment, they can still experience delusions. However, if they are experiencing a severe psychotic episode there is often little you can do to alter their beliefs and they may need urgent help or treatment. If you are in this situation our factsheet '**Getting help in a crisis**' may be useful to you.

How to help someone with delusions and paranoid beliefs

The key to helping your relative deal with their delusions is being able to communicate with them and listen empathetically[1].

- Avoid laughing at them, ignoring them or telling them their thoughts are stupid.
- Remember that to your loved one the delusions seem totally real and are also likely to be make them feel very anxious.
- You can acknowledge your relative's feelings without reinforcing the actual belief. You can communicate that you are on their side and want to help. This may give you a chance to discuss the delusions and how to try and deal with them. For example -

"….this must be very frightening for you, maybe if we talk about it you may feel less anxious…."

- Try to avoid agreeing with the beliefs as this may reinforce them.
- It is also unhelpful to challenge the delusions too directly as this can backfire. Research shows that if a person is confronted about their belief, they may end up believing in it more[2].
- It can help to reassure them clearly and calmly. You can let them know that you understand they may see things in a particular way but you believe there is no problem or threat in the situation. This draws a line between his/her reality and your own[3]. For example -

"I know you think the police are following you, but I don't think this is true…."

- If their belief causes certain emotions, try to respond to these emotions with a rational explanation about why they should not worry. For example-

"….you have no need to worry, you have done nothing wrong, so the police would not be interested in you"

- Sometimes you can try to explore the evidence for a particular belief. This is not the same as challenging it. You could encourage your relative to consider the evidence for their belief by asking questions and being non judgmental. Try to highlight the difference between a guess and a fact and try to work with them to provide alternative explanations for what they believe. It is important that discussing the evidence is done sympathetically and carefully to avoid challenging their beliefs too strongly[4].

"You say that man was following you but can you be sure? How many times have you seen him? Did you see where he walked to? He could have just been walking in the same direction a few times because he lives nearby."

If your relative is hearing voices you may be able to help them develop ways of dealing with them. You can find more information about how to do this in our factsheet **'Coping with hearing voices'**.

2. Lack of motivation and loss of interest and/or pleasure in things

Lack of motivation and a loss of interest in pleasurable activities can be symptoms of mental illness. Many people are a lot less active than they were before they became unwell. This can be very upsetting for those around them and can be some of the most frustrating behaviour to deal with.

How can I help someone with a loss of motivation and interest?

- You could first explore whether this is a part of the illness. Sometimes what can appear to be symptoms of mental illness may be side effects of medication[5]. You can find more information about dealing with the problematic side effects of medications in our factsheet **'Medication – choice and managing problems'**.
- The next important step is to accept that this may be a part of your relative's illness, at least for now, and not to put too much pressure on your relative.

- Include your relative in daily activities such as shopping or housework as well as fun activities. Do not put any expectations on them and simply invite them to take part however they feel comfortable. This may increase the chances of them joining you again.
- Organise specific fun activities each week. If your relative gets into a habit of taking part in a certain activity regularly, their enjoyment of this activity may eventually grow. You could explore activities your relative used to enjoy doing or suggest new activities.
- Try to focus on the future and not the past. Your relative may have lost interest in life because they are aware of how things have changed. Reminding your relative of how they used to be may add to this feeling. Instead talk about the range of opportunities available to your relative now.
- Your relative may want their life to improve but may not feel it is possible. Work with your relative to break down goals into small steps. Progress may be slow but reassure and encourage them by noting and praising each small success made.[6]
- It may be important for your relative to think about their life goals and what motivates and interests them. This can be important for their person recovery. They may also find it helpful to see examples of what helped other people recover from mental illness. You can find more information about recovery in our factsheet **'Recovery'** .

3. Withdrawing from other people

Withdrawing from other people can be another symptom of mental illness. You might hear this called 'social withdrawal'. It can also be caused by other symptoms that your relative is experiencing. For example, your relative may start to see themselves as different, feeling unable to 'fit in' with friends and family and so they may withdraw. It can start with staying at home and not socialising, not speaking or even not showing emotions.

It is important to remember that someone with mental illness can experience a blow to their self-confidence and sense of who they are. They may not feel confident enough to manage even ordinary day-to-day social situations. To cope with this, they may cut themselves off from these sorts of situations. Contact with people inside and outside the family is likely to decrease.

How can I help someone who is becoming socially isolated?

- To deal with your relative withdrawing from other people you may need to accept it. Lower your expectation to a realistic level and do not put too much pressure on them.

- Provide uncomplicated and undemanding social activity to help rebuild their confidence. Keep the number of people to a minimum and keep conversations short and avoid issues that can become too emotional.
- Understand that your relative might feel vulnerable in social situations. Simply invite them along and allow them to take part however they feel comfortable
- Ask your relative where they would feel most comfortable. Often people with mental illness feel isolated by society because of stigma they may have experienced or think they will experience. If your relative is concerned about this, you could encourage them to socialise with other people who have mental illness. They could attend a day centre or a support group. This can be helpful in the short term.[7]

5. Problems with thinking and speech

Problems with thinking and speech can be seen in a number of mental illnesses. They are most commonly associated with schizophrenia. When we think and communicate, we usually put one related idea after another in a logical order. If your relative has problems with this, it is known as 'disordered thinking'.

People with disordered thinking find it difficult to keep a logical order to their ideas. Their thoughts and speech may be jumbled and disconnected. In disordered thinking, thoughts jump between completely unrelated topics or may be blocked altogether. The person may appear to talk nonsense, make up words or replace words with sounds or rhymes.

How can I help someone with disordered thought and speech?

- Try to be patient and listen to your relative.
- If they start drifting off onto unrelated subjects try to steer them back onto the subject.
- If you don't understand something that you think is important to the conversation, ask them to explain it.[8]

6. Aggression

Most people with mental illness are no more aggressive or violent than anyone else. However, there is a small group of people who experience problems with controlling their impulses, aggression and paranoia. This can make them more likely to strike out violently if they are not receiving adequate treatment[9]. Remember that most of the anger and aggression directed against you is likely to be because you are the closest person to them and it is not necessarily a personal attack.

How can I minimise or stop aggressive behaviour?[10]

- If you can figure out which situations make your relative aggressive (perhaps by keeping a diary), you may be able to work out ways of

avoiding these situations. For example, there may be certain topics of conversation you wish to avoid. Changing arrangements at short notice might make your relative frustrated which then turns into anger, so you may want to avoid this if possible.
- Listen to your relative and try to work out why they are angry or upset by putting yourself in their shoes. Try to understand what they are saying. You could ask them to explain or you could summarise what you think they mean and ask them if this is correct. Be prepared to repeat yourself and be patient.
- Use your relative's name, speak to them like an adult, respect their feelings and don't be dismissive.
- Try not to get upset or angry yourself. Use a calm voice and keep a neutral facial expression. If you give the impression you are not going to respond angrily, your relative may feel the situation is under control.
- If all your efforts to listen or communicate have failed and/or the situation is escalating, remove yourself and other people from the situation.
- Do not put your own safety at risk. If you feel under immediate threat of violence call the police.
- If you have regular contact with your relative and they are showing more aggressive behaviour, you should inform their care team (if they have one) and discuss the situation. If you live with your relative and they are being regularly aggressive towards you, you may wish to review the living arrangements.
- Aggressive behaviour can be a sign that your relative is becoming very unwell and needs treatment.[11] You may want to consider your options to try and arrange this. Our factsheet '**Getting help in a crisis**' may help.

7. Risky behaviour

A number of mental illnesses can cause people to engage in risky behaviour.

Risky behaviour can vary. Someone who is behaving riskily usually cannot see the consequences of their actions, has reduced boundaries and is more uninhibited and impulsive. They increase the risks they will take. Risky behaviour can include -

- Spending beyond means.
- Increased drinking and drug taking.
- Increased sexual activity and sexual practices.

How can I help someone who is engaging in risky behaviour?

It can be difficult to get a balance between protecting someone who is showing risky behaviour and taking control.

- Try to help your relative see the consequences of what they are doing.
- Reassure them so that your relative knows that you will support them until they regain control over the situation.
- Urge your relative to seek help. Engaging in risky behaviour is often a sign of deteriorating mental health in someone with mental illness.
- Try to understand why your relative is showing a particular risky behaviour.
- If your relative has little control over their behaviour, suggest ways in which they could be more safe. For instance, if their sex drive is greatly increased, suggest they practise safe sex. Sexually transmitted diseases are higher in people with mental illness and it is important to make your relative aware of the risks[12].
- If your relative finds it difficult to manage their money sensibly when they become unwell, you may wish to consider options for taking control of the situation. For example, if your relative has capacity they can authorise you to have Lasting Power Of Attorney over their financial affairs. You may want to contact the Court of Protection if you feel your relative lacks capacity and is putting their assets at risk. You can find more information on this in our factsheet **'Options for dealing with someone else's financial affairs'**.
- If your relative's behaviour is putting either you or them in any danger it is important that you consider seeking help. You may want to contact their GP or their mental health team. You can find more information on possible options in our factsheets **'Getting help in a crisis'** and **'Are you worried about someone's mental health?'**.

8. Becoming over-dependent

When someone you care about has mental illness, you often want or need to help them through difficult periods. This could be by listening, encouraging and supporting them, taking them to appointments or making sure they take their medication, pay their bills and eat properly. However, you may start out helping with small tasks and end up doing a lot more.

If your relative has been unable to cope alone, they may not feel confident enough to go back to coping the way they did before they became unwell. It is important for both yourself and your relative that your relative does not become over-dependent on you.

Over-dependence can affect self-esteem and confidence in a person with mental illness. In addition, it can lead you to being less able to support your relative if you are tired and cannot make time for yourself.

How can I stop someone becoming over-dependent?

- Decide early on how much you can do and how much you want to do and set boundaries. Make sure you let your relative know these boundaries as diplomatically as possible and explain the reasons why they are needed.
- Work with your relative to gradually build up their independence. Discuss the skills they need to focus on and agree goals. If necessary show them how to do the skill first and agree to practice it with them until they feel confident to do it on their own [13].
- If you find yourself having to do more than you want to do because your relative is particularly unwell, contact your local social care team for a carer's assessment. They may be able to arrange additional help or a respite break for you and your relative. You can find more information in our factsheet **'Carers Assessments'**.
- If your relative is under the Community Mental Health Team, you could talk to your relative's care coordinator about how their care plan helps them develop independent living skills. Possible options could include a referral to an occupational therapist or considering supported living options if they are needed.

You can download our factsheets for free from www.rethink.org/factsheets.

Complete Family Guide to Schizophrenia. Helping Your Loved One Get the Most Out of Life ~ Kim T. Mueser PhD and Susan Gingerich MSW (2006).
Based on of research and therapeutic experience, this book offers pragmatic suggestions for dealing with depression, psychosis, and other symptoms. They show the reader how to prioritise needs, resolve everyday problems, and encourage your relative to set life goals.

Living with Mental Illness: A Book for Relatives and Friends: A Book for Relatives and Friends - Liz Kuipers and Paul Bebbington (Human Horizons 2005).
This book provides advice for families on how to cope day-to-day with different mental illness.

Back to Life, Back to Normality: Cognitive Therapy, Recovery and Psychosis by Douglas Turkington et al. (Cambridge University Press, 2009)
An informational self-help guide designed for people who have psychotic symptoms and their carers. It helps the reader use Cognitive Therapy techniques to control their symptoms and delay or prevent relapse.

[1] Mueser KT, Gingerich S. *Complete Family Guide to Schizophrenia. Helping Your Loved One Get the Most Out of Life.* Guildford Press; 2006 Page 259

[2] Mueser KT, Gingerich S. *Complete Family Guide to Schizophrenia. Helping Your Loved One Get the Most Out of Life.* Guildford Press; 2006 Page 261

[3] Kuipers L, Bebbington P. *Living with Mental Illness: A Book for Relatives and Friends*, Souvenir Press Ltd; 1987. Page 38

[4] Kuipers L, Bebbington P. *Living with Mental Illness: A Book for Relatives and Friends*, Souvenir Press Ltd; 1987. Page 39

[5] Holloway, F and Tracy D. *Being positive about negative symptoms.* Your Voice, Rethink Mental Illness 2007.

[6] Mueser KT, Gingerich S. *Complete Family Guide to Schizophrenia. Helping Your Loved One Get the Most Out of Life.* Guildford Press; 2006 Page 411

[7] Mueser KT, Gingerich S. *Complete Family Guide to Schizophrenia. Helping Your Loved One Get the Most Out of Life.* Guildford Press; 2006 Page 414 - 415

[8] Mueser KT, Gingerich S. *Complete Family Guide to Schizophrenia. Helping Your Loved One Get the Most Out of Life.* Guildford Press; 2006 Page 414 - 415

[9] Mullen PE. A Reassessment of the Link between Mental Disorder and Violent Behaviour, and its Implications for Clinical Practice. *Aust N Z J Psychiatry* 1997; 31(1):3-11

[10] Queensland Health. *Preventing and managing anger*. http://www.health.qld.gov.au/abios/behaviour/family_sup_worker/defusing_anger_fsw.pdf[Accessed November 2012]

[11] Kuipers L, Bebbington P. *Living with Mental Illness: A Book for Relatives and Friends*, Souvenir Press Ltd; 1987. Page 52 - 56

[12] Senn TE, Carey MP.HIV testing among individuals with a severe mental illness: review, suggestions for research, and clinical implications; *Psychological Medicine* 2009;, 39:355-363

[13] Mueser KT, Gingerich S. *Complete Family Guide to Schizophrenia. Helping Your Loved One Get the Most Out of Life.* Guildford Press; 2006 Page 414 - 415

10 Tips From the Depression Alliance
What you want to tell someone you love who is depressed

I'm here for you
- » What to say: You're not alone in this.
- » What NOT to say: There's always someone worse off than you are.

You matter
- » What to say: You are important to me.
- » What NOT to say: No one ever said that life was fair.

Let me help
- » What to say: Do you want a hug?
- » What NOT to say: Stop feeling sorry for yourself.

Depression is real
- » What to say: You are not going crazy.
- » What NOT to say: So you're depressed. Aren't you always?

There is hope
- » What to say: We are not on this earth to see through one another, but to see one another through.
- » What NOT to say: Try not to be so depressed.

You can survive this
- » What to say: When all this is over, I'll still be here and so will you.
- » What NOT to say: It's your own fault.

I'll do my best to understand
- » What to say: I can't really understand what you are feeling, but I can offer my compassion.
- » What NOT to say: Believe me, I know how you feel. I was depressed once for several days.

You won't drive me away
- » What to say: I'm not going to leave you or abandon you.
- » What NOT to say: I think your depression is a way of punishing us.

I care about you
- » What to say: I love you. (Say this only if you mean it.)
- » What NOT to say: Haven't you grown tired of all this "me, me, me" stuff yet?

We'll get through this together
- » What to say: I'm sorry that you're in so much pain. I am not going to leave you. I am going to take care of myself, so you don't need to worry that your pain might hurt me.
- » What NOT to say: Have you tried chamomile tea?

Reference Forms

The following forms are included for reference purposes:

1. NC Form for Advance Instruction For Mental Health Treatment (235)
2. Alternative Psychiatric Advanced Directive Form (243)
3. NC Form for Healthcare Power of Attorney (253)
4. Alternative Healthcare Power of Attorney Form (259)
5. Affidavit and Petition for Involuntary Commitment (267)
6. HIPAA Authorization for Use or Disclosure of Health Information (269)

STATE OF NORTH CAROLINA

ADVANCE INSTRUCTION FOR MENTAL HEALTH TREATMENT

COUNTY OF _____

(NOTICE TO PERSON MAKING AN INSTRUCTION FOR MENTAL HEALTH TREATMENT)

This is an important legal document. It creates an instruction for mental health treatment. You should consider filing it with the Advanced Health Care Directive Registry maintained by the North Carolina Secretary of State: http://www.secretary.state.nc.us/ahcdr/thepage.aspx

Before signing this document you should know these important facts:
This document allows you to make decisions in advance about certain types of mental health treatment. The instructions you include in this declaration will be followed if a physician or eligible psychologist determines that you are incapable of making and communicating treatment decisions. Otherwise, you will be considered capable to give or withhold consent for the treatments. Your instructions may be overridden if you are being held in accordance with civil commitment law. Under the Health Care Power of Attorney you may also appoint a person as your health care agent to make treatment decisions for you if you become incapable. You have the right to revoke this document at any time you have not been determined to be incapable. YOU MAY NOT REVOKE THIS ADVANCE INSTRUCTION WHEN YOU ARE FOUND INCAPABLE BY A PHYSICIAN OR OTHER AUTHORIZED MENTAL HEALTH TREATMENT PROVIDER. A revocation is effective when it is communicated to your attending physician or other provider. The physician or other provider shall note the revocation in your medical record. To be valid, this advance instruction must be signed by two qualified witnesses, personally known to you, who are present when you sign or acknowledge your signature. It must also be acknowledged before a notary public.

NOTICE TO PHYSICIAN OR OTHER MENTAL HEALTH TREATMENT PROVIDER
Under North Carolina law, a person may use this advance instruction to provide consent for future mental health treatment if the person later becomes incapable of making those decisions. Under the Health Care Power of Attorney the person may also appoint a health care agent to make mental health treatment decisions for the person when incapable. A person is "incapable"

when in the opinion of a physician or eligible psychologist the person currently lacks sufficient understanding or capacity to make and communicate mental health treatment decisions. This document becomes effective upon its proper execution and remains valid unless revoked. Upon being presented with this advance instruction, the physician or other provider must make it a part of the person's medical record. The attending physician or other mental health treatment provider must act in accordance with the statements expressed in the advance instruction when the person is determined to be incapable, unless compliance is not consistent with G.S. 122C-74(g). The physician or other mental health treatment provider shall promptly notify the principal and, if applicable, the health care agent, and document noncompliance with any part of an advance instruction in the principal's medical record. The physician or other mental health treatment provider may rely upon the authority of a signed, witnessed, dated and notarized advance instruction, as provided in G.S. 122C-75.)

I, _____, being an adult of sound mind, willfully and voluntarily make this advance instruction for mental health treatment to be followed if it is determined by a physician or eligible psychologist that my ability to receive and evaluate information effectively or communicate decisions is impaired to such an extent that I lack the capacity to refuse or consent to mental health treatment. "Mental health treatment" means the process of providing for the physical, emotional, psychological, and social needs of the principal. "Mental health treatment includes electroconvulsive treatment (ECT), commonly referred to as "shock treatment", treatment of mental illness with psychotropic medication, and admission to and retention in a facility for care or treatment of mental illness.

I understand that under G.S. 122C-57, other than for specific exceptions stated there, mental health treatment may not be administered without my express and informed written consent or, if I am incapable of giving my informed consent, the express and informed consent of my legally responsible person, my health care agent named pursuant to a valid health care power of attorney, or my consent expressed in this advance instruction for mental health treatment. I understand that I may become incapable of giving or withholding informed consent for mental treatment due to the symptoms of a diagnosed mental disorder. These symptoms may include:

_____

_____

PSYCHOACTIVE MEDICATIONS

If I become incapable of giving or withholding informed consent for mental health treatment, my instructions regarding psychoactive medications are as follows: *(Place initials beside choice.)*

_____ I consent to the administration of the following medications:

_____ I do not consent to the administration of the following medications:
_____

Conditions or limitations: _____

ADMISSION TO AND RETENTION IN FACILITY

If I become incapable of giving or withholding informed consent for mental health treatment, my instructions regarding admission to and retention in a health care facility for mental health treatment are as follows: *(Place initials beside choice.)*

I consent to being admitted to a health care facility for mental health treatment. My facility preference is
_____

I do not consent to being admitted to a health care facility for mental health treatment.

This advance instruction cannot, by law, provide consent to retain me in a facility for more than ten (10) days.

Conditions or limitations: _____

ADDITIONAL INSTRUCTIONS

These instructions shall apply during the entire length of my incapacity. In case of mental health crisis, please contact:

1. Name: _____
   Home Address: _____
   Home Telephone Number: _____
   Work Telephone Number: _____
   Relationship to Me: _____

2. Name:
   Home Address: _____
   Home Telephone Number: _____
   Work Telephone Number: _____
   Relationship to Me: _____
3. My Physician:
   Name: _____
   Telephone Number:
4. My Therapist:
   Name:
   Telephone Number: _____

The following may cause me to experience a mental health crisis:

The following help me avoid a hospitalization:

I generally react to being hospitalized as follows:
_____
Staff of the hospital or crisis unit can help me by doing the following:

I give permission for the following person or people to visit me:
_____
Instructions concerning any other medical interventions, such as electroconvulsive (ECT) treatment (commonly referred to as "shock treatment"):
_____
Other instructions:
_____
_____

_____ *(Initial if applicable)* I have attached an additional sheet of instructions to be followed and considered part of this advance instruction.

SHARING OF INFORMATION BY PROVIDERS

I understand that the information in this document may be shared by my mental health treatment provider with any other mental health treatment provider who may serve me when necessary to provide treatment in accordance with this advance instruction.

Other instructions about sharing of information:

SIGNATURE OF PRINCIPAL

By signing here, I indicate that I am mentally alert and competent, fully informed as to the contents of this document, and understand the full impact of having made this advance instruction for mental health treatment.

_____   _____
Date   Signature of Principal

NATURE OF WITNESSES

I hereby state that the principal is personally known to me, that the principal signed or acknowledged the principal's signature on this advance instruction for mental health treatment in my presence, that the principal appears to be of sound mind and not under duress, fraud, or undue influence, and that I am not:

a. The attending physician or mental health service provider or an employee of the physician or mental health treatment provider;

b. An owner, operator, or employee of an owner or operator of a health care facility in which the principal is a patient or resident; or

c. Related within the third degree to the principal or to the principal's spouse.

AFFIRMATION OF WITNESS

We affirm that the principal is personally known to us, that the principal signed or acknowledged the principal's signature on this advance instruction for mental health treatment in our presence, that the principal appears to be of sound mind and not under duress, fraud, or undue influence, and that neither of us is:

    a.   A person appointed as an attorney-in-fact by this document;

    b.   The principal's attending physician or mental health service provider or a relative of the physician or provider;

    c.   The owner, operator, or relative of an owner or operator of a facility in which the principal is a patient or resident; or

    d.   A person related to the principal by blood, marriage or adoption.

Witnessed by:

_____   _____
Witness   Witness

_____   _____
Date   Date

STATE OF NORTH CAROLINA
COUNTY OF _____

CERTIFICATION OF NOTARY PUBLIC

I, _____ , a Notary Public for the County cited above in the State of North Carolina, hereby certify that _____ appeared before me and swore or affirmed to me and to the witnesses in my presence that this instrument is an advance instruction for mental health treatment, and that he/she willingly and voluntarily made and executed it as his/her free act and deed for the purposes expressed in it.

I further certify that _____ and _____ _____, witnesses, appeared before me and swore or affirmed that they witnessed _____ sign the attached advance instruction for mental health treatment, believing him/her to be of sound mind; and also swore that at the time they witnessed the signing they were not (i) the attending physician or mental health treatment provider or an employee of the physician or mental health treatment provider and (ii) they were not an owner, operator, or employee of an owner or operator of a health care facility in which the principal is a patient or resident, and (iii) they were not related within the third degree to the principal or to the principal's spouse. I further certify that I am satisfied as to the genuineness and due execution of the instrument.

This the _____ day of _____, 20_____.

_____
Notary Public
My Commission Expires:_____

Principal Name: _____

Advance Directives for Mental Health Treatment

(Please refer to the Psychiatric Advance Directives Toolkit for instructions to complete this worksheet.)

1. Symptom(s) I might experience during a period of crisis:

_____
_____
_____
_____
_____
_____
_____

2. Medication instructions.

A. I agree to administration of the following medication(s):

_____
_____
_____
_____
_____
_____
_____

B. I do not agree to administration of the following medication(s):

_____
_____
_____

Principal Name: _____

_____
_____
_____
_____

C. Other information about medications (allergies, side effects)

_____
_____
_____
_____
_____
_____

3. Facility Preferences.

A. I agree to admission to the following hospital(s):

_____
_____
_____
_____

B. I do not agree to admission to the following hospital(s):

_____
_____

Principal Name: _____

_____
_____
_____

Other information about hospitalization:

_____
_____
_____
_____
_____

Emergency Contacts in case of mental health crisis:

Name: _____

Address: _____

Home Phone # _____

Work Phone # _____

Relationship to Me: _____

Name: _____

Address: _____

Home Phone # _____

Work Phone # _____

Relationship to Me: _____

Principal Name: _____

Psychiatrist: _____

Work Phone # _____

Case Manager/Therapist: _____

Work Phone # _____

5. Crisis Precipitants. The following may cause me to experience a mental health crisis:

_____
_____
_____
_____
_____
_____
_____

6. Protective Factors. The following may help me avoid a mental health crisis:

_____
_____
_____
_____
_____

Principal Name: _____

. **Response to Hospital.** I usually respond to the hospital as follows:

. **Preferences for Staff Interactions.**

. Staff of the hospital or crisis unit can help me by doing the following:

. Staff can minimize use of restraint and seclusion by doing the following:

Principal Name: _____

_____
_____
_____
_____

9. I give permission for the following people to visit me in the hospital:

_____
_____
_____
_____
_____

10. The following are my preferences about ECT:

_____
_____
_____
_____
_____
_____

11. Other Instructions.

a. If I am hospitalized, I want the following to be taken care of at my home:

_____
_____

Principal Name: _____

_____
_____
_____
_____
_____
_____

I understand that the information in this document may be shared by my mental health treatment provider with any other mental health treatment provider who may serve me when necessary to provide treatment in accordance with this advance instruction. Other instructions about sharing of information are as follows:

_____
_____
_____
_____
_____
_____
_____
_____

Principal Name: _____

12. Legal documentation for Advance Directives:

a. Signature of Principal

By signing here, I indicate that I am mentally alert and competent, fully informed as to the contents of this document, and understand the full impact of having made this advance instruction for mental health treatment.

Signature of Principal _____ Date _____

Nature of Witnesses

I hereby state that the principal is personally known to me, that the principal signed or acknowledged the principal's signature on this advance instruction for mental health treatment in my presence, that the principal appears to be of sound mind and not under duress, fraud, or undue influence, and that I am not:

- The attending physician or mental health service provider or an employee of the physician or mental health treatment provider;
- An owner, operator, or employee of an owner or operator of a health care facility in which the principal is a patient or resident; or
- Related within the third degree to the principal or to the principal's spouse.

b. Affirmation of Witnesses

We affirm that the principal is personally known to us, that the principal signed or acknowledged the principal's signature on this advance instruction for mental health treatment in our presence, that the principal appears to be of sound mind and not under duress, fraud, or undue influence, and that neither of us is: A person appointed as an attorney-in-fact by this document; The principal's attending physician or mental health service provider or a relative of the physician or provider; The owner, operator, or relative of an owner or operator of a facility in which the principal is a patient or resident; or A person related to the principal by blood, marriage, or adoption.

Witnessed by:

Witness:_____ Date: _____

Witness:_____ Date: _____

STATE OF NORTH CAROLINA, COUNTY OF _____

Principal Name: _____

Certification of Notary Public

STATE OF NORTH CAROLINA
COUNTY OF

_____, a Notary Public for the County cited above in the State of North Carolina, hereby certify that _____ appeared before me and swore or affirmed to me and to the witnesses in my presence that this instrument is an advance instruction for mental health treatment, and that he/she willingly and voluntarily made and executed it as his/her free act and deed for the purposes expressed in _____.

I further certify that _____ and _____, witnesses, appeared before me and swore or affirmed that they witnessed _____ sign the attached advance instruction for mental health treatment, believing him/her to be of sound mind; and also swore that at the time they witnessed the signing they were not (i) the attending physician or mental health treatment provider or an employee of the physician or mental health treatment provider and (ii) they were not an owner, operator, or employee of an owner or operator of a health care facility in which the principal is a patient or resident, and (iii) they were not related within the third degree to the principal or to the principal's spouse. I further certify that I am satisfied as to the genuineness and due execution of the instrument.

This is the _____ day of _____, 20___.

Notary Public

My Commission expires:

Statutory Notices

Notice to Person Making an Instruction For Mental Health Treatment. This is an important legal document. It creates an instruction for mental health treatment. Before signing this document you should know these important facts: This document allows you to make decisions in advance about certain types of mental health treatment. The instructions you include in this declaration will be followed if a physician or eligible psychologist determines that you are incapable of making and communicating treatment decisions. Otherwise you will be

Principal Name: _____

considered capable to give or withhold consent for the treatments. Your instructions may be overridden if you are being held in accordance with civil commitment law. Under the Health Care Power of Attorney you may also appoint a person as your health care agent to make treatment decisions for you if you become incapable. You have the right to revoke this document at any time you have not been determined to be incapable. YOU MAY NOT REVOKE THIS ADVANCE INSTRUCTION WHEN YOU ARE FOUND INCAPABLE BY A PHYSICIAN OR OTHER AUTHORIZED MENTAL HEALTH TREATMENT PROVIDER. A revocation is effective when it is communicated to your attending physician or other provider. The physician or other provider shall note the revocation in your medical record. To be valid, this advance instruction must be signed by two qualified witnesses, personally known to you, who are present when you sign or acknowledge your signature. It must also be acknowledged before a notary public.

Notice to Physician or Other Mental Health Treatment Provider. Under North Carolina law, a person may use this advance instruction to provide consent for future mental health treatment if the person later becomes incapable of making those decisions. Under the Health Care Power of Attorney the person may also appoint a health care agent to make mental health treatment decisions for the person when incapable. A person is "incapable" when in the opinion of a physician or eligible psychologist the person currently lacks sufficient understanding or capacity to make and communicate mental health treatment decisions. This document becomes effective upon its proper execution and remains valid unless revoked. Upon being presented with this advance instruction, the physician or other provider must make it a part of the person's medical record. The attending physician or other mental health treatment provider must act in accordance with the statements expressed in the advance instruction when the person is determined to be incapable, unless compliance is not consistent with G.S. 122C-74(g). The physician or other mental health treatment provider shall promptly notify the principal and, if applicable, the health care agent, and document noncompliance with any part of an advance instruction in the principal's medical record. The physician or other mental health treatment provider may rely upon the authority of a signed, witnessed, dated, and notarized advance instruction, as provided in G.S. 122C-75. (1997-442, s. 2; 1998-198, s. 2; 1998-217, s. 53(a)(5).)

32A-25. Statutory form health care power of attorney.

The use of the following form in the creation of a health care power of attorney is lawful and, when used, it shall meet the requirements of and be construed in accordance with the provisions of this Article:

Notice: This document gives the person you designate your health care agent broad powers to make health care decisions, including mental health treatment decisions, for you. Except to the extent that you express specific limitations or restrictions on the authority of your health care agent, this power includes the power to consent to your doctor not giving treatment or stopping treatment necessary to keep you alive, admit you to a facility, and administer certain treatments and medications. This power exists only as to those health care decisions for which you are unable to give informed consent.

This form does not impose a duty on your health care agent to exercise granted powers, but when a power is exercised, your health care agent will have to use due care to act in your best interests and in accordance with this document. For mental health treatment decisions, your health care agent will act according to how the health care agent believes you would act if you were making the decision. Because the powers granted by this document are broad and sweeping, you should discuss your wishes concerning life-sustaining procedures, mental health treatment, and other health care decisions with your health care agent.

Use of this form in the creation of a health care power of attorney is lawful and is authorized pursuant to North Carolina law. However, use of this form is an optional and nonexclusive method for creating a health care power of attorney and North Carolina law does not bar the use of any other or different form of power of attorney for health care that meets the statutory requirements.)

Designation of health care agent.

I, _____, being of sound mind, hereby appoint

Name: _____

Home Address: _____

Home Telephone Number _____ Work Telephone Number _____

as my health care attorney-in-fact (herein referred to as my "health care agent") to act for me and in my name (in any way I could act in person) to make health care decisions for me as authorized in this document.

If the person named as my health care agent is not reasonably available or is unable or unwilling to act as my agent, then I appoint the following persons (each to act alone and successively, in the order named), to serve in that capacity: (Optional)

    A.   Name: _____
           Home Address: _____
           Home Telephone Number _____ Work Telephone Number _____

    B.   Name: _____
           Home Address: _____
           Home Telephone Number _____ Work Telephone Number _____

Each successor health care agent designated shall be vested with the same power and duties as if originally named as my health care agent.

2. Effectiveness of appointment.

(Notice: This health care power of attorney may be revoked by you at any time in any manner by which you are able to communicate your intent to revoke to your health care agent and your attending physician.)

Absent revocation, the authority granted in this document shall become effective when and if the physician or physicians designated below determine that I lack sufficient understanding or capacity to make or communicate decisions relating to my health care and will continue in effect during my incapacity, until my death, except if I authorize my health care agent to exercise my rights with respect to anatomical gifts, autopsy, or disposition of my remains, this authority will continue after my death to the extent necessary to exercise the authority granted in this document for these purposes.

This determination shall be made by the following physician or physicians. For decisions related to mental health treatment, this determination shall be made by the following physician or eligible psychologist. (You may include here a designation of your choice, including your attending physician or eligible psychologist, or any other physician or eligible psychologist. You may also name two or more physicians or eligible psychologists, if desired, both of whom must make this determination before the authority granted to the health care agent becomes effective.):

_____
_____
_____
_____

3. General statement of authority granted.

Except as indicated in section 4 below, I hereby grant to my health care agent named above full power and authority to make health care decisions, including mental health treatment decisions, on my behalf, including, but not limited to, the following:

- A. To request, review, and receive any information, verbal or written, regarding my physical or mental health, including, but not limited to, medical and hospital records, and to consent to the disclosure of this information.
- B. To employ or discharge my health care providers.
- C. To consent to and authorize my admission to and discharge from a hospital, nursing or convalescent home, or other institution.
- D. To consent to and authorize my admission to and retention in a facility for the care or treatment of mental illness.
- E. To consent to and authorize the administration of medications for mental health treatment and electroconvulsive treatment (ECT) commonly referred to as "shock treatment".
- F. To give consent for, to withdraw consent for, or to withhold consent for, X ray, anesthesia, medication, surgery, and all other diagnostic and treatment procedures ordered by or under the authorization of a licensed physician, dentist, or podiatrist. This authorization

specifically includes the power to consent to measures for relief of pain.

G. To authorize the withholding or withdrawal of life-sustaining procedures when and if my physician determines that I am terminally ill, permanently in a coma, suffer severe dementia, or am in a persistent vegetative state. Life-sustaining procedures are those forms of medical care that only serve to artificially prolong the dying process and may include mechanical ventilation, dialysis, antibiotics, artificial nutrition and hydration, and other forms of medical treatment which sustain, restore or supplant vital bodily functions. Life-sustaining procedures do not include care necessary to provide comfort or alleviate pain.

> I DESIRE THAT MY LIFE NOT BE PROLONGED BY LIFE-SUSTAINING PROCEDURES IF I AM TERMINALLY ILL, PERMANENTLY IN A COMA, SUFFER SEVERE DEMENTIA, OR AM IN A PERSISTENT VEGETATIVE STATE.

H. To exercise any right I may have to make a disposition of any part or all of my body for medical purposes; to authorize an autopsy; to make an anatomical gift of my organs or body, or part thereof, and to direct the disposition of my remains.

I. To take any lawful actions that may be necessary to carry out these decisions, including the granting of releases of liability to medical providers.

Special provisions and limitations.

(Notice: The above grant of power is intended to be as broad as possible so that your health care agent will have authority to make any decisions you could make to obtain or terminate any type of health care. If you wish to limit the scope of your health care agent's powers, you may do so in this section.)

A. In exercising the authority to make health care decisions on my behalf, the authority of my health care agent is subject to the following special provisions and limitations (Here you may include any specific limitations you deem appropriate such as: your own definition of when life-sustaining treatment should be withheld or discontinued, or instructions to refuse any specific types of treatment that are inconsistent with your religious beliefs, or unacceptable to you for any other reason.):

_____
_____
_____

B. In exercising the authority to make mental health decisions on my behalf, the authority of my health care agent is subject to the following special provisions and limitations. (Here you may include any specific limitations you deem appropriate such as: limiting the grant of authority to make only mental health treatment decisions, your own instructions regarding the administration or withholding of psychotropic medications and electroconvulsive treatment (ECT), instructions regarding your admission to and retention in a health care facility for mental health treatment, or instructions to refuse any specific types of treatment that are unacceptable to you):

_____
_____
_____
_____

C. (Notice: This health care power of attorney may incorporate or be combined with an advance instruction for mental health treatment, executed in accordance with Part 2 of Article 3 of Chapter 122C of the General Statutes, which you may use to state your instructions regarding mental health treatment in the event you lack sufficient understanding or capacity to make or communicate mental health treatment decisions. Because your health care agent's decisions about decisions must be consistent with any statements you have expressed in an advance instruction, you should indicate here whether you have executed an advance instruction for mental health treatment.):

_____
_____
_____
_____

D. In exercising the authority to make decisions regarding autopsy, anatomical gifts and disposition of remains on my behalf, the authority of my health care agent is subject to the following special provisions and limitations. (Here you may include any specific limitations you deem appropriate such as: limiting the grant of authority and the scope of authority, instructions regarding gifts of the body or body part, or instructions regarding burial or cremation):

_____
_____
_____
_____

5. Guardianship provision.

If it becomes necessary for a court to appoint a guardian of my person, I nominate my health care agent acting under this document to be the guardian of my person, to serve without bond or security. The guardian shall act consistently with G.S. 35A-1201(a)(5).

6. Reliance of third parties on health care agent.

A. No person who relies in good faith upon the authority of or any representations by my health care agent shall be liable to me, my estate, my heirs, successors, assigns, or personal representatives, for actions or omissions by my health care agent.

B. The powers conferred on my health care agent by this document may be exercised by my health care agent alone, and my health care agent's signature or act under the authority granted in this document may be accepted by persons as fully authorized by me and with the same force and effect as if I were personally present, competent, and acting on my own behalf. All acts performed in good faith by my health care agent pursuant to this power of attorney are done with my consent and shall have the same validity and effect as if I were present and exercised the powers myself, and shall inure to the benefit of and bind me, my estate, my heirs, successors, assigns, and personal representatives. The authority of my health care agent pursuant to this power of attorney shall be superior to and binding upon my family, relatives, friends, and others.

7. Miscellaneous provisions.

A. I revoke any prior health care power of attorney.

B. My health care agent shall be entitled to sign, execute, deliver, and acknowledge any contract or other document that may be necessary, desirable, convenient, or proper in order to exercise and carry out any of the powers described in this document and to incur reasonable costs on my behalf incident to the exercise of these powers; provided, however, that except as shall be necessary in order to exercise the powers described in this document relating to my health care, my health care agent shall not have any authority over my property or financial affairs.

C. My health care agent and my health care agent's estate, heirs, successors, and assigns are hereby released and forever discharged by me, my estate, my heirs, successors, and assigns and personal representatives from all liability and from all claims or demands of all kinds arising out of the acts or omissions of my health care agent pursuant to this document, except for willful misconduct or gross negligence.

D. No act or omission of my health care agent, or of any other person, institution, or facility acting in good faith in reliance on the authority of my health care agent pursuant to this health care power of attorney shall be considered suicide, nor the cause of my death for any civil or criminal purposes, nor shall it be considered unprofessional conduct or as lack of professional competence. Any person, institution, or facility against whom criminal or civil liability is asserted because of conduct authorized by this health care power of attorney may interpose this document as a defense.

Signature of principal.

By signing here, I indicate that I am mentally alert and competent, fully informed as to the contents of this document, and understand the full import of this grant of powers to my health care agent.

_____ (SEAL)   _____
Signature of Principal   Date

9. Signatures of Witnesses.

I hereby state that the Principal, _____, being of sound mind, signed the foregoing health care power of attorney in my presence, and that I am not related to the principal by blood or marriage, and I would not be entitled to any portion of the estate of the principal under any existing will or codicil of the principal or as an heir under the Intestate Succession Act, if the principal died on this date without a will. I also state that I am not the principal's attending physician, nor an employee of the principal's attending physician, nor an employee of the health facility in which the principal is a patient, nor an employee of a nursing home or any group care home where the principal resides. I further state that I do not have any claim against the principal.

Witness: _____ Date: _____
Witness: _____ Date: _____

STATE OF NORTH CAROLINA
COUNTY OF _____

CERTIFICATE

I, _____, a Notary Public for _____ County, North Carolina, hereby certify that _____ appeared before me and swore to me and to the witnesses in my presence that this instrument is a health care power of attorney, and that he/she willingly and voluntarily made and executed it as his/her free act and deed for the purposes expressed in it.

I further certify that _____ and _____, witnesses, appeared before me and swore that they witnessed _____ sign the attached health care power of attorney, believing him/her to be of sound mind; and also swore that at the time they witnessed the signing (i) they were not related within the third degree to him/her or his/her spouse, and (ii) they did not know nor have a reasonable expectation that they would be entitled to any portion of his/her estate upon his/her death under any will or codicil thereto then existing or under the Intestate Succession Act as it provided at that time, and (iii) they were not a physician attending him/her, nor an employee of an attending physician, nor an employee of a health facility in which he/she was a patient, nor an employee of a nursing home or any group-care home in which he/she resided, and (iv) they did not have a claim against him/her. I further certify that I am satisfied as to the genuineness and due execution of the instrument.

This the _____ day of _____, _____.

_____
Notary Public

My Commission Expires:
_____

(A copy of this form should be given to your health care agent and any alternate named in this power of attorney, and to your physician and family members.)

Principal Name: _____

Health Care Power of Attorney

(Please refer to the Health Care Power of Attorney Toolkit for instructions to complete this worksheet.)

Assign Health Care Agent(s).

I, _____, appoint

Name: _____

Address: _____

Home Phone # _____

Work Phone # _____

as my health care attorney-in-fact (herein referred to as my "health care agent") to act for me and in my name (in any way I could act in person) to make health care decisions for me as authorized in this document.

If the person named as my health care agent is not reasonably available or is unable or unwilling to act as my agent, then I appoint the following persons (each to act alone and successively, in the order named), to serve in that capacity:

(Optional)

Name: _____

Address: _____

Home Phone # _____

Work Phone # _____

Principal Name: _____

If the preceding persons named as my health care agent are not reasonably available or is unable or unwilling to act as my agent, then I appoint the following persons (each to act alone and successively, in the order named), to serve in that capacity: (Optional)

Name:_____

Address:_____

Home Phone # _____

Work Phone #_____

2. Designate Physicians for Crisis Evaluation. I wish the following doctor to evaluate whether I lack sufficient understanding to make or communicate treatment decisions:

Name:_____

Home Phone # _____

Work Phone #_____

3. Grant Authorities to Health Care Agent. Below, my initial signifies I grant the following powers to my Health Care Agent:

_____ A. To request, review, and receive any information, verbal or written, regarding my physical or mental health, including, but not limited to, medical and hospital records, and to consent to the disclosure of this information.

Principal Name: _____

_____ B. To employ or discharge my health care providers.

_____ C. To consent to and authorize my admission to and discharge from a hospital, nursing or convalescent home, or other institution.

_____ D. To consent to and authorize my admission to and retention in a facility for the care or treatment of mental illness.

_____ E. To consent to and authorize the administration of medications for mental health treatment and electroconvulsive treatment (ECT) commonly referred to as "shock treatment".

_____ F. To give consent for, to withdraw consent for, or to withhold consent for, X ray, anesthesia, medication, surgery, and all other diagnostic and treatment procedures ordered by or under the authorization of a licensed physician, dentist, or podiatrist. This authorization specifically includes the power to consent to measures for relief of pain.

_____ G. To authorize the withholding or withdrawal of life-sustaining procedures when and if my physician determines that I am terminally ill, permanently in a coma, suffer severe dementia, or am in a persistent vegetative

Principal Name: _____

state. Life-sustaining procedures are those forms of medical care that only serve to artificially prolong the dying process and may include mechanical ventilation, dialysis, antibiotics, artificial nutrition and hydration, and other forms of medical treatment which sustain, restore or supplant vital bodily functions. Life-sustaining procedures do not include care necessary to provide comfort or alleviate pain.

_____ H. To exercise any right I may have to make a disposition of any part or all of my body for medical purposes, to donate my organs, to authorize an autopsy, and to direct the disposition of my remains.

_____ I. To take any lawful actions that may be necessary to carry out these decisions, including the granting of releases of liability to medical providers.

4. Special Provisions. The health care agent is subject to the following limitations when making decisions about my:

A. Physical Health

_____
_____
_____
_____
_____

Principal Name: _____

3. Mental Health

_____
_____
_____
_____
_____
_____
_____
_____

Provision on Guardianship. My initial here signifies I would like to nominate our health care agent as a guardian, should the need arise: _____

Legal Documentation
Miscellaneous Provisions

. I revoke any prior health care power of attorney.

. My health care agent shall be entitled to sign, execute, deliver, and acknowledge any contract or other document that may be necessary, desirable, convenient, or proper in order to exercise and carry out any of the powers described in this document and to incur reasonable costs on my behalf incident to the exercise of these powers; provided, however, that except as shall be necessary in order to exercise the powers described in this document relating to my health care, my health care agent shall not have any authority over my property or financial affairs.

. My health care agent and my health care agent's estate, heirs, successors, and assigns are hereby released and forever discharged by me, my estate, my heirs, successors, and assigns and personal representatives from all liability and

Principal Name: _____

from all claims or demands of all kinds arising out of the acts or omissions of my health care agent pursuant to this document, except for willful misconduct or gross negligence.

4. No act or omission of my health care agent, or of any other person, institution, or facility acting in good faith in reliance on the authority of my health care agent pursuant to this health care power of attorney shall be considered suicide, nor the cause of my death for any civil or criminal purposes, nor shall it be considered unprofessional conduct or as lack of professional competence. Any person, institution, or facility against whom criminal or civil liability is asserted because of conduct authorized by this health care power of attorney may interpose this document as a defense.

B. Signature

By signing here, I indicate that I am mentally alert and competent, fully informed as to the contents of this document, and understand the full import of this grant of powers to my health care agent.

Signature of Principal_____

Date _____   (SEAL)

C. Witnesses

I hereby state that the Principal, _____, being of sound mind, signed the foregoing health care power of attorney in my presence, and that I am not related to the principal by blood or marriage, and I would not be entitled to any portion of the estate of the principal under any existing will or codicil of the principal or as an heir under the Intestate Succession Act, if the principal died on this date without a will. I also state that I am not the principal's attending physician, nor an employee of the principal's attending physician, nor an employee of the health facility in which the principal is a patient,

Principal Name: _____

...or an employee of a nursing home or any group care home where the principal resides. I further state that I do not nave any claim against the principal.

Witness: _____ Date: _____

Witness: _____ Date: _____

D. Notarization

STATE OF NORTH CAROLINA COUNTY OF _____

CERTIFICATE

I, _____, a Notary Public for _____ County, North Carolina, hereby certify that _____ appeared before me and swore to me and to the witnesses in my presence that this instrument is a health care power of attorney, and that he/she willingly and voluntarily made and executed it as his/her free act and deed for the purposes expressed in it.

I further certify that _____ and _____, witnesses, appeared before me and swore that they witnessed _____ sign the attached health care power of attorney, believing him/her to be of sound mind; and also swore that at the time they witnessed the signing (i) they were not related within the third degree to him/her or his/her spouse, and (ii) they did not know nor have a reasonable expectation that they would be entitled to any portion of his/her estate upon his/her death under any will or codicil thereto then existing or under the Intestate Succession Act as it provided at that time, and (iii) they were not a physician attending him/her, nor an employee of an attending physician, nor an employee of a health facility in which he/she was a patient, nor an employee of a nursing home or any group-care home in which he/she resided, and (iv) they did

Principal Name: _____

not have a claim against him/her. I further certify that I am satisfied as to the genuineness and due execution of the instrument.

This the _____ day of _____, 20____.

_____
Notary Public

My Commission Expires: _____

STATE OF NORTH CAROLINA

_____ County

IN THE MATTER OF

Name And Address Of Respondent

File No. _____

In The General Court Of Justice
District Court Division

**AFFIDAVIT AND PETITION FOR
INVOLUNTARY COMMITMENT**

G.S. 122C-261, 122C-281

Social Security No. Of Respondent (if available)	Date Of Birth	Drivers License No. Of Respondent	State

The undersigned affiant, being first duly sworn, and having sufficient knowledge to believe that the respondent is a proper subject for involuntary commitment, allege that the respondent is a resident of, or can be found in the above named county, and is:

(check all that apply)

1. mentally ill and dangerous to self or others or mentally ill and in need of treatment in order to prevent further disability or deterioration that would predictably result in dangerousness.
   ☐ in addition to being mentally ill, respondent is also "mentally retarded" pursuant to G.S. 122C-261.

2. a substance abuser and dangerous to self or others.

The facts upon which this opinion is based are as follows: *(State facts, not conclusions, to support ALL blocks checked.)*

Name And Address Of Nearest Relative Or Guardian	Name And Address Of Person Other Than Petitioner Who May Testify
Home Telephone No. / Business Telephone No.	Home Telephone No. / Business Telephone No.

Petitioner requests the court to issue an order to a law enforcement officer to take the respondent into custody for examination by a person authorized by law to conduct the examination for the purpose of determining if the respondent should be involuntarily committed.

SWORN/AFFIRMED AND SUBSCRIBED TO BEFORE ME

Signature	Signature Of Petitioner
☐ Deputy CSC ☐ Assistant CSC ☐ Clerk Of Superior Court ☐ Magistrate	Name And Address Of Petitioner (type or print)
☐ Notary (use only with physician or psychologist petitioner)	Date Notary Commission Expires	Relationship To Respondent
SEAL	County Where Notarized	Home Telephone No.	Business Telephone No.

Original-File   Copy-Hospital   Copy-Special Counsel   Copy-Attorney General
(Over)

AOC-SP-300, Rev. 5/17
© 2017 Administrative Office of the Courts

PETITIONER'S WAIVER OF NOTICE OF HEARING

I voluntarily waive my right to notice of all hearings and rehearings in which the Court may commit the respondent or extend the respondent' commitment period, or discharge the respondent from the treatment facility.

Signature Of Witness	Date
	Signature Of Petitioner

NOTE: *"Upon the request of the legally responsible person or the minor admitted or committed, and after that minor has both been released and reached adulthood, the court records of that minor made in proceedings pursuant to Article 5 of [Chapter 122C] may be expunged from the files of the court."* G.S. 122C-54(e).

HIPAA AUTHORIZATION FOR USE OR DISCLOSURE OF HEALTH INFORMATION

This form is for use when such authorization is required and complies with the Health Insurance Portability and Accountability Act of 1996 (HIPAA) Privacy Standards.

Print Name of Patient: _____

Date of Birth: _____ SSN: _____

My Authorization

I authorize the following using or disclosing party:

_____

To use or disclose the following health information.

[ ] - All of my health information

[ ] - My health information relating to the following treatment or condition:

_____

[ ] - My health information covering the period from _____ (date) to _____ (date)

[ ] - Other: _____

The above party may disclose this health information to the following recipient:

Name (or title) and organization _____

Address _____

City _____ State _____ Zip _____

Phone _____ Fax _____ Email _____

The purpose of this authorization is (check all that apply):

[ ] - At my request

[ ] - Other: _____

[ ] - To authorize the using or disclosing party to communicate with me for marketing purposes when they receive payment from a third party to do so.

[ ] - To authorize the using or disclosing party to sell my health information. I understand that the seller will receive compensation for my health information and will stop any future sales if I revoke this authorization.

This authorization ends:

[ ] - On (date)_____

[ ] - When the following event occurs: _____

II. My Rights

I understand that I have the right to revoke this authorization, in writing, at any time, except where uses or disclosures have already been made based upon my original permission. I may not be able to revoke this authorization if its purpose was to obtain insurance. In order to revoke this authorization, I must do so in writing and send it to the appropriate disclosing party.

I understand that uses and disclosures already made based upon my original permission cannot be taken back.

I understand that it is possible that information used or disclosed with my permission may be re-disclosed by the recipient and is no longer protected by the HIPAA Privacy Standards.

I understand that treatment by any party may not be conditioned upon my signing of this authorization (unless treatment is sought only to create health information for a third party or to take part in a research study) and that I may have the right to refuse to sign this authorization.

I will receive a copy of this authorization after I have signed it. A copy of this authorization is as valid as the original.

Signature of Patient: _____

Date: _____

If the patient is a minor or unable to sign, please complete the following:

☐ - Patient is a minor: _____ years of age

☐ - Patient is unable to sign because: _____

Signature of Authorized Representative: _____

Date: _____

Print Name of Authorized Representative: _____

Authority of representative to sign on behalf of the patient:

☐ - Parent   ☐ - Legal Guardian   ☐ - Court Order   ☐ - Other: _____

Additional Consent for Certain Conditions

This medical record may contain information about **physical or sexual abuse, alcoholism, drug abuse, sexually transmitted diseases, abortion, or mental health treatment**. Separate consent must be given before this information can be released.

_ - I consent to have the above information released.

_ - I do not consent to have the above information released.

Signature of Patient or Authorized Representative: _____

Date: _____   Time: _____

Additional Consent for HIV/AIDS

This medical record may contain information concerning **HIV testing and/or AIDS diagnosis or treatment**. Separate consent must be given to have this information released.

_ - I consent to have the above information released.

_ - I do not consent to have the above information released.

Signature of Patient or Authorized Representative: _____

Date: _____   Time: _____

RESOURCES

No list of resources can be comprehensive or provide something for every concern. We have tried to offer a wide range of resources, covering a swathe of perspectives on mental illnesses: living with these illnesses and learning to manage them. We have provided resources written by professionals and by those with lived experience. Some of the resources listed come strongly recommended by those who developed this guide or by people we know. Others were discovered by search and research.

We advise you to do your own research—both on the resources provided here and for other resources that may be available. Before choosing, read the comments of others who have used the resource and consider what the support or information offers. Keep in mind always that there are many perspectives on mental illnesses, their treatment, and those who live with them. The more you learn, the better equipped you will be to sort through the pile and find the information that will be most helpful to you, your family, and the person you love.

*<u>Inclusion in this guide should NOT alone indicate our endorsement.
Resources in **BOLD PRINT** are recommended.</u>*

Resources: Books

72 Hour Hold: Bebe Moore Campbell

A Beautiful Mind: Sylvia Nasar

A Night in Jail: A Story About Drugs and Mental Illness, Inspired by True Events: H.A. Swan and K. Anderson

Addict in the House: A No-Nonsense Family Guide Through Addiction and Recovery: Robin Barnett, EdD, LCSW and Darren Kavinosky

***An Unquiet Mind*, Kay Redfield Jamison**

Another Kind of Madness: A Journey Through the Stigma and Hope of Mental Illness: Stephen P. Hinshaw, Sean Pratt

Atmospheric Disturbances: Scenes From a Marriage: Maggie May Etheridge

Beautiful Boy: A Father's Journey Through His Son's Meth Addiction: **David Sheff**

Behind the Wall, The True Story of Mental Illness as Told by Parents: Mary Widdefield and Ellen Widdefield, MA

Between Breaths: A Memoir of Panic and Addiction: Elizabeth Vargas

Bipolar Disorder, A Guide for Patients and Families: Francis Mark Mondimore, MD

Birth of a New Brain: Healing from Postpartum Bipolar Disorder: Dyane Harwood and Dr. Carol Henshaw

Broken: My Story of Addiction and Redemption: Scott Brick and William Cope Moyers

Broken Brain, Fortified Faith: Lessons of Hope Through a Child's Mental Illness: Virginia Pillars and Catherine Force

Coming Out Proud, Stories and Essays of Solidarity: Editors, Patrick W. Corrigan, John E. Larson, and Patrick J. Michaels

Detour: My Bi-polar Road Trip: Lizzie Simon

Different: The Story of an Outside-the-Box Kid and the Mom Who Loved Him: Sally Clarkson

***First Person Accounts of Mental Illness and Recovery*: Editors, Craig Winston LeCroy and Jane Holschuh**

Hurry Down Sunshine, A Memoir: Michael Greenburg

I am Not Sick. I Don't Need Help: How to Help Someone with Mental Illness Accept Treatment: Xavier Amador, Ph.D

I'll Run Till the Sun Goes Down: A Memoir About Depression and Discovering Art: David Sandum

Informed Consent to Psychoanalysis: The Law, the Theory, and the Data: Elyn R Saks and Shahrokh Golshan

In My Skin: A Memoir of Addiction: Kate Holden and Christie Lynn

Insane Consequences: How the Mental Halth Industry Fails the Mentally Ill: DJ Chaffee

Interpreting Interpretation: The Limits of Hermeneutic Psychoanalysis, Elyn R. Saks

Lori: The Disintegration of My Ordinary Reality: Anne Crowe and Lori Morrison

Love is the Drug: A Mother and Son Memoir: Dane Jacobs and Jodi Dale

Mental Health: Policies, Laws and Attitudes: A Conversation With Elyn Saks: Ideas Roadshow and Howard Burton

Mind Estranged: My Journey from Schizophrenia and Homelessness to Recovery: Bethany Yeiser

Mothering Addiction: A Parent's Story of Heartache, Healing, and Keeping the Door Open: Lynda Harrison Hatcher

My Age of Anxiety: Fear, Hope, Dread and the Search for Peace of Mind: Scott Stossel

Night Falls Fast: Understanding Suicide: Kay Redfield Jamison

Nothing Was the Same: A Memoir: Kay Refield Jamison and Renee Raudman

Opiate Addiction—The Painkiller Addiction Epidemic, Heroin Addiction and the Way Out: Taite Adams

Refusing Care: Forced Treatment and the Rights of the Mentally Ill: Elyn R. Saks

Rescuing Patty Hearst: Growing Up Sane in a Decade Gone Mad: Virgina Holman

Robert Lowell, Setting the River on Fire: A Study of Genius, Mania, and Character: Kay Refield Jamison and Jefferson Mays

Saving Jake: When Addiction Hits Home: D'Anne Burwell

Show Me All Your Scars: True Stories of Living with Mental Illness: Lee Gutkind

Still Life: A Memoir of Living Fully With Depression: Gillian Marchenko

Surviving Manic Depression: E. Fuller Torrey, MD and Michael B. Knable, D.O.

The Bipolar Disorder Survival Guide, Second Edition: What You and Your Family Need to Know: David J. Miklowitz

The Center Cannot Hold, My Journey Through Madness: Elyn R. Saks

The Essential Family Guide to Borderline Personality Disorder: Randi Kreger

The Flawed Ones: Jay Chirino

The Journey of the Heroic Parent: Your Child's Struggles and the Road Home: Brad Reedy, Tom Parks

The Mindfulness Workbook for Addiction: A Guide to Coping With the Grief, Stress and Anger That Trigger Addictive Behaviors: Rebecca E. Williams and Julie S. Kraft, MA

This Stranger My Son: A Mother's Story: Louise Wilson

Touched With Fire: Manic Depressive Illness and the Artistic Temperament: Kay Redfield Jamison
Turtles All the Way Down (Young Adult): John Green

We Heard the Angels of Madness, A Family Guide to Coping With Manic Depression: Diane and Lisa Berger

When Someone You Love Has a Mental Illness: A Handbook for Family, Friends, and Caregivers: Rebecca Woolis

When Your Adult Child Breaks Your Heart: Coping With Substance Abuse, Mental Illness, and The Problems That Tear Families Apart: Joel Young and Christine Adamec

Resources: Online
Information, Blogs, Community, etc.
This list was accurate at the time of publication—
but websites change and some sites may no longer be active.

Active Minds: http://www.activeminds.org/ - Changing the conversation about mental health on college campuses.

ADA National Network: http://adata.org/ - Provides information, guidance and training on how to implement the Americans With Disabilities Act.

Anxiety United: https://anxietyunited.com/ - An independent mental health and anxiety content sharing hub and social network platform. Helpful information and resources.

BeThe1To: https://www.bethe1to.com - Comprehensive website dedicated to suicide prevention.

Black Dog Tribe: http://www.sane.org.uk/what_we_do/bdt - Online community for anyone affected by mental illness. Run by Charity Sane.

Bring Change To Mind: https://bringchange2mind.org/ - Ending the stigma and discrimination surrounding mental illness. Videos, stories, and resources.

Buddy Project: http://www.buddy-project.org/ - Non-profit movement aiming to prevent suicide and self harm by paring people as buddies and raising awareness for mental health.

Canadian Alliance on Mental Illness and Mental Health: http://www.camimh.ca/

Canadian Mental Health Alliance: https://cmha.ca/ - Promoting mental health and supports for people recovering from mental illness.

Conquer Worry: http://www.conquerworry.org/ - Site which inspires, educates, and advocates for those who struggle with stress or mental health issues.

Freedom House Recovery: http://freedomhouserecovery.org

Headspace: https://headspace.org.au/ - Australia's national Youth Mental Health Foundation. Online support.

MedCircle Depression: https://www.medcircle.com/ - Verified and up-to-date information on depression.

Mental Health America: http://www.mentalhealthamerica.net/ Resources and Information

Mental Health Channel: http://www.mentalhealthchannel.tv/ - Films, documentaries, ideas, voices. Free mental health and mental illness videos.

Mind Charity: https://www.mind.org.uk/ - Working to ensure support and respect for all who experience mental health problems.

National Alliance on Mental Illness—National: https://www.nami.org/ - Offers programs and resources for families and those diagnosed with mental illness.

National Alliance on Mental Illness -NC: https://naminc.org/ Includes link to local NAMI office in NC as well as resources. Promote recovery and optimize the quality of life for those affected by mental illness.

National Institute on Mental Health: https://www.nimh.nih.gov/

Open Sourcing Mental Illness: https://osmihelp.org/ - Raising awareness and ending the stigma of mental illness in the tech community.

Pathways RTC: https://www.pathwaysrtc.pdx.edu/ - Improving the lives of youth and young adults with serious mental health conditions.

Recovery: https://www.recovery.org/ - Sharing hope, encouragement, and support to help people struggling with substance abuse and behavioral addictions. Resources and information.

Relief From Anxiety: http://reliefromanxiety.blogspot.com/
Personal Mental Health blog

Rethink Depression: http://rethinkdepression.com/community/
Articles, information, stories about living with depression and ways to manage.

Rethink Mental Illness: https://www.rethink.org/ - Excellent resources. Leading the way to a better life for everyone affected by mental illness.

SAMHSA: https://www.samhsa.gov/ - Substance Abuse and Mental Health Services Administration

Sick Not Weak: https://www.sicknotweak.com/ - Helping people understand that mental illness is a sickness, not a weakness. Shared stories.

Sooner Than Tomorrow: http://www.soonerthantomorrow.com/ A Safe Space to Talk About Mental Illness in Our Families. Stories. Blog. Resources.

Spreading the Love: https://www.spreadingthelove.us/ - A nonprofit aimed to end bullying, the stigma surrounding mental illness, and suicide.

The Depression Files Podcast: http://podcast.thedepressionfiles.com/

The Mental Elf: https://www.nationalelfservice.net/mental-health/ UK-based website that provides up-to-date information, blogs, and highlights publications relevant to mental health from 500 sources, updated weekly. *"No Bias. No Misinformation. No Spin. Just what you need."*

The Mighty: https://themighty.com/ - Community-based resource for dealing with mental illness and other disabling conditions and illnesses. Blogs. Stories. *"We face disability, disease, and mental illness together."*

The Thought Hackers: http://thethoughthackers.com/ - Podcast which focuses on trauma, PTSD, Depression and Anxiety.

Time to Change: https://www.time-to-change.org.uk/ - Raising awareness of mental health and reducing stigma. Personal stories.

Transitions: https://www.umassmed.edu/TransitionsACR - Young adult mental health research, resources, technical assistance, news in the field, and collaborations.

TU Collaborative: http://tucollaborative.org/ A research center at Temple University focused on community and inclusion for people with psychiatric disabilities.

Resources: NC Agencies & Organizations

Coordinated Specialty Care: Treatment for young people experiencing their first episode of psychosis.

- Carrboro: https://www.med.unc.edu/psych/oasis
- Wilmington: http://www.myrha.org/news/rha-behavioral-health-shore-program-opens-in-wilmington

Disability Rights Bar: http://disabilityrights-law.org/ - The Disability Rights Bar Association is an online national network of attorneys who specialize in disability civil rights law.

Disability Rights NC: http://www.disabilityrightsnc.org/ - Protects the legal rights of people with disabilities through both individual and systems advocacy

Easter Seals: Children's Mental Health Services: 1-800-662-7119 http://www.easterseals.com/NCVA/our-programs/childrens-services/childrens-behaviorial-health.html

National Alliance on Mental Illness—National: https://www.nami.org/ - Offers programs and resources for families and those diagnosed with mental illness

National Alliance on Mental Illness -NC: 919-788-0801 https://naminc.org/ - Includes link to local NAMI office in NC as well as resources. Promote recovery and optimize the quality of life for those affected by mental illness

North Carolina Department of Health and Human Services: https://www.ncdhhs.gov/

> NCDHHS Adult Mental Health Services: https://www.ncdhhs.gov/divisions/mhddsas/adultmentalhealth
>
> NCDHHS Mental Health and Substance Abuse: https://www.ncdhhs.gov/assistance/mental-health-substance-abuse
>
> NC Mental Health, Developmental Disabilities and Substance Abuse Services: 919-733-7011, https://www.ncdhhs.gov/divisions/mhddsas

North Carolina Families United: 1-336-395-8828, https://www.ncfamiliesunited.org/ - Support and advocacy organization for children, youth, and families with emotional, behavioral, or mental health needs.

North Carolina Health Advocacy/NC Justice Center: http://www.ncjustice.org/ - Project of the NC Justice Center working to ensure that all people can access quality, affordable healthcare

Psychiatric Foundation of NC: http://www.ncpsychiatry.org/foundation

Social Security Disability Resource Center: Mental Disability Benefits NC: http://www.ssdrc.com/state-north-carolina-nc-9.html

Treatment Advocacy Center NC: http://www.treatmentadvocacycenter.org/north-carolina Eliminating Barriers to the Treatment of Mental Illness

Classes, Workshops, Information Sessions

Family to Family, offered by NAMI in most counties in NC, is an intensive 12 session program aimed at providing families with the information they need to support their loved one with mental illness and maintain their own health.

Mental Health First Aid for Adults and *Mental Health First Aid for Adolescents* are day long classes which provide important information on mental illness. They are often offered through *Mental Health America*. *QPR* (Question, Persuade, Refer) http://www.qprinstitute.com QPR is a widely taught class on suicide prevention. It is also available on-line.

Resources: NC Facilities

This list may not be comprehensive. For more information you can call DHHS, your local LME/MCO, or do an online search: psychiatric or mental health, or substance abuse treatment: inpatient, NC

Alcohol and Drug Abuse Treatment Centers. State centers serving adults in need of substance abuse disorder treatment .Offer a variety of specialized programs.
    Julian F. Keith, Black Mountain, NC 828-257-6200
    R.J. Blackley, Butner, NC 919-575-7928
    Walter B. Jones, Greenville, NC 252-830-3426

Broughton Hospital, Morganton, NC: 828-433-2111
    Regional psychiatric hospital operating as part of DHHS. Serves the western 37 counties of North Carolina. Adult/Geriatric/Adult extended treatment/Adolescent/Deaf consumers

Brynn Marr, Jacksonville, NC 910-577-1400
    Inpatient child/adolescent/adult behavioral health services. Passages psychiatric residential treatment facility

Cape Fear Valley Behavioral Health Care, Fayetteville, NC 910-615-3600
    Inpatient adult services. Outpatient children/adolescent/adult services. Substance Abuse treatment also available
        Outpatient detox and crisis stabilization: 910-615-3370
        Community Mental Health Center: 910-615-3333
        Community Mental health, Children's Services: 910-615-3333
        Military Family Clinic: 910-615-3737
        Inpatient Unit: 910-615-3610

Carolinas Medical Center, Behavioral Health Center, Randolph, NC 704-444-2400
    Outpatient services for adult/adolescent/children. Partial Hospitalization program for psychiatric and substance abuse. The only 24/7 psychiatric emergency department in the region staffed by psychiatrists, and psychiatric nurses. The Emergency department also has telemedicine capability.

Central Regional Hospital, Butner, NC: 919-764-2000
    Operated by DHHS. Regional facility serving 25 counties in central NC. Inpatient and medical services to adults/adolescents.

Cherry Hospital, Goldsboro, NC: 919-947-7000
> Inpatient regional referral psychiatric hospital managed by DHHS. Provides services to 38 counties in eastern region of NC. Adults/adolescents/geriatric. Short and long-term care.

Cone Behavioral Health Hospital, Greensboro, NC: 800-711-2635
> Inpatient adults/children/adolescent. Outpatient services in several locations for children/adolescent/adult

Coastal Plain Hospital (UNC), Nash and Edgecombe County, Rocky Mount, NC: 252-962-5000
> Adult inpatient: psychiatric and substance abuse
> 24 hour crisis line: 800-234-0234

Crossroads Mental Health, Carolina East Health System, New Bern, NC: 252-633-8204
> Inpatient: Adult Mental Health

Duke University Hospital Williams Psychiatric Hospital and Durham Regional Hospital, Durham, NC: 919-970-0519
> Inpatient adult psychiatric.

High Point Regional, Smith Psychiatric Center, High Point, NC: 336-878-6098
> 24/7 assessment/crisis stabilization Adult mental health and substance abuse, inpatient psychiatric and detox. Outpatient treatment programs.

Holly Hill, Raleigh, NC: 919-250-7000 or 10800-447-1860
> Adult/Children/Adolescent inpatient units/outpatient programs, Mental Health, Substance Abuse, Detox, Dual Diagnosis.

New Hanover Regional Medical Center, Behavioral Health Hospital, Wilmington, NC: 910-667-7787
> Inpatient psychiatric, co-occurring diagnosis: adult/Geriatric

Novant Health, Forsyth Medical Center, Winston Salem, NC: 800-718-3550, 336-718-3550
> Inpatient and outpatient psychiatric: children/adult Telepsychiatry, mobile crisis team, 24 hour assessment and triage. Adult/Women/Geriatric
>> Crisis Response Team: 800-718-3550

Old Vineyard Behavioral Health Services, Winston Salem, NC: 336-794-3550
 Adult, acute inpatient psychiatric

Psychiatric Center at Gaston, Gastonia, NC: 704-834-2834

University of North Carolina, Memorial Hospital Psychiatric Unit, Chapel Hill NC: 984-974-1000
 Assessment, inpatient: adult. Outpatient Adult/child, Inpatient Geriatric Evaluation and Behavior management program
  Adult Outpatient Psychiatry: 984-974-5217
  Child Outpatient Psychiatry: 984-974-2199
  Women's Mood Disorders: 984-974-5217
  UNC Mental Health Specialists Faculty Practice: 919-445-0770
  Weekend, after hours, holidays: 984-974-5217
  Gender Equality Psychiatry Clinic: 984-974-5217
  Outpatient Mental Health Clinics: 919-843-7075

University of North Carolina, Wakebrook, Raleigh, NC 984-974-4800
 Adult: Psychiatric, substance abuse, crisis and assessment, detox, inpatient, facility-based crisis unit, psychiatric and rehabilitation. Outpatient services

Whitaker Psychiatric Residential Treatment Facility, Butner, NC: 919-575-7927
 State funded, non-acute treatment program for adolescents

Wright School, Durham, NC: 919-560-5790
 Residential mental health treatment for children

Strategic Behavioral Health, Garner, Wilmington, Charlotte: 855-537-2262
 Children, adolescent and geriatric services. Acute inpatient, partial day programs, intensive outpatient, psychiatric residential treatment options.

About the Authors

Donna Kay Smith has a BA in Psychology, a Masters in Rehabilitation Counseling, and a Masters of Divinity. She is a former Certified Rehabilitation Counselor, United Methodist Clergy, and is currently an institutional chaplain. Much of her professional life has been spent in crisis counseling, including work with victims of sexual assault, domestic violence, those who are homeless, and those suffering mental health crises. In 2003 her only child developed a severe persistent mental illness. This changed the course of both of their lives. She was able to bring her many years as a case manager and rehabilitation specialist to assisting her adult child. She came to understand that the experience of having a loved one who lives with a mental illness is wholly different than that depicted by professionals. She also recognized that if she, with her years of training and experience, found this overwhelming and desperately difficult at times, the challenges faced by those with no expertise in these illnesses or the treatment system sometimes seem insurmountable. She came to believe that those who live with these illnesses and the people who love them are best able to help others facing the same challenges.

"This book is dedicated to the bravest, wisest, strongest, and most successful person I know – my child. You not only taught me how to love, you have taught me how to persevere – and to thrive."

****

Susan Willey Spalt is a retired nurse and health educator who spent her career serving as the first Health Coordinator of the Chapel Hill-Carrboro Schools. During that time she worked to establish programs aimed at supporting students affected by mental illness and substance abuse. She also developed and taught units on mental illness and substance abuse and often worked directly with students to help them access the help they needed. She has also had personal experience with mental illness in her family and her community. She knows what it is like to try and support loved ones who angrily reject help, and how difficult it is to balance hope and heartbreak in an on-going struggle.

Since her retirement Susan has volunteered with numerous community programs related to mental illness awareness and advocacy. In addition, she has pursued her life long love of poetry and serves on the Carrboro Poetry Council. Her chapbook, *Longer If It's Raining* was published by Red Dashboard Press. Her poems, many of which address mental illness, have appeared in several anthologies and journals. She is married to Allen Spalt and has two adult children. She is currently discovering the joys of being a grandmother to two grandchildren.

"This book is dedicated to the families who struggle, with courage and love to support their loved ones as they strive to live a life, affected but not destroyed by, mental illness."